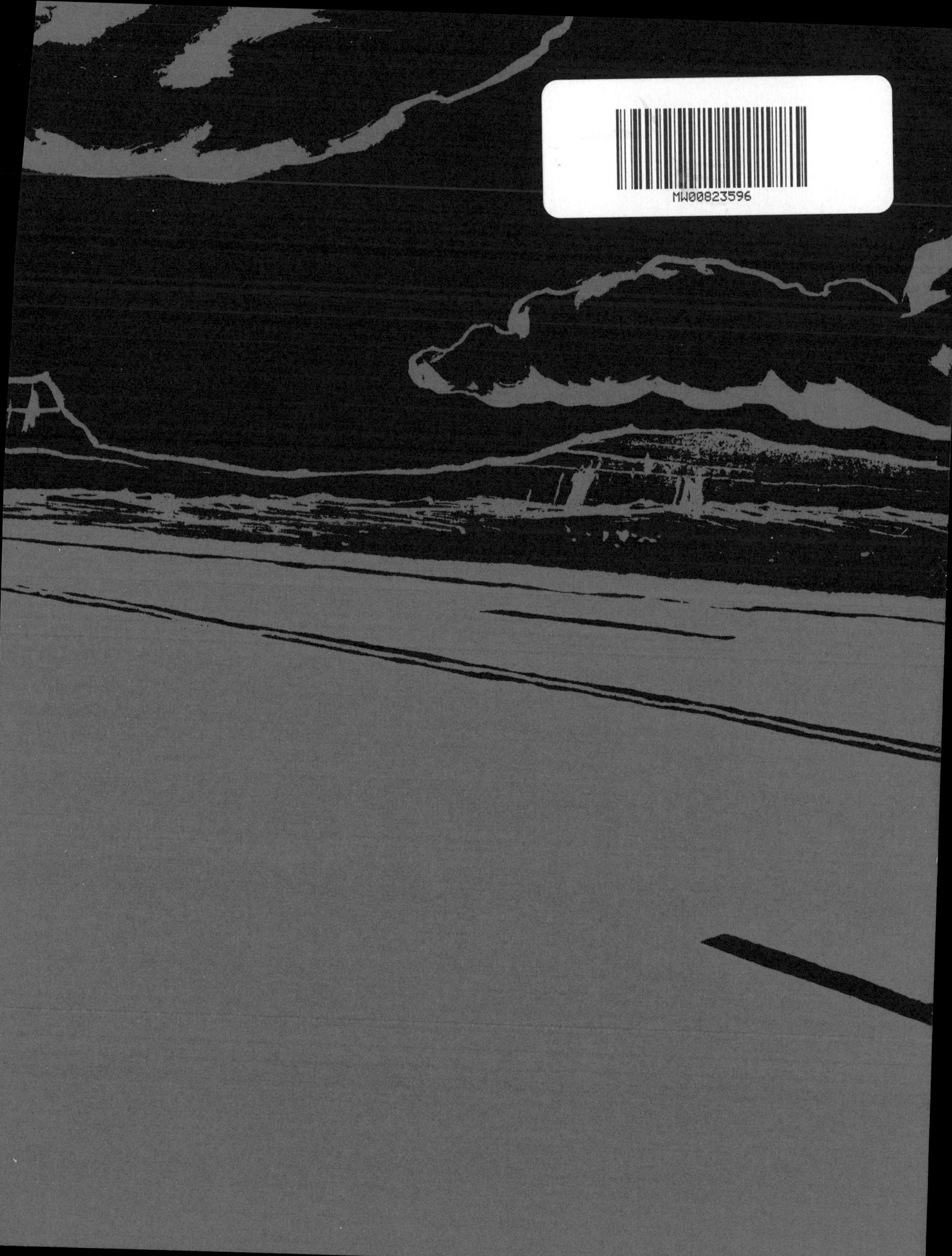

DISTRIBUTED IN THE U.S. BY W.W. NORTON AND COMPANY. INC. (212-354-5500) / DISTRIBUTED IN CANADA BY T
CANADIAN MANDA GROUP (416-516-0911) / DISTRIBUTED TO COMICS STORES BY DIAMOND COMICS DISTRII
TORS (800-452-6642) / DISTRIBUTED IN THE UNITED KINGDOM BY TURNAROUND DISTRIBUTION (108-829-30

FANTAGRAPHICS BOOKS 7563 LAKE CITY WAY NE, SEATTLE, WA 98115 / FIRST FANTAGRAPHICS PRINTING: MARCH 2010 / ISBN 978-1-56097-321-7 / PRINTED IN HONG KONG /
CHE ANDERSON CAN BE REACHED AT DOGEATSMAN@GMAIL.COM / PLEASE VISIT HOCHEANDERSONART.C

"I AM THAT WHICH LIVETH AND WAS DEAD; AND BEHOLD, I AM ALIVE FOR EVERMORE, AND HOLD THE KEYS OF HELL AND OF DEATH."

–*REVELATIONS 1:18*

# BIEN
# SIDHE

FANTAGRAPHICS

**NOUN (IN IRISH LEGEND):** A FEMALE SPIRIT WHOSE WAILING WARNS OF DEATH IN A HOUSE. ORIGIN LATE 17TH CENTURY; ALSO KNOWN AS BANSHEE, "WOMAN OF THE FAIRIES."

*–FROM THE NEW OXFORD DICTIONARY*

FIRST THE ANCIENT ONES SANG. UNTIL THE WAR WITH THE MEN FROM THE SOUTH. IN DEFEAT A COVENANT WAS ARRANGED: THE ANCIENTS WOULD LIVE IN A NEW REALM UNDERGROUND, CLOSER TO THE DARK ONES BORN OF WATER. A FEW REMAINED AS SERFS OF MAN, TO MIND THEM AND PRESAGE DEATH. ALONE AND BANISHED FROM MEMORY—THEIR VOICES TRANSFORMED FROM A SONG TO A WAIL.

*–FROM FOLKLORE*

BOOKS PRESENTS

HO CHE ANDERSON'S

# SAND & FURY

&

# FURY

A SCREAM QUEEN ADVENTURE

# WHAT'S MY NAME?

# CHAPTER ONE SCREAM QUEEN

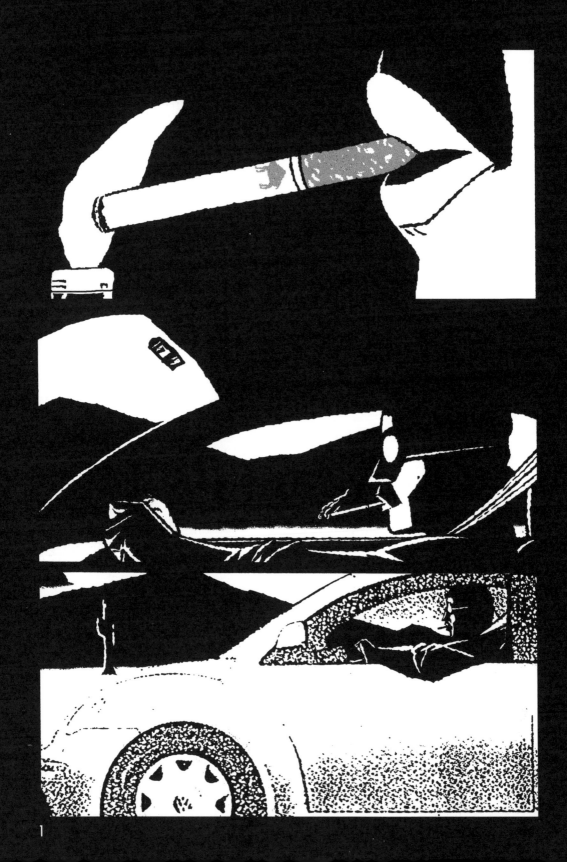

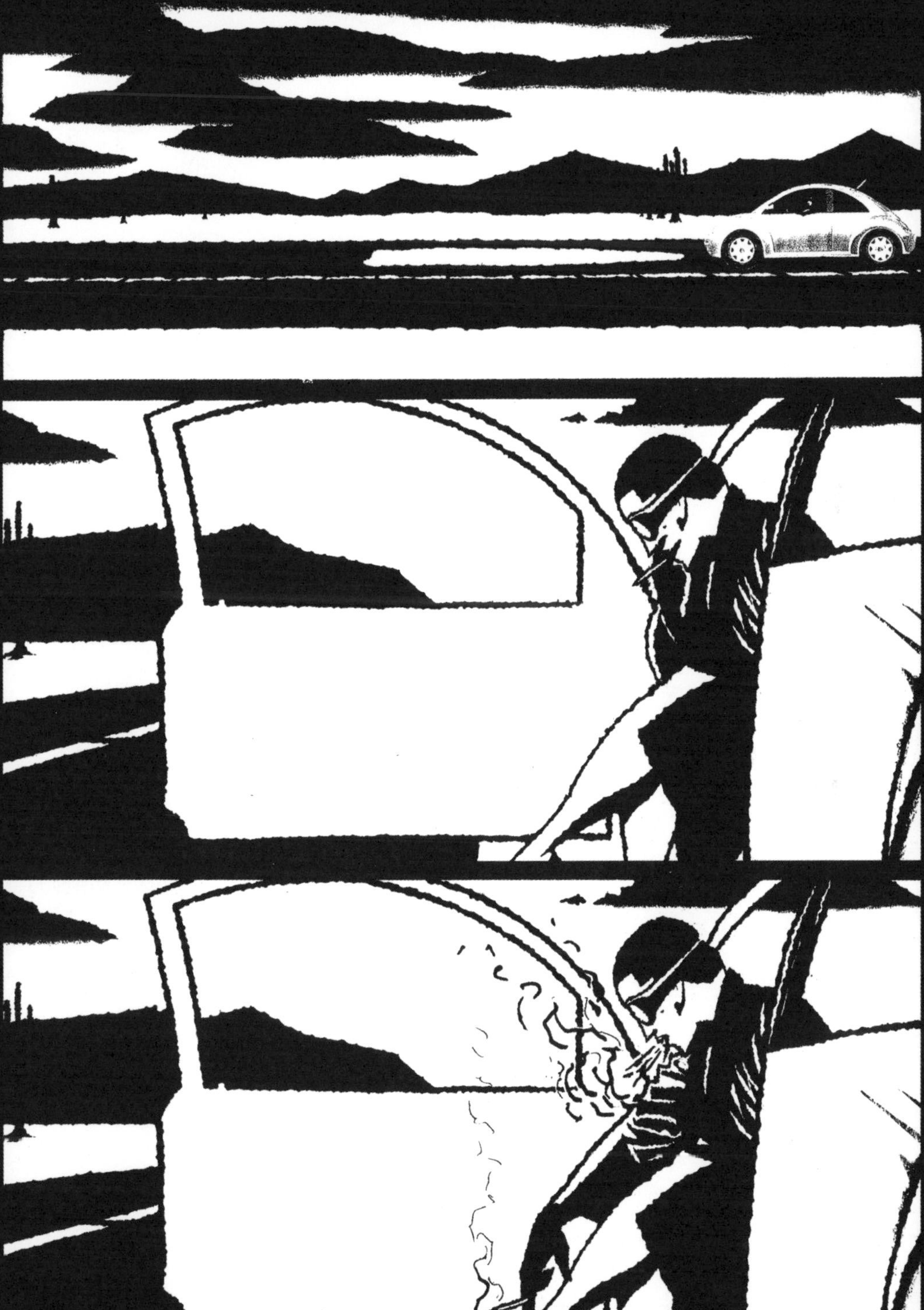

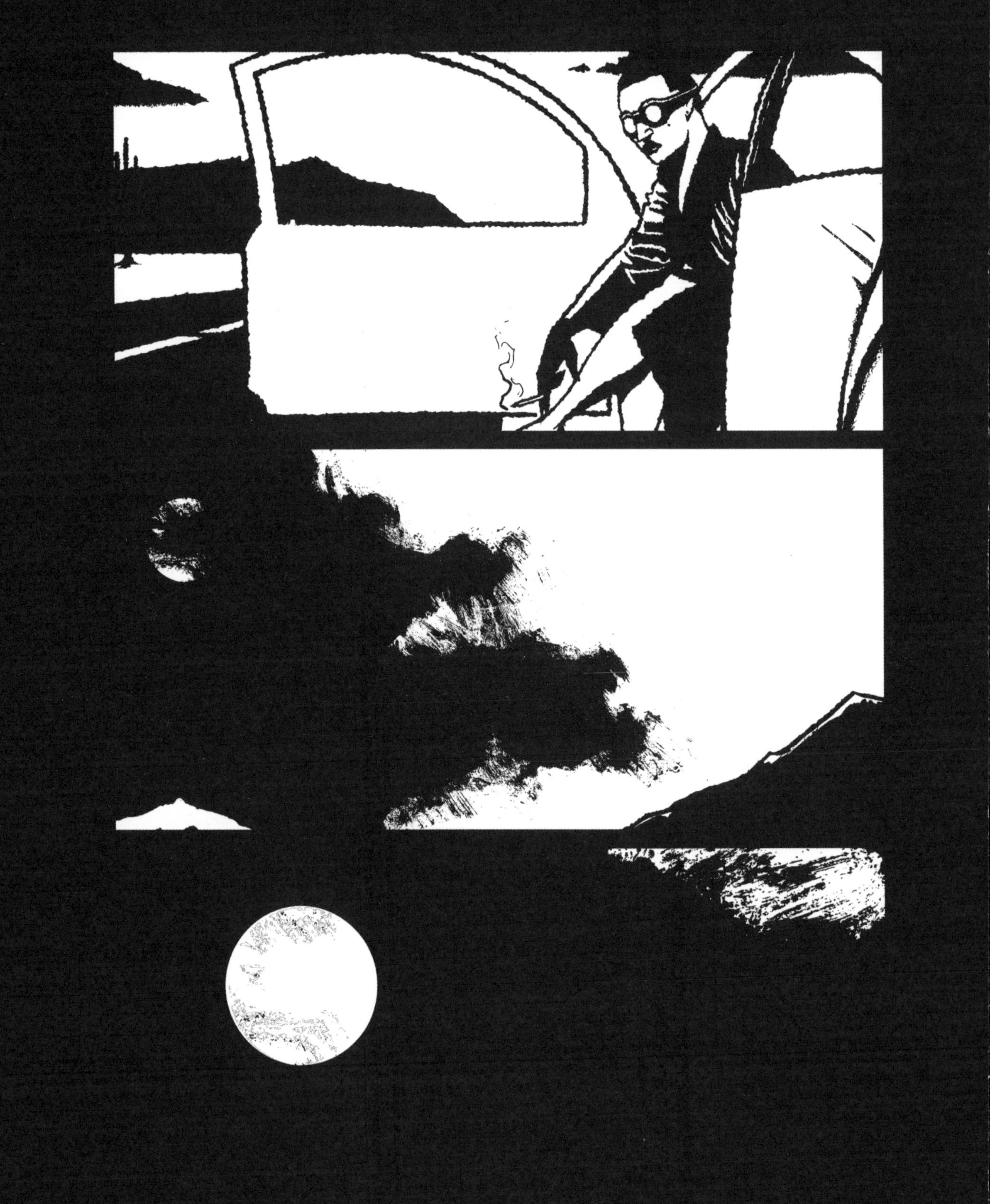

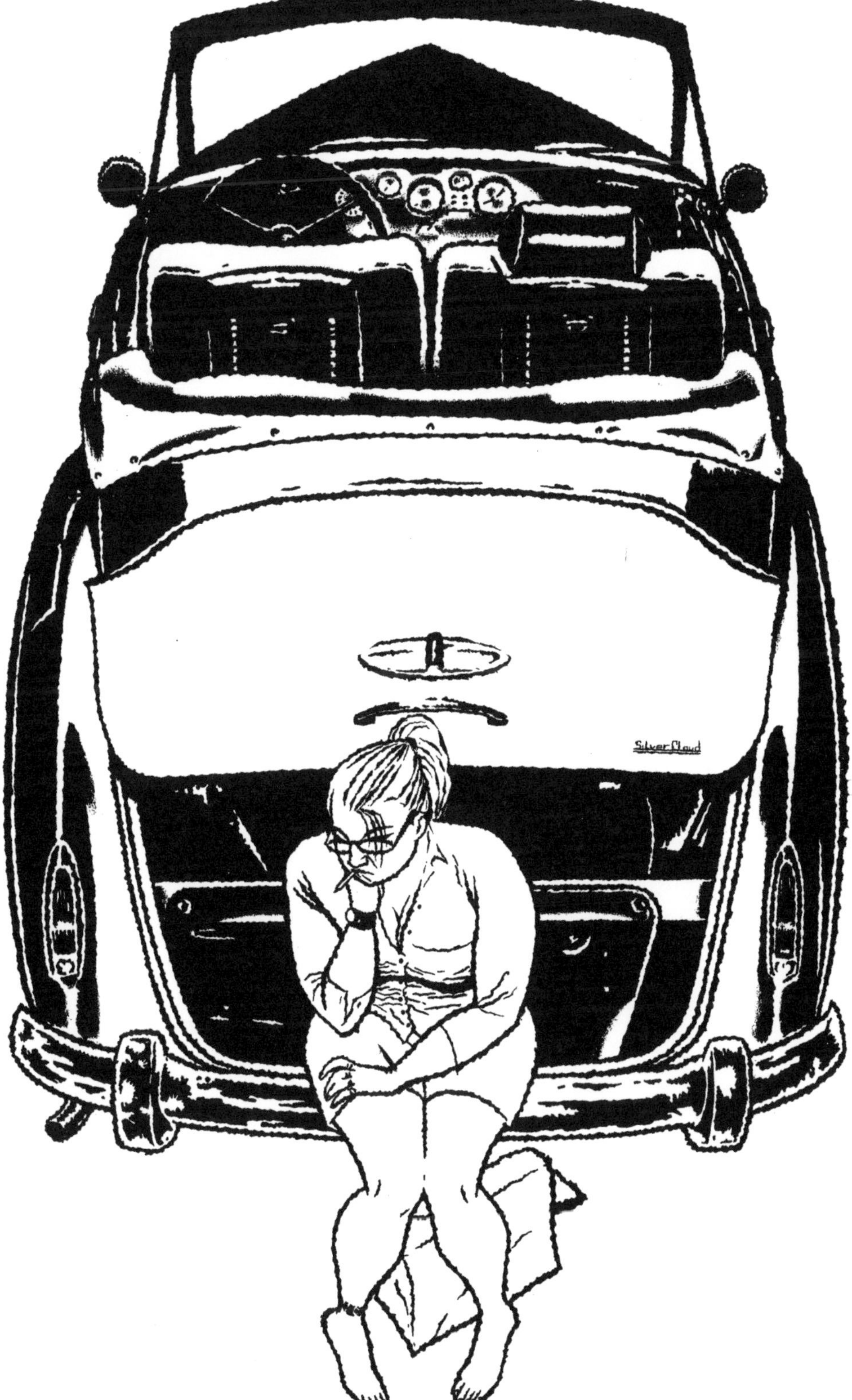
Silver Cloud

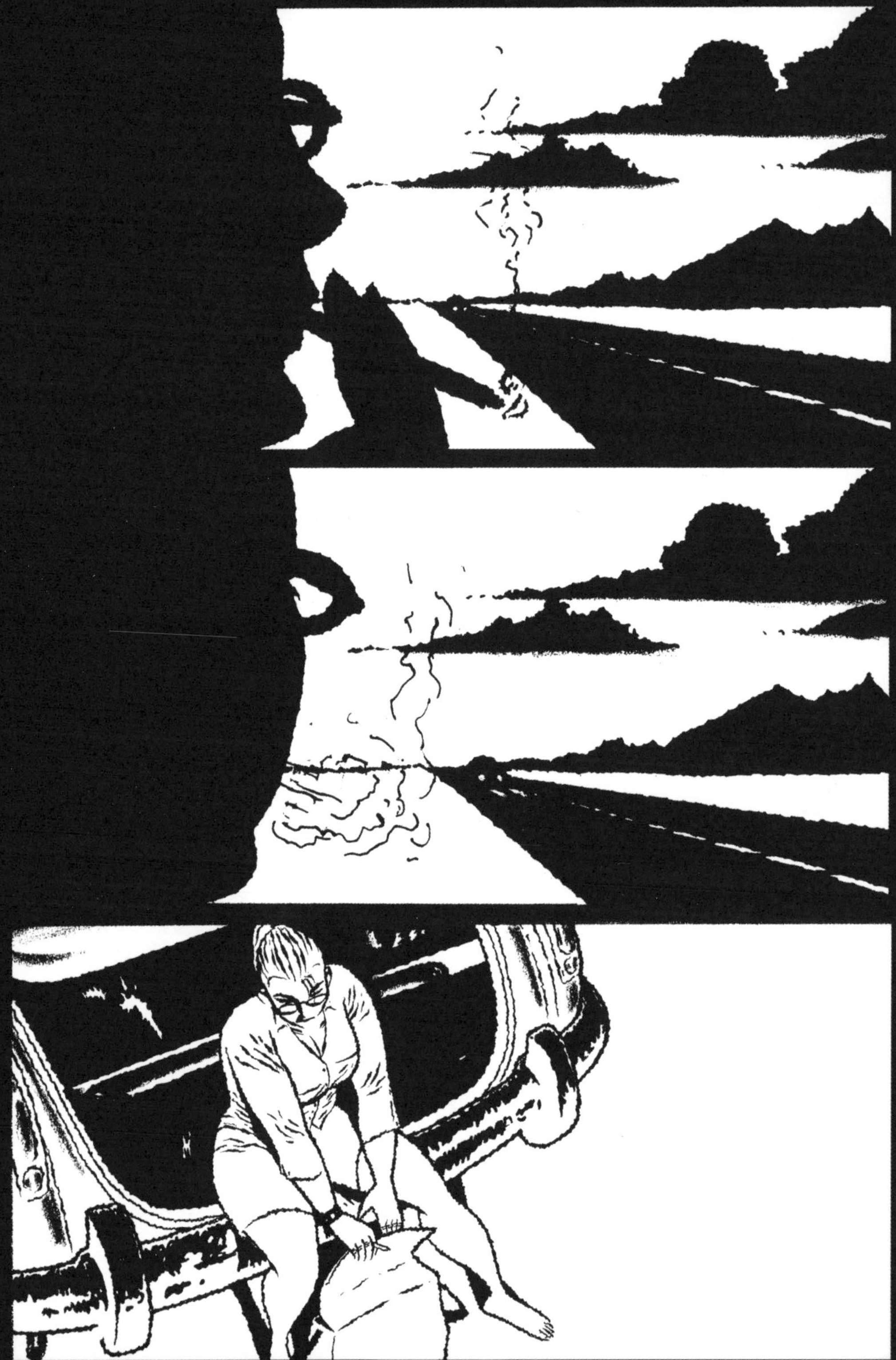

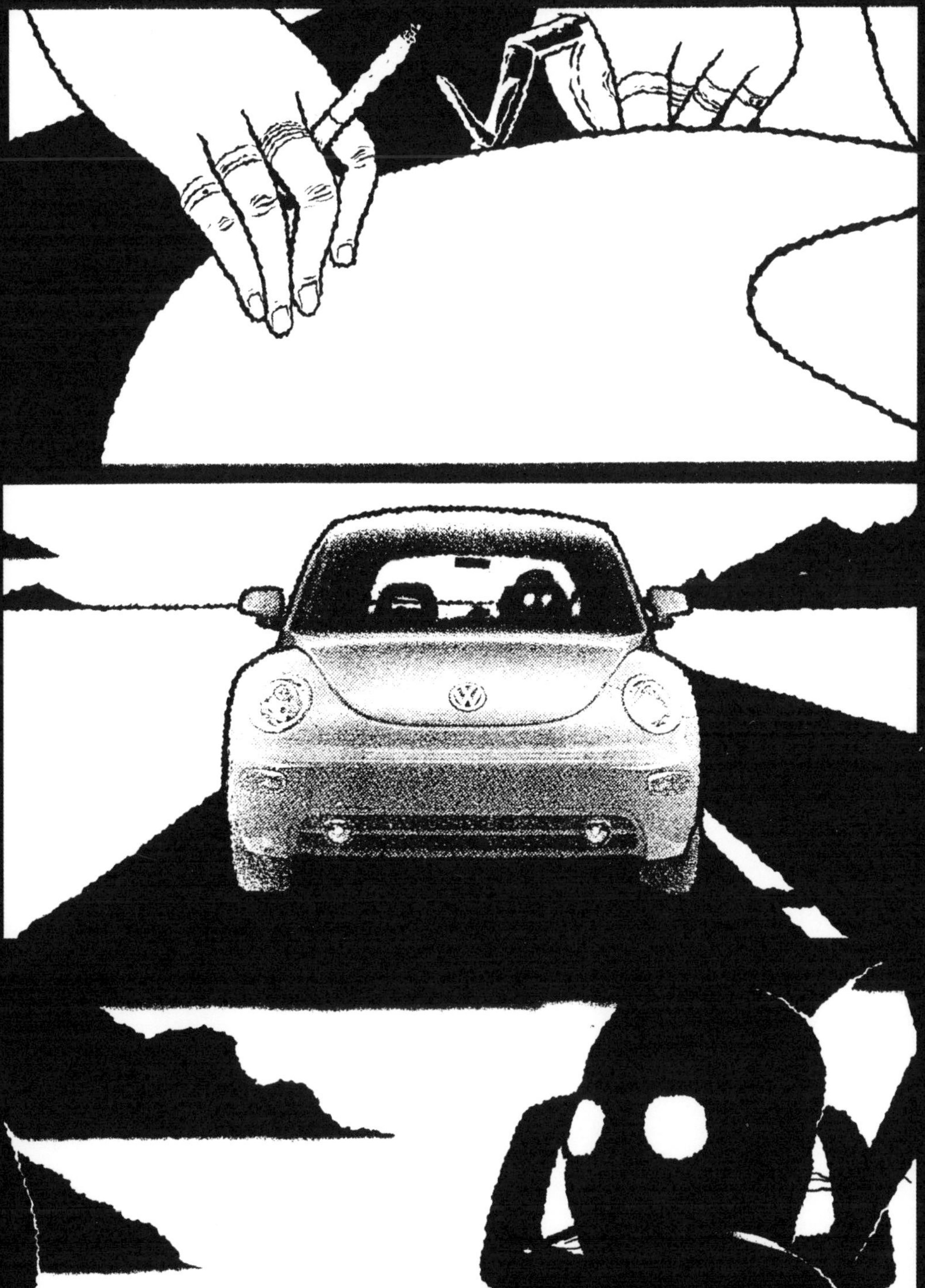

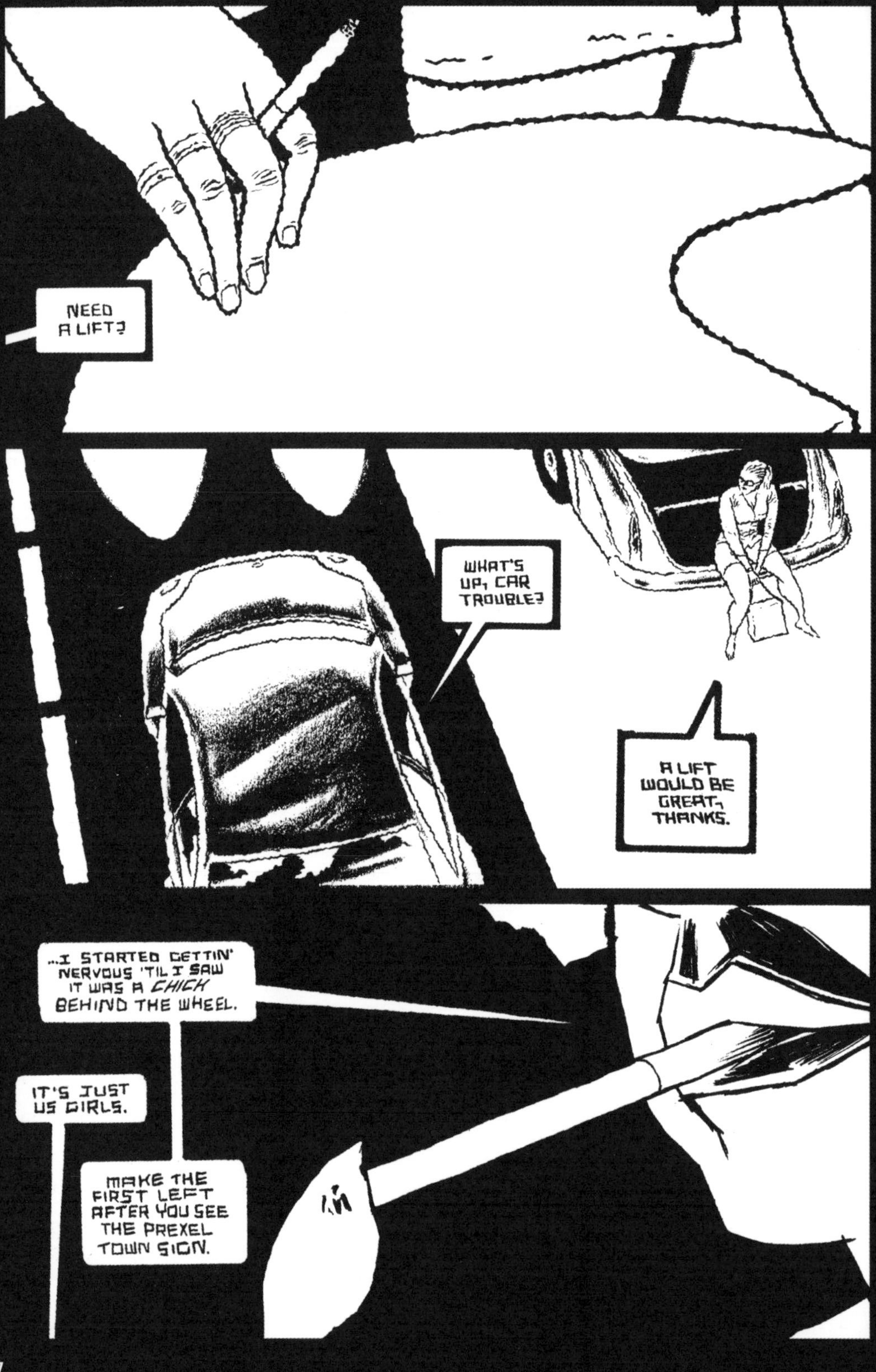

NEED A LIFT?
WHAT'S UP, CAR TROUBLE?
A LIFT WOULD BE GREAT, THANKS.
...I STARTED GETTIN' NERVOUS 'TIL I SAW IT WAS A *CHICK* BEHIND THE WHEEL.
IT'S JUST US GIRLS.
MAKE THE FIRST LEFT AFTER YOU SEE THE PREXEL TOWN SIGN.

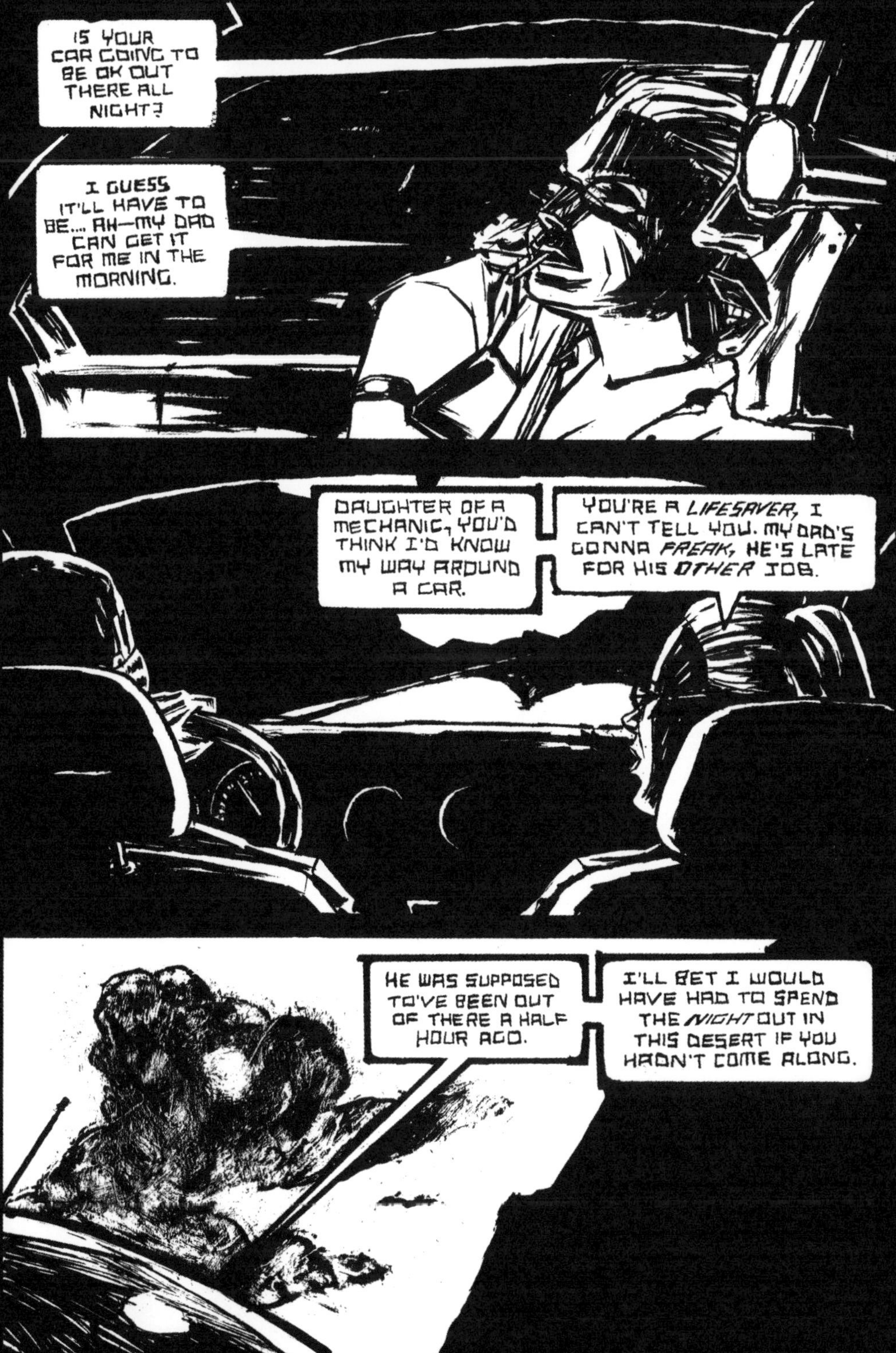
IS YOUR CAR GOING TO BE OK OUT THERE ALL NIGHT?
I GUESS IT'LL HAVE TO BE... AH—MY DAD CAN GET IT FOR ME IN THE MORNING.
DAUGHTER OF A MECHANIC, YOU'D THINK I'D KNOW MY WAY AROUND A CAR.
YOU'RE A LIFESAVER, I CAN'T TELL YOU. MY DAD'S GONNA FREAK, HE'S LATE FOR HIS OTHER JOB.
HE WAS SUPPOSED TO'VE BEEN OUT OF THERE A HALF HOUR AGO.
I'LL BET I WOULD HAVE HAD TO SPEND THE NIGHT OUT IN THIS DESERT IF YOU HADN'T COME ALONG.

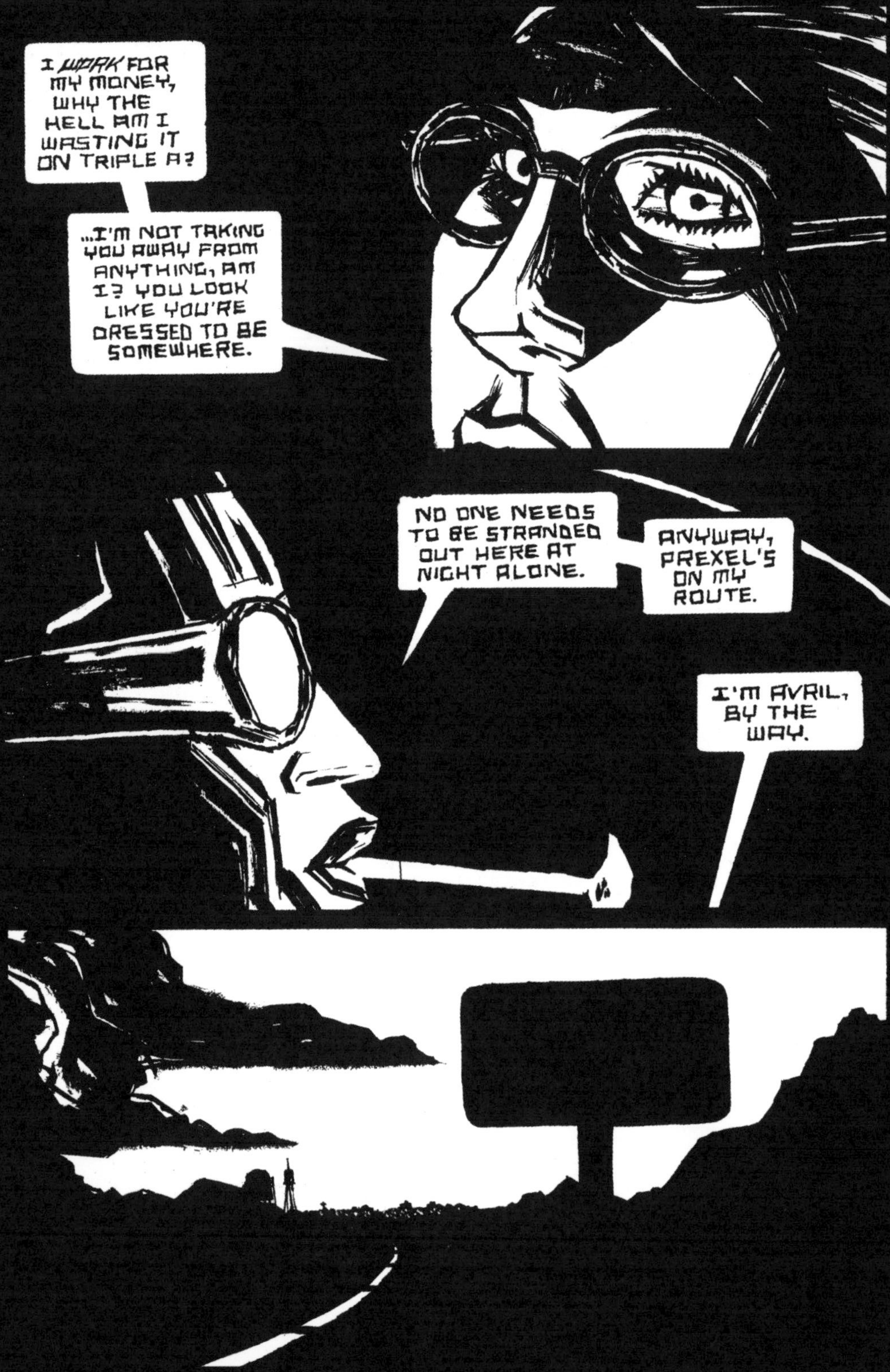
I WORK FOR MY MONEY, WHY THE HELL AM I WASTING IT ON TRIPLE A?
...I'M NOT TAKING YOU AWAY FROM ANYTHING, AM I? YOU LOOK LIKE YOU'RE DRESSED TO BE SOMEWHERE.
NO ONE NEEDS TO BE STRANDED OUT HERE AT NIGHT ALONE.
ANYWAY, PREXEL'S ON MY ROUTE.
I'M AVRIL, BY THE WAY.

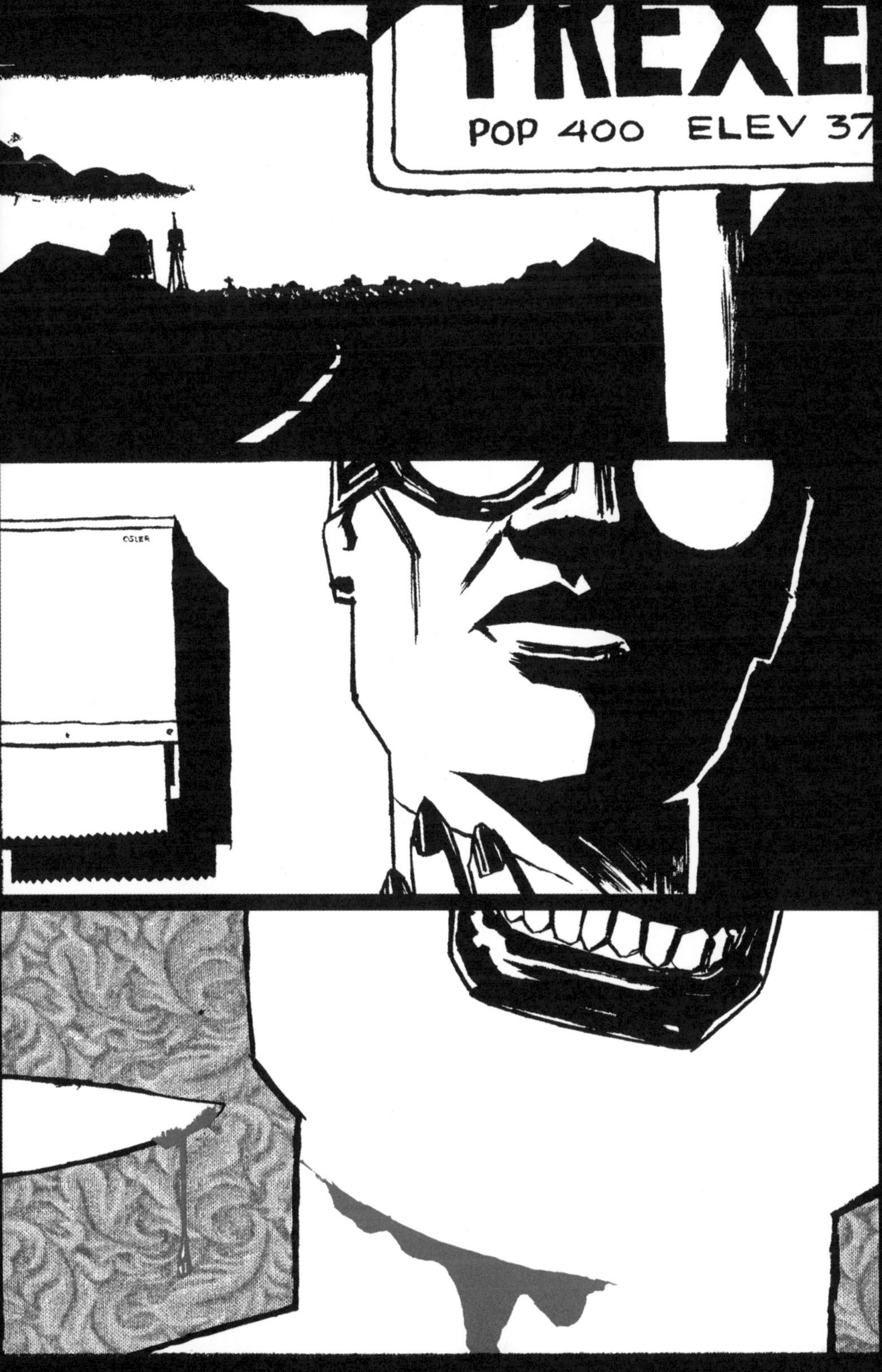
PREXE
POP 400 ELEV 37
OSLER

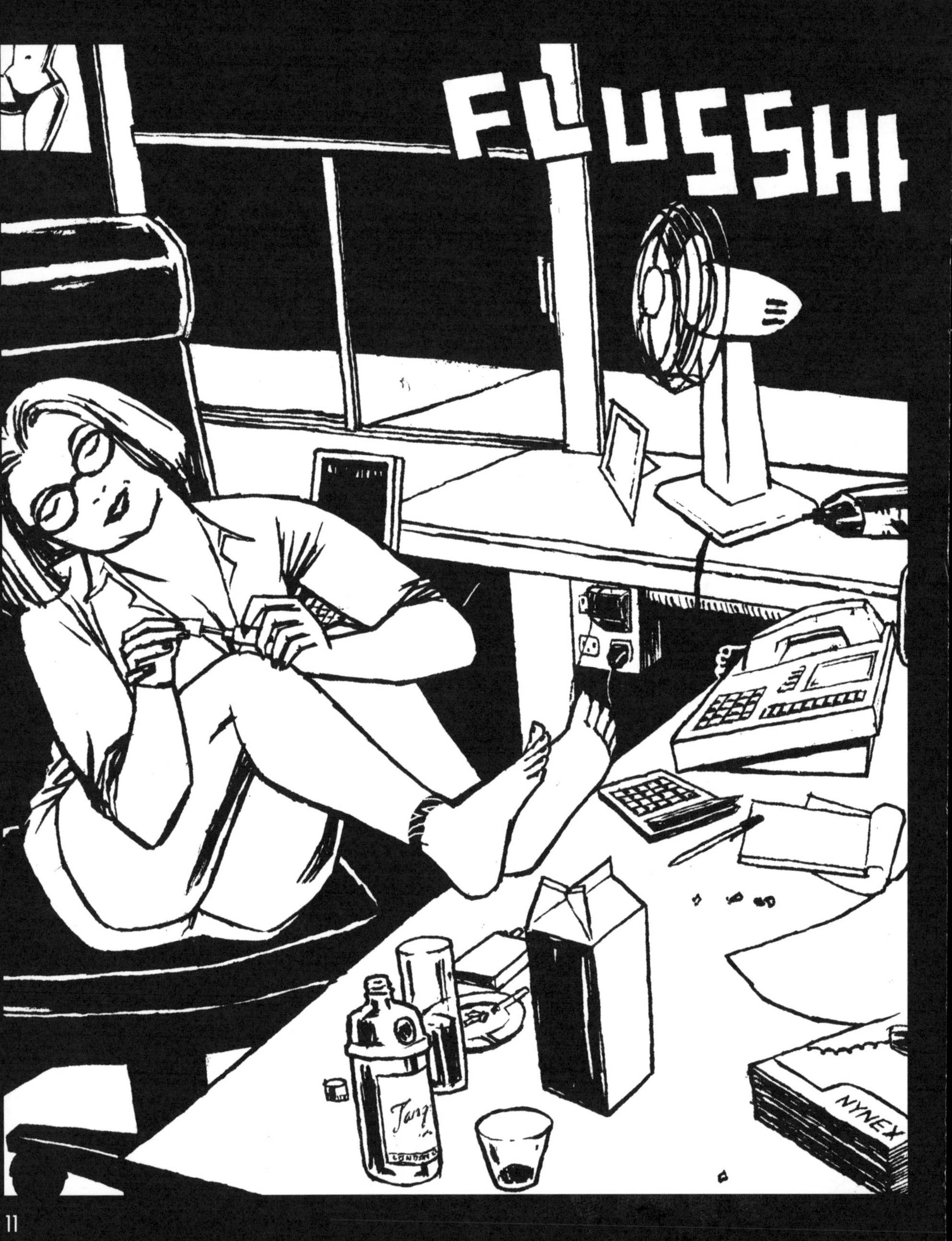
FLUSSH
NYNEX

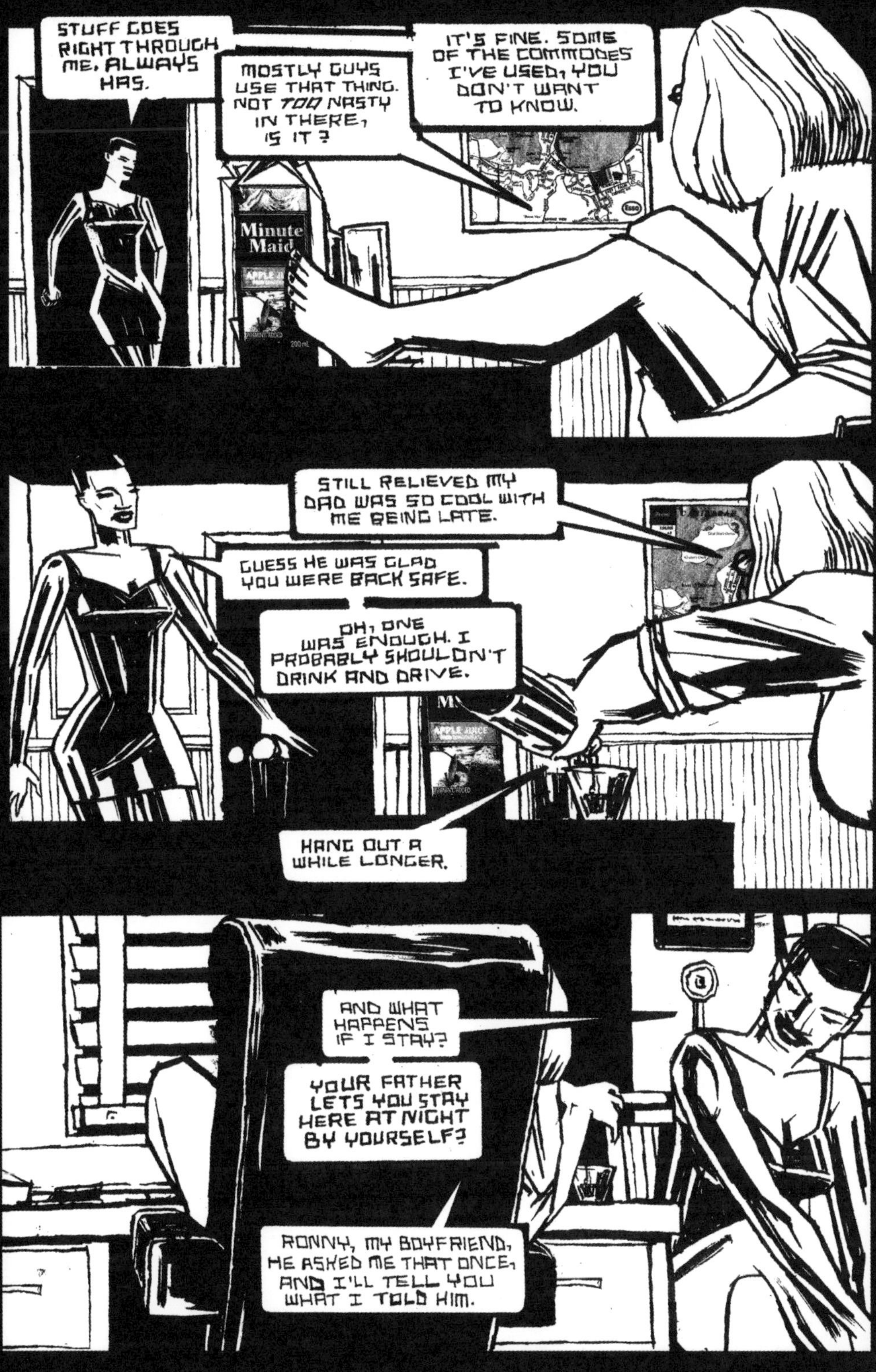
STUFF GOES RIGHT THROUGH ME, ALWAYS HAS.
MOSTLY GUYS USE THAT THING. NOT TOO NASTY IN THERE, IS IT?
IT'S FINE. SOME OF THE COMMODES I'VE USED, YOU DON'T WANT TO KNOW.
Minute Maid
APPLE JUICE
STILL RELIEVED MY DAD WAS SO COOL WITH ME BEING LATE.
GUESS HE WAS GLAD YOU WERE BACK SAFE.
OH, ONE WAS ENOUGH. I PROBABLY SHOULDN'T DRINK AND DRIVE.
HANG OUT A WHILE LONGER.
AND WHAT HAPPENS IF I STAY?
YOUR FATHER LETS YOU STAY HERE AT NIGHT BY YOURSELF?
RONNY, MY BOYFRIEND, HE ASKED ME THAT ONCE, AND I'LL TELL YOU WHAT I TOLD HIM.

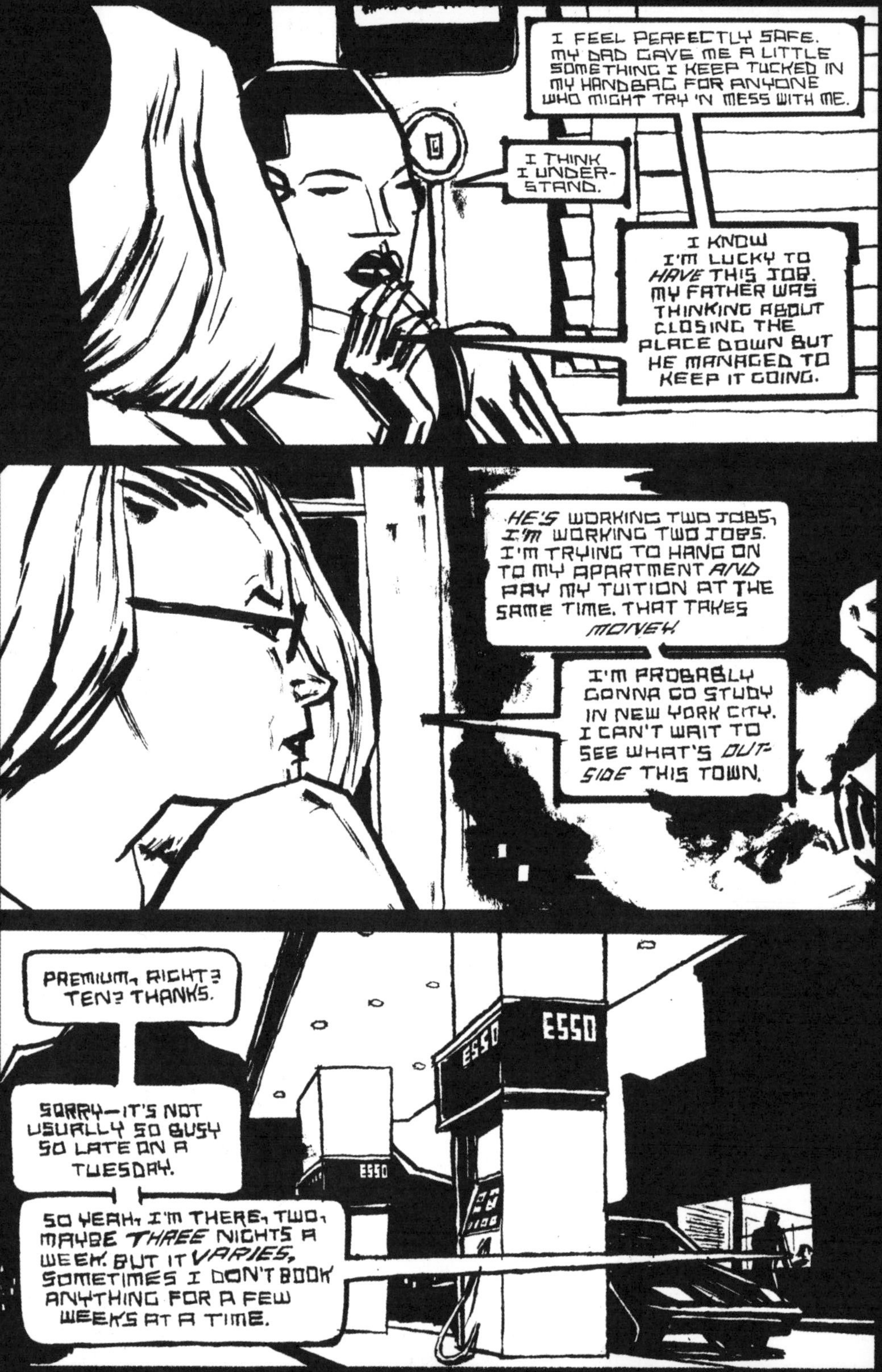

I FEEL PERFECTLY SAFE. MY DAD GAVE ME A LITTLE SOMETHING I KEEP TUCKED IN MY HANDBAG FOR ANYONE WHO MIGHT TRY 'N MESS WITH ME.
I THINK I UNDER-STAND.
I KNOW I'M LUCKY TO *HAVE* THIS JOB. MY FATHER WAS THINKING ABOUT CLOSING THE PLACE DOWN BUT HE MANAGED TO KEEP IT GOING.
*HE'S* WORKING TWO JOBS, *I'M* WORKING TWO JOBS. I'M TRYING TO HANG ON TO MY APARTMENT *AND* PAY MY TUITION AT THE SAME TIME. THAT TAKES *MONEY.*
I'M PROBABLY GONNA GO STUDY IN NEW YORK CITY. I CAN'T WAIT TO SEE WHAT'S *OUT-SIDE* THIS TOWN.
PREMIUM, RIGHT? TEN? THANKS.
ESSO
SORRY—IT'S NOT USUALLY SO BUSY SO LATE ON A TUESDAY.
SO YEAH, I'M THERE, TWO, MAYBE *THREE* NIGHTS A WEEK. BUT IT *VARIES,* SOMETIMES I DON'T BOOK ANYTHING FOR A FEW WEEKS AT A TIME.

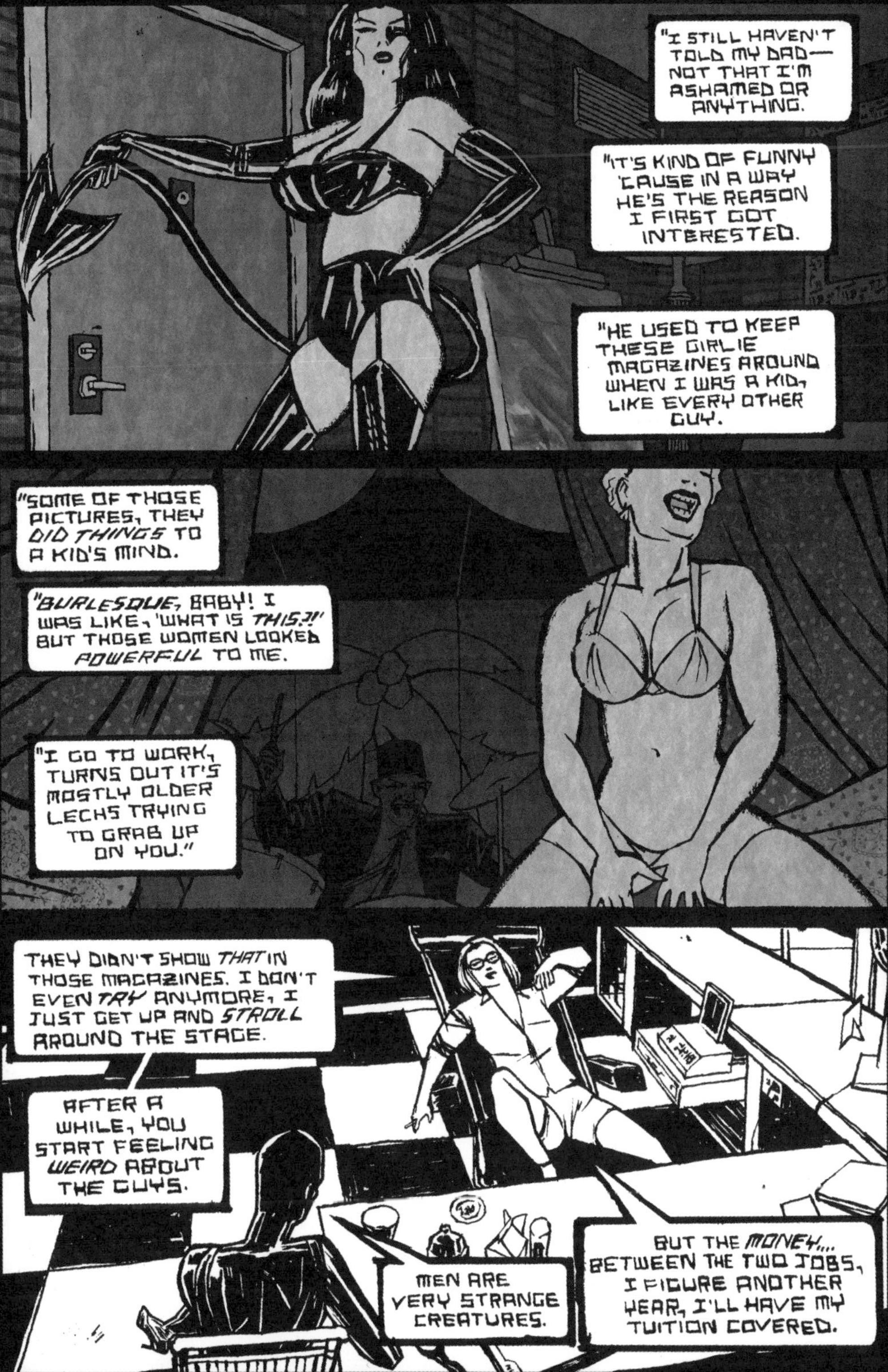
"I STILL HAVEN'T TOLD MY DAD— NOT THAT I'M ASHAMED OR ANYTHING.
"IT'S KIND OF FUNNY 'CAUSE IN A WAY HE'S THE REASON I FIRST GOT INTERESTED.
"HE USED TO KEEP THESE GIRLIE MAGAZINES AROUND WHEN I WAS A KID, LIKE EVERY OTHER GUY.
"SOME OF THOSE PICTURES, THEY DID THINGS TO A KID'S MIND.
"BURLESQUE, BABY! I WAS LIKE, 'WHAT IS THIS?!' BUT THOSE WOMEN LOOKED POWERFUL TO ME.
"I GO TO WORK, TURNS OUT IT'S MOSTLY OLDER LECHS TRYING TO GRAB UP ON YOU."
THEY DIDN'T SHOW THAT IN THOSE MAGAZINES. I DON'T EVEN TRY ANYMORE, I JUST GET UP AND STROLL AROUND THE STAGE.
AFTER A WHILE, YOU START FEELING WEIRD ABOUT THE GUYS.
MEN ARE VERY STRANGE CREATURES.
BUT THE MONEY.... BETWEEN THE TWO JOBS, I FIGURE ANOTHER YEAR, I'LL HAVE MY TUITION COVERED.

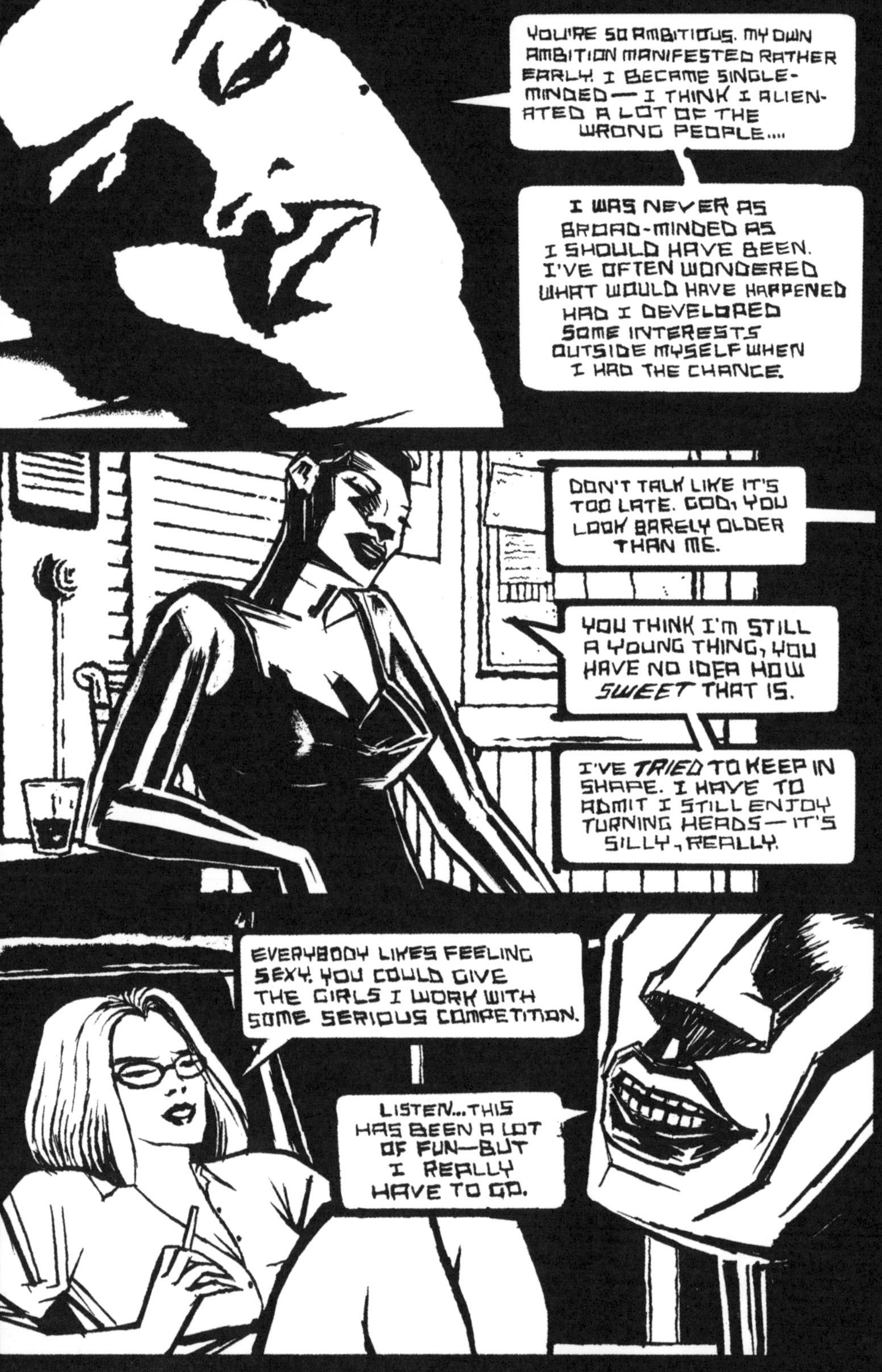
YOU'RE SO AMBITIOUS. MY OWN AMBITION MANIFESTED RATHER EARLY. I BECAME SINGLE-MINDED — I THINK I ALIENATED A LOT OF THE WRONG PEOPLE....
I WAS NEVER AS BROAD-MINDED AS I SHOULD HAVE BEEN. I'VE OFTEN WONDERED WHAT WOULD HAVE HAPPENED HAD I DEVELOPED SOME INTERESTS OUTSIDE MYSELF WHEN I HAD THE CHANCE.
DON'T TALK LIKE IT'S TOO LATE. GOD, YOU LOOK BARELY OLDER THAN ME.
YOU THINK I'M STILL A YOUNG THING, YOU HAVE NO IDEA HOW *SWEET* THAT IS.
I'VE *TRIED* TO KEEP IN SHAPE. I HAVE TO ADMIT I STILL ENJOY TURNING HEADS — IT'S SILLY, REALLY.
EVERYBODY LIKES FEELING SEXY. YOU COULD GIVE THE GIRLS I WORK WITH SOME SERIOUS COMPETITION.
LISTEN...THIS HAS BEEN A LOT OF FUN—BUT I REALLY HAVE TO GO.

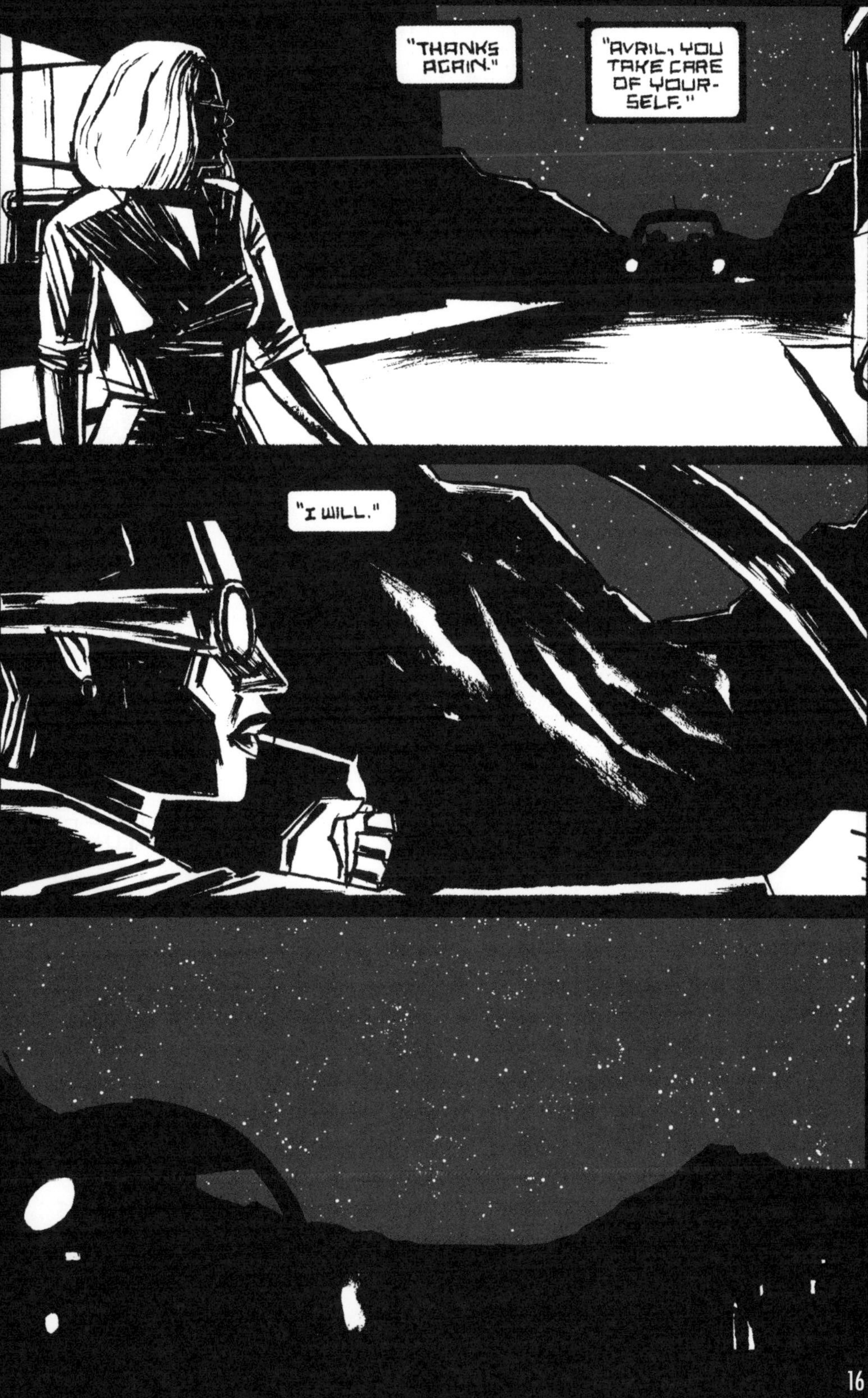
"THANKS AGAIN."
"AVRIL, YOU TAKE CARE OF YOURSELF."
"I WILL."

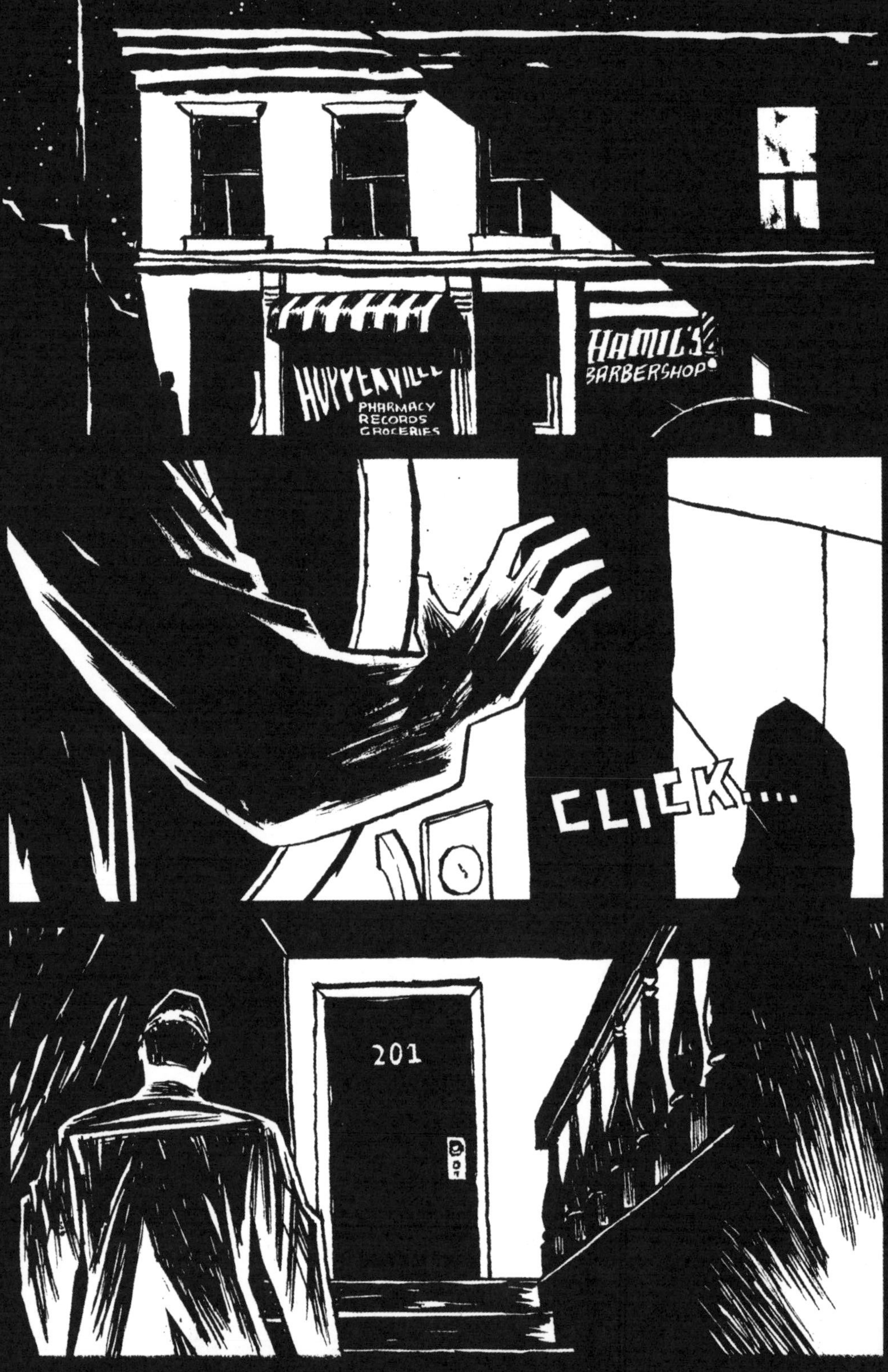
HOPPERVILLE
PHARMACY
RECORDS
GROCERIES
HAMIL'S
BARBERSHOP
CLICK....
201

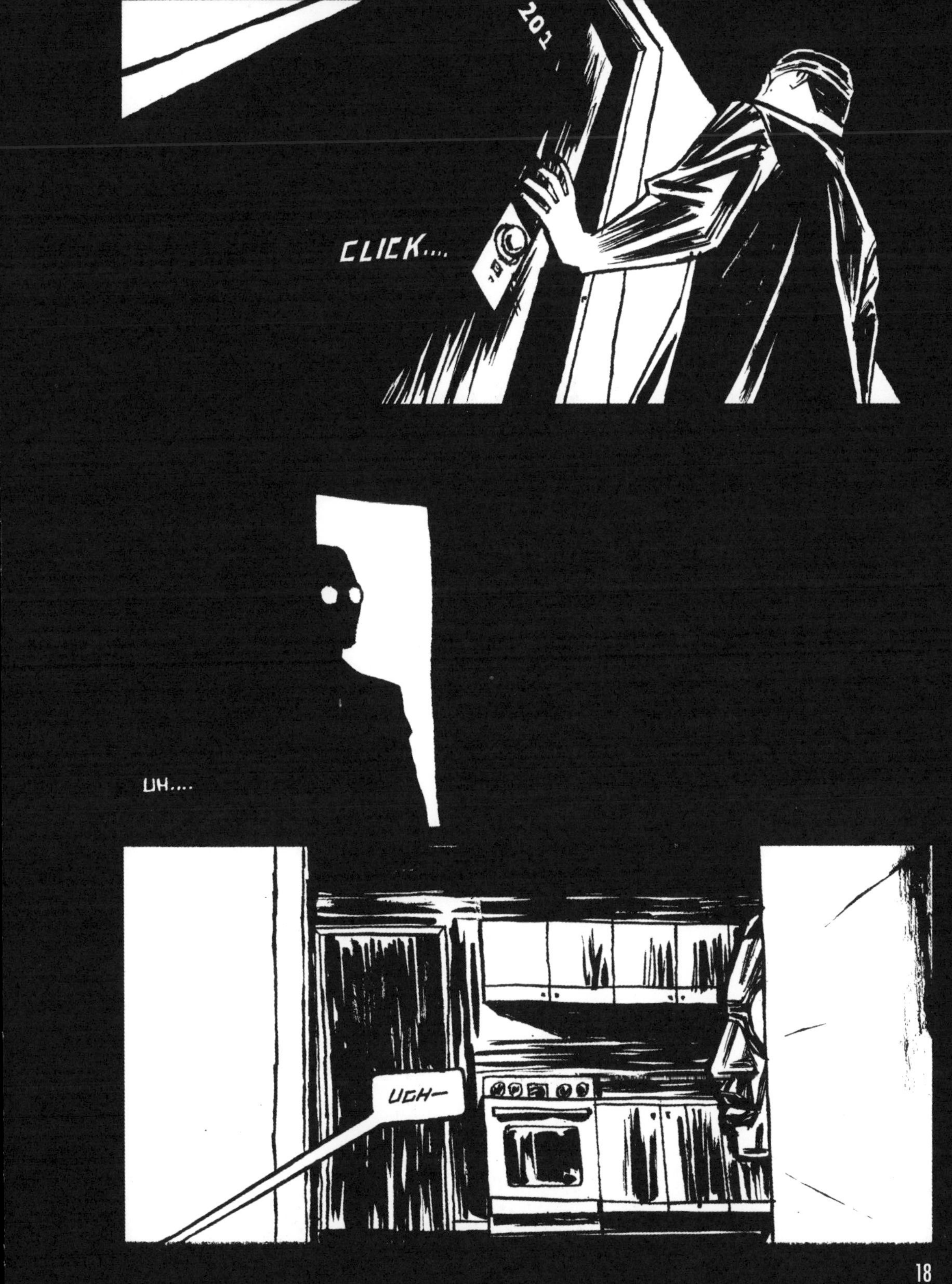
201
CLICK....
UH....
UGH—

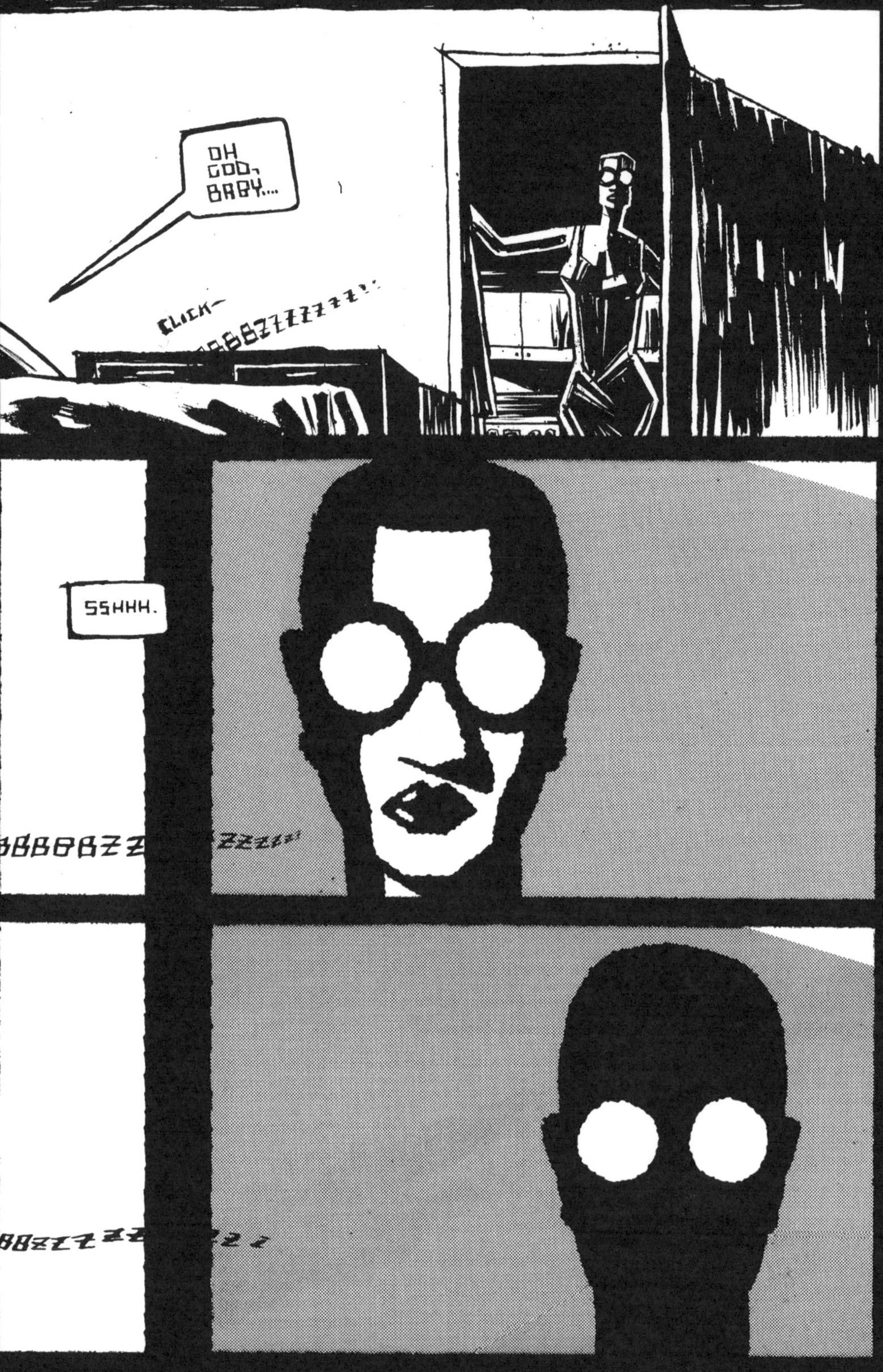

OH GOD, BABY....
CLICK—
BBBZZZZZZZZ
SSHHH.
BBBBBZZZZZZZ
BBZZZZZZZZZ

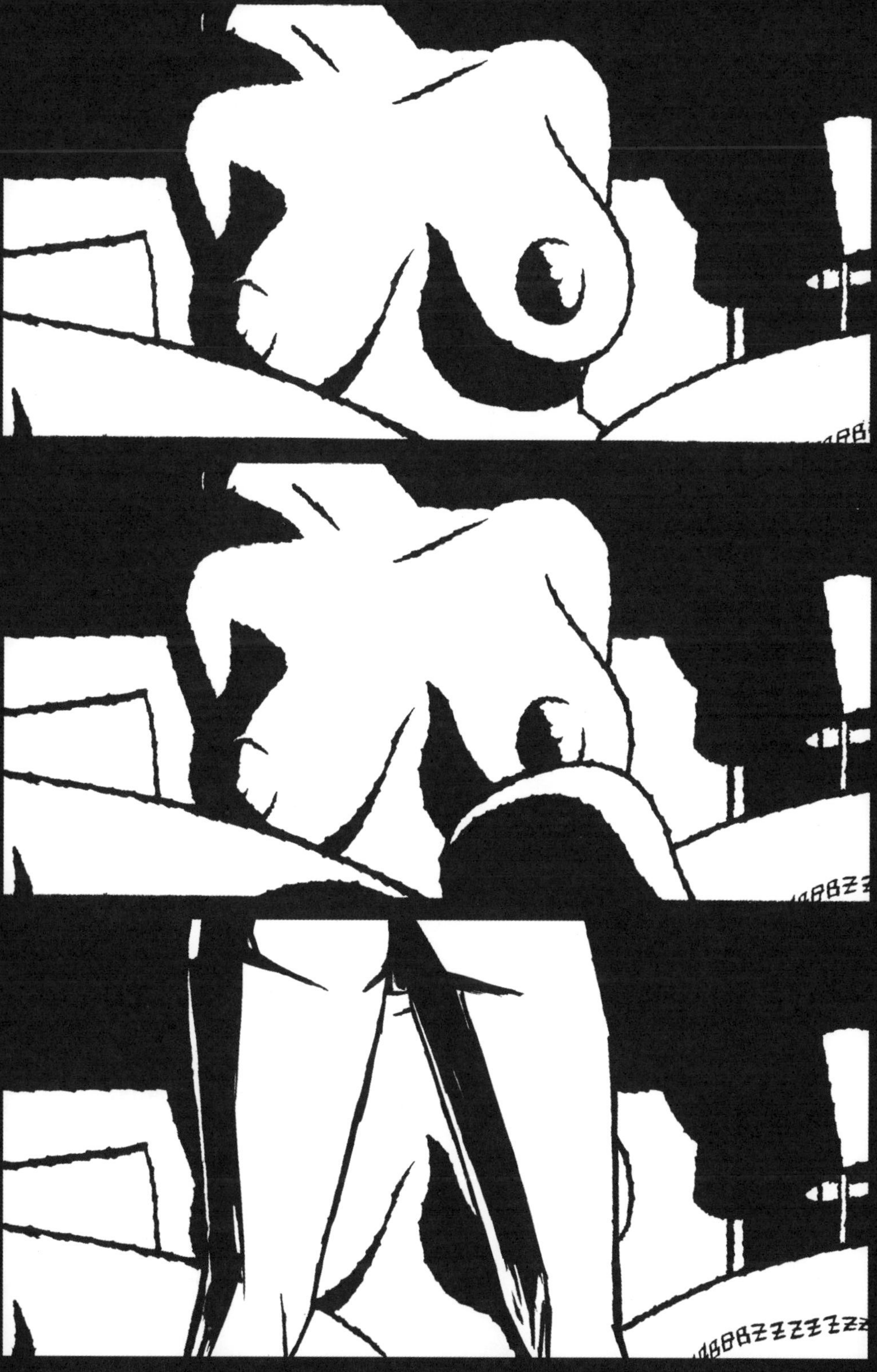
BBBZZZZZZZ

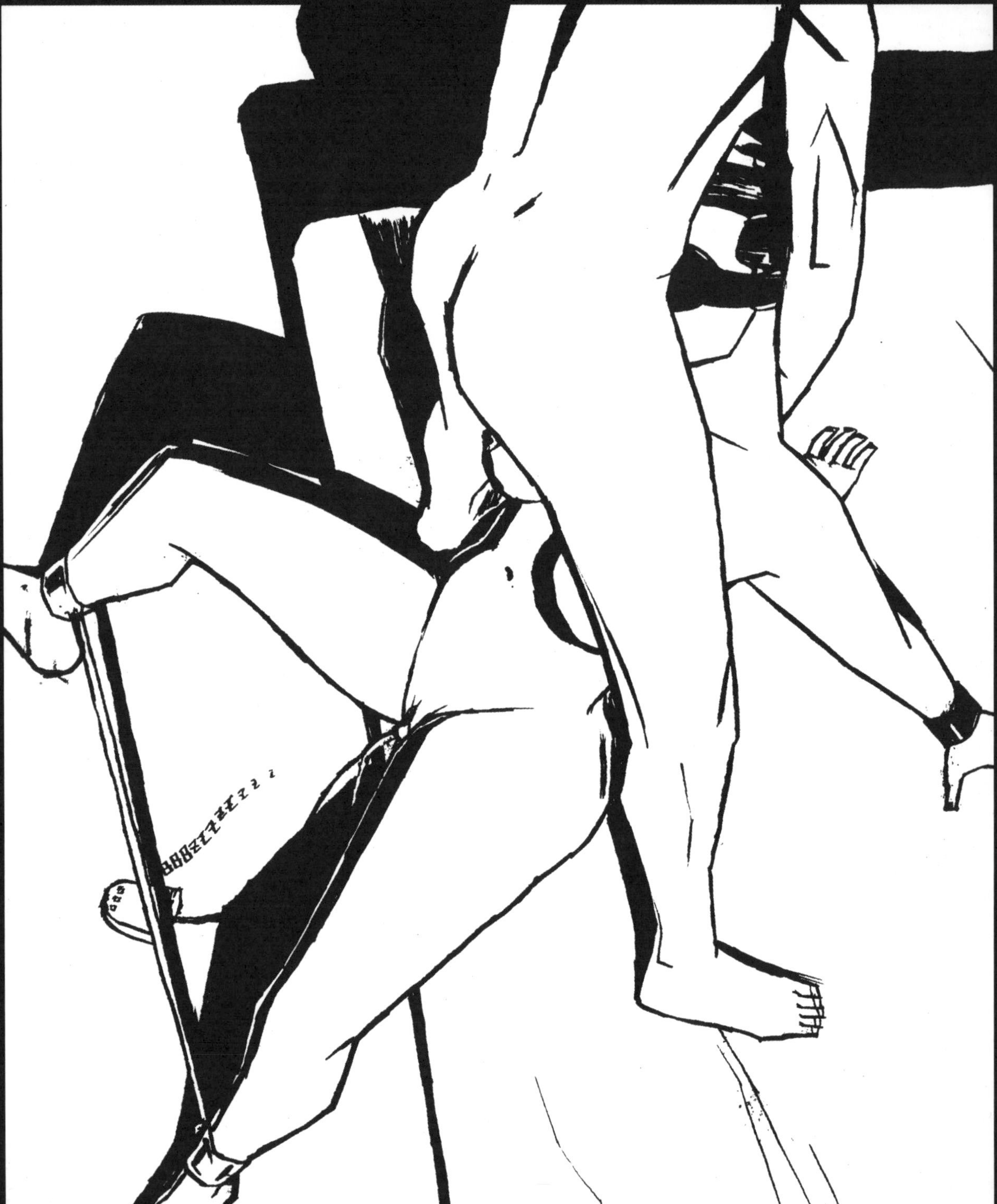
BBBzzzzzzzz

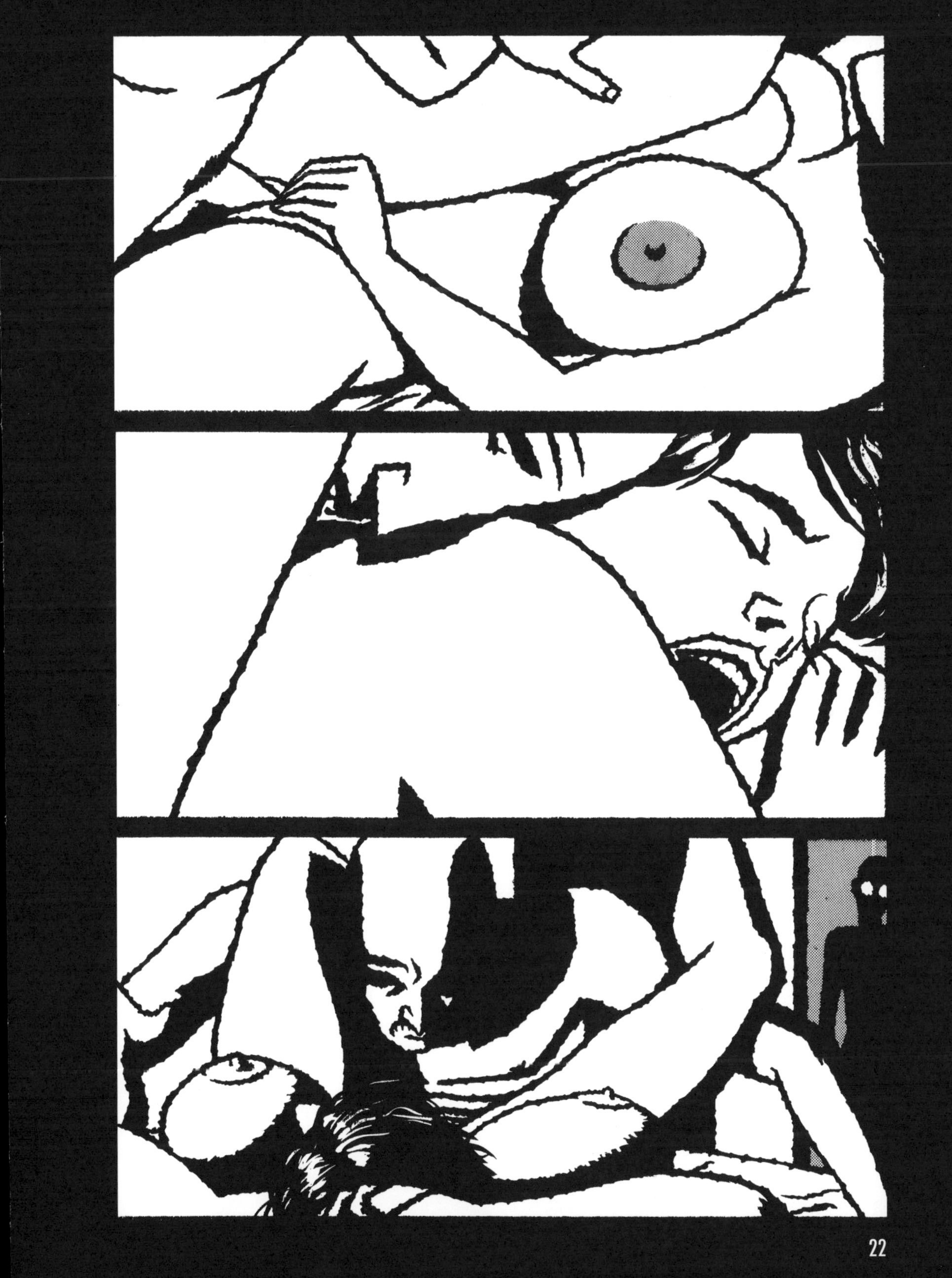

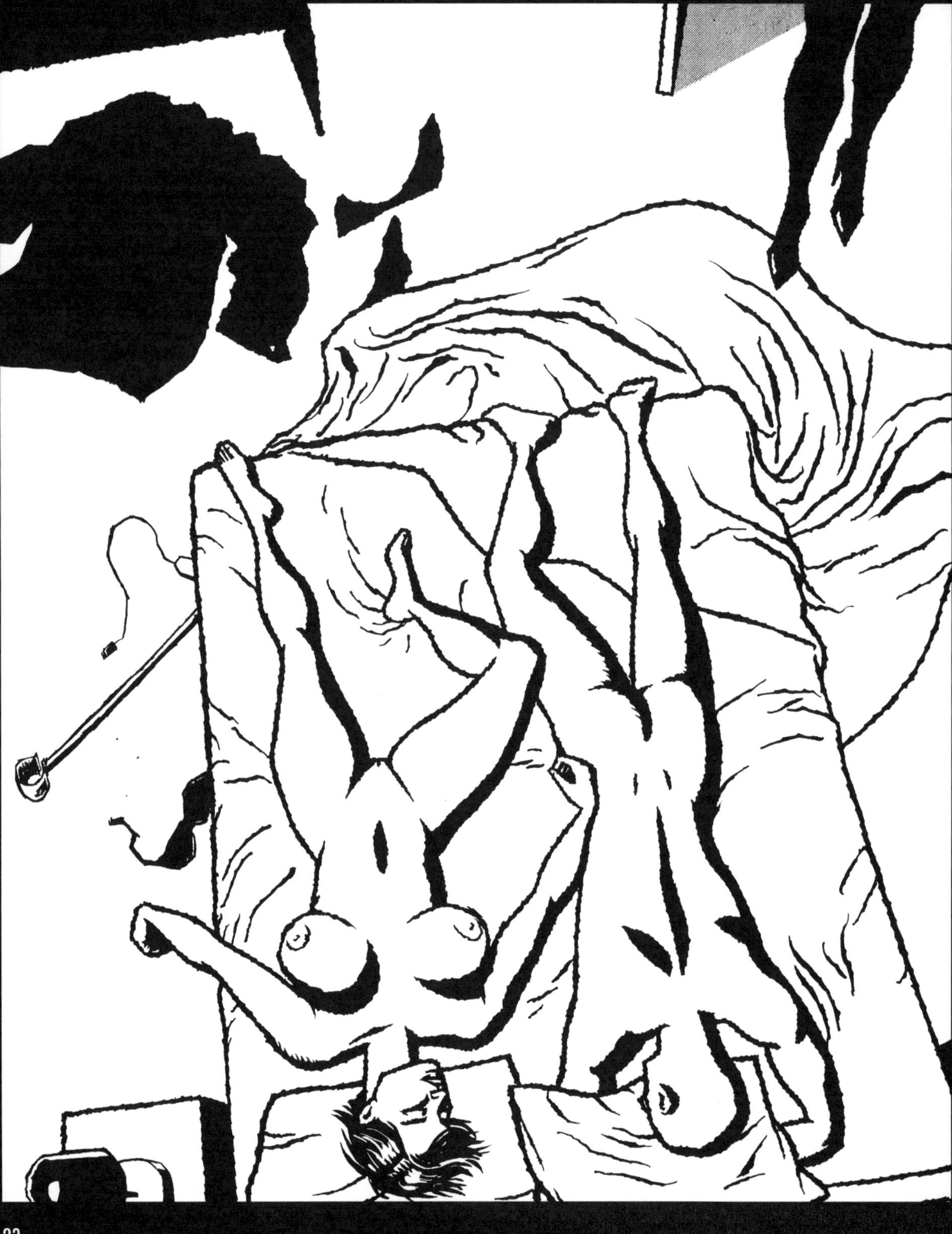

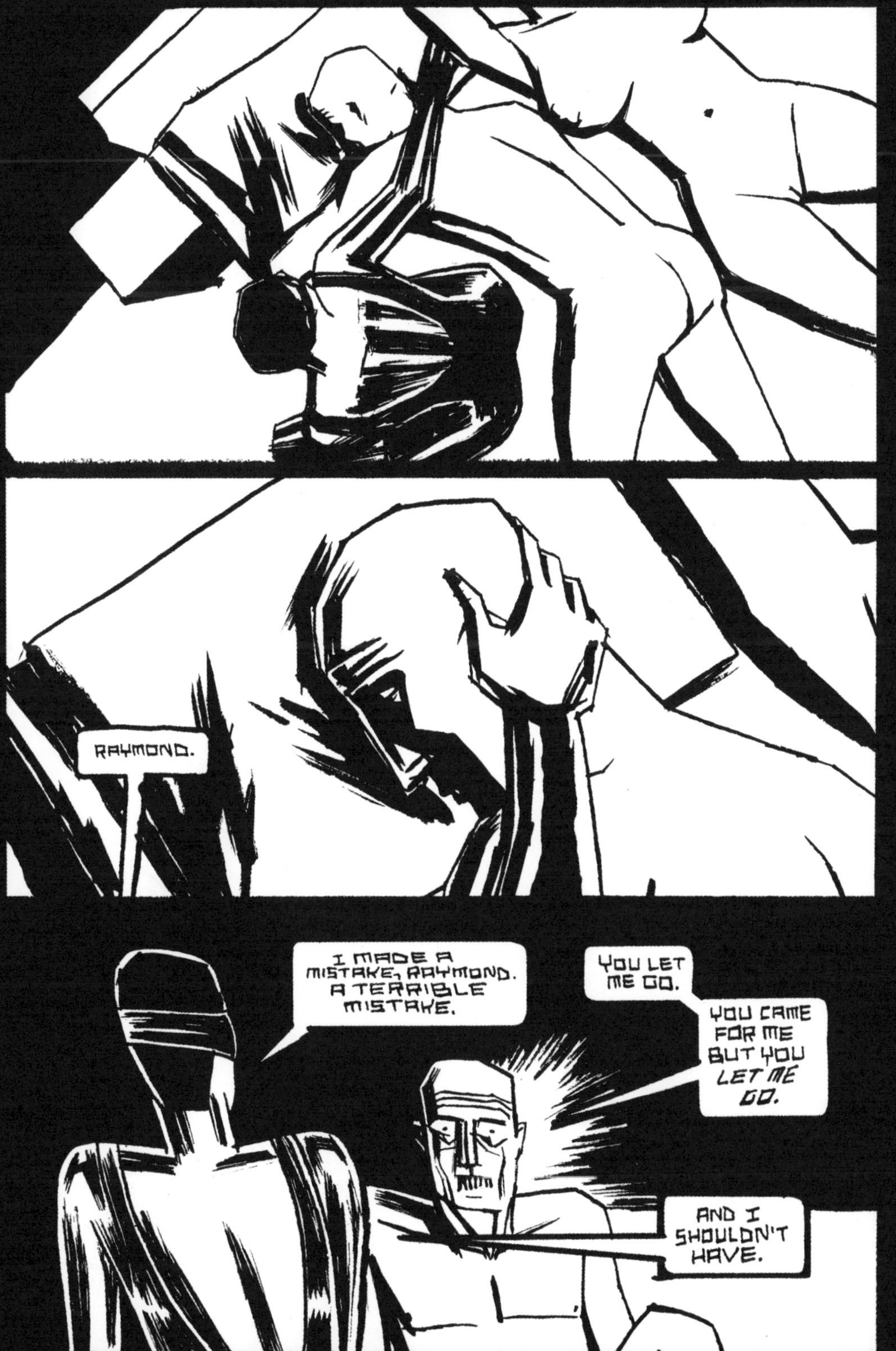
RAYMOND.
I MADE A MISTAKE, RAYMOND. A TERRIBLE MISTAKE.
YOU LET ME GO.
YOU CAME FOR ME BUT YOU *LET ME GO.*
AND I SHOULDN'T HAVE.

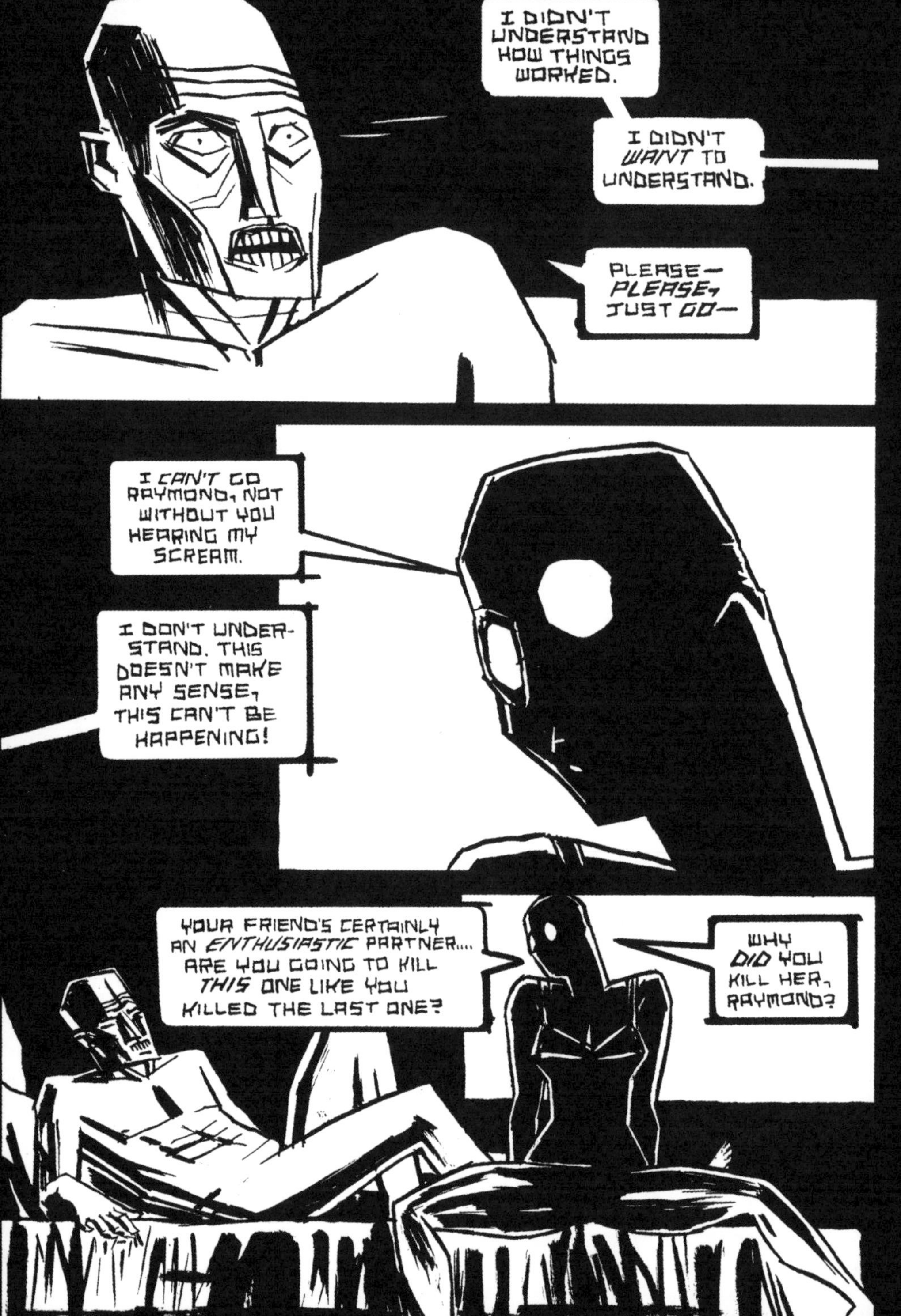

I DIDN'T UNDERSTAND HOW THINGS WORKED.
I DIDN'T WANT TO UNDERSTAND.
PLEASE— PLEASE, JUST GO—
I CAN'T GO RAYMOND, NOT WITHOUT YOU HEARING MY SCREAM.
I DON'T UNDER-STAND. THIS DOESN'T MAKE ANY SENSE, THIS CAN'T BE HAPPENING!
YOUR FRIEND'S CERTAINLY AN ENTHUSIASTIC PARTNER.... ARE YOU GOING TO KILL THIS ONE LIKE YOU KILLED THE LAST ONE?
WHY DID YOU KILL HER, RAYMOND?

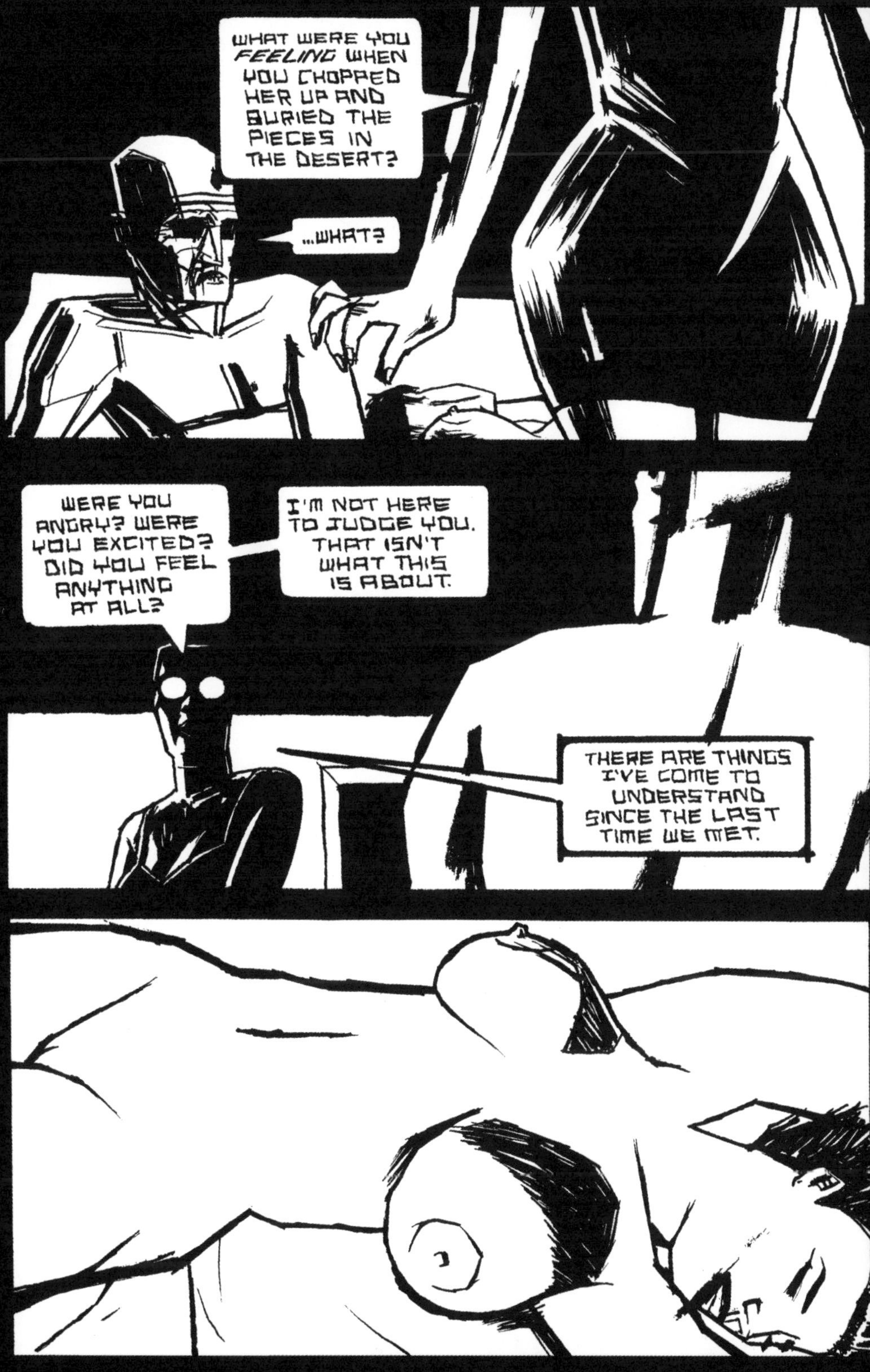
WHAT WERE YOU *FEELING* WHEN YOU CHOPPED HER UP AND BURIED THE PIECES IN THE DESERT?
...WHAT?
WERE YOU ANGRY? WERE YOU EXCITED? DID YOU FEEL ANYTHING AT ALL?
I'M NOT HERE TO JUDGE YOU. THAT ISN'T WHAT THIS IS ABOUT.
THERE ARE THINGS I'VE COME TO UNDERSTAND SINCE THE LAST TIME WE MET.

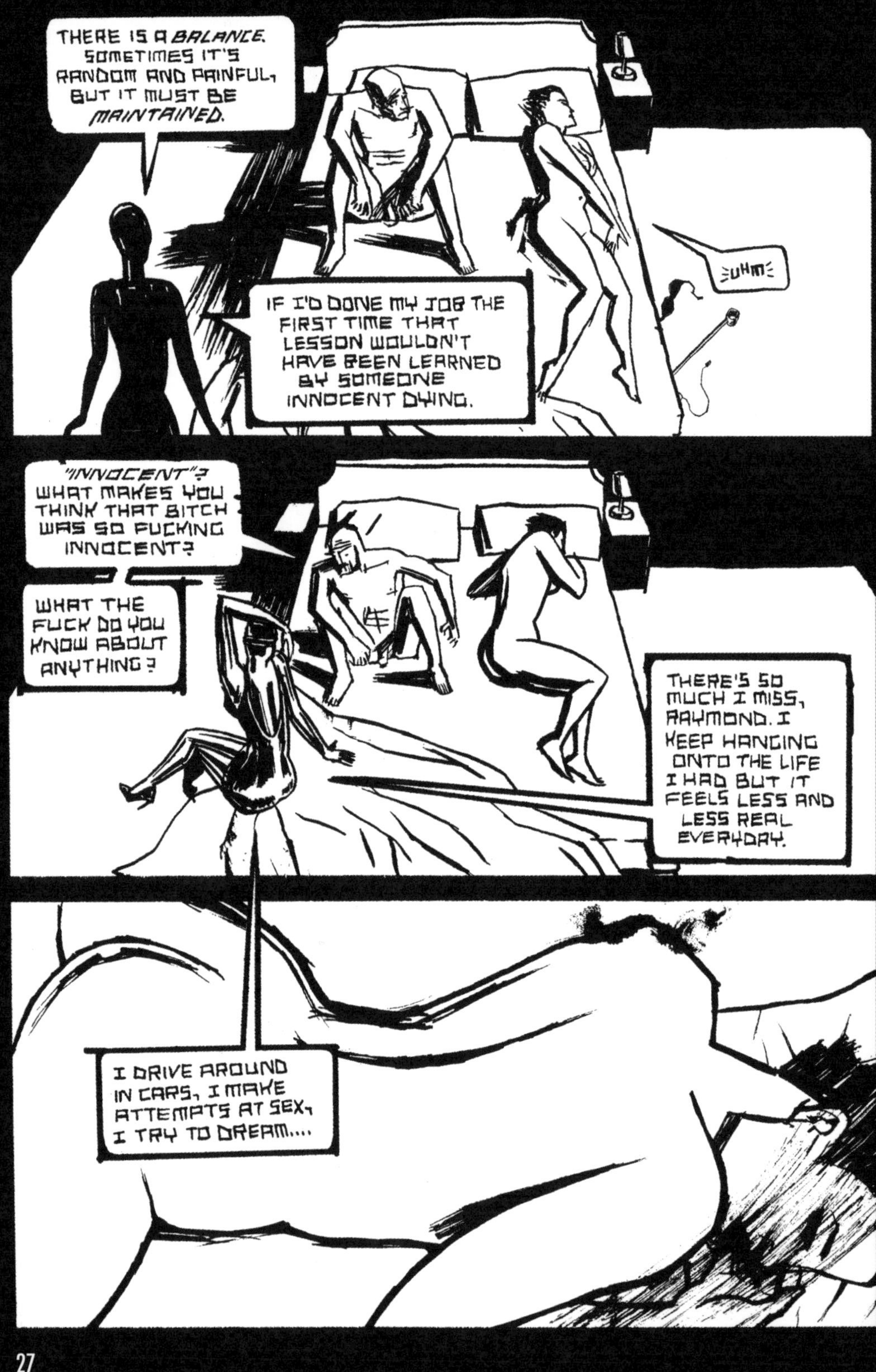
THERE IS A BALANCE. SOMETIMES IT'S RANDOM AND PAINFUL, BUT IT MUST BE MAINTAINED.
UHM
IF I'D DONE MY JOB THE FIRST TIME THAT LESSON WOULDN'T HAVE BEEN LEARNED BY SOMEONE INNOCENT DYING.
"INNOCENT"? WHAT MAKES YOU THINK THAT BITCH WAS SO FUCKING INNOCENT?
WHAT THE FUCK DO YOU KNOW ABOUT ANYTHING?
THERE'S SO MUCH I MISS, RAYMOND. I KEEP HANGING ONTO THE LIFE I HAD BUT IT FEELS LESS AND LESS REAL EVERYDAY.
I DRIVE AROUND IN CARS, I MAKE ATTEMPTS AT SEX, I TRY TO DREAM....

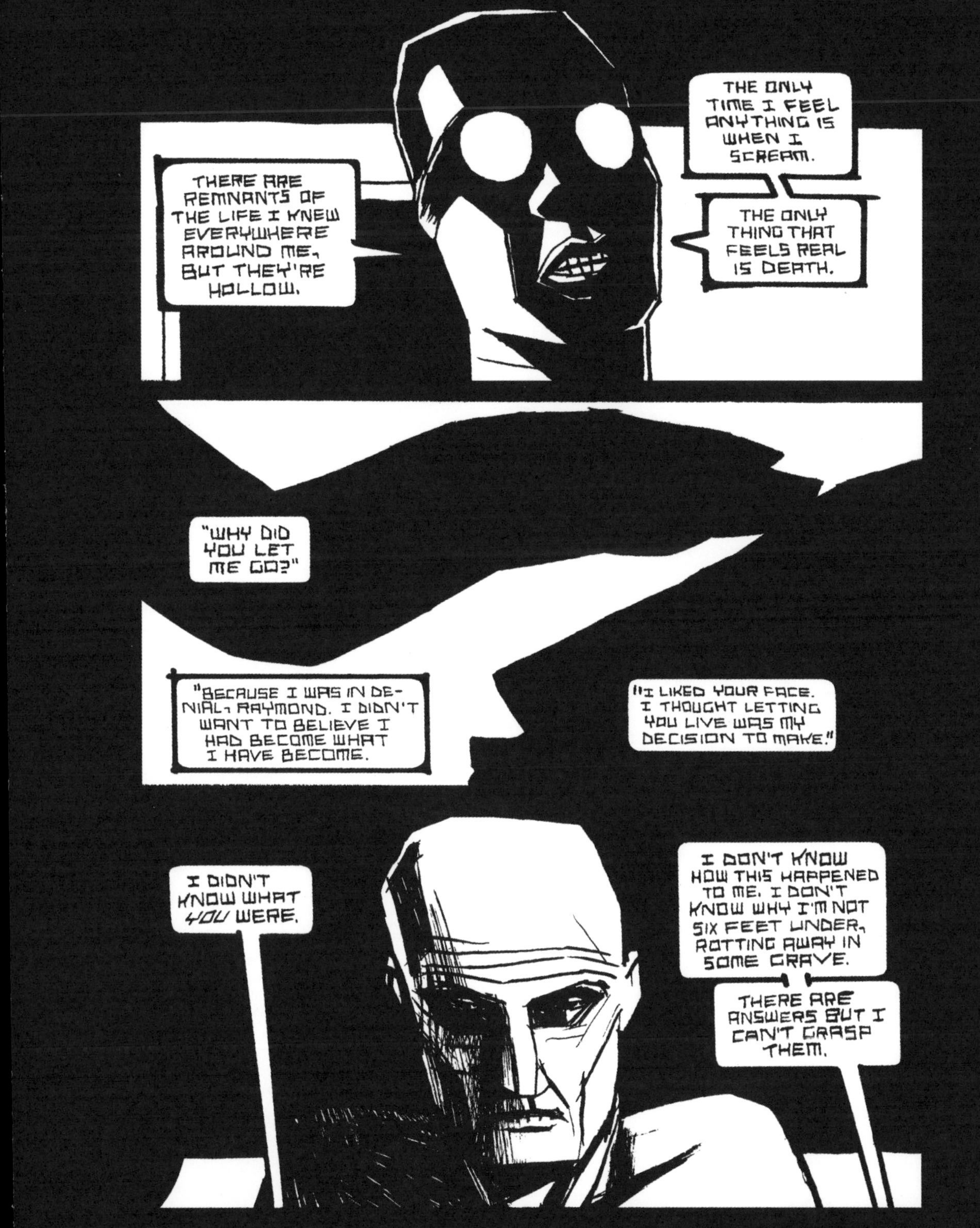
THERE ARE REMNANTS OF THE LIFE I KNEW EVERYWHERE AROUND ME, BUT THEY'RE HOLLOW.
THE ONLY TIME I FEEL ANYTHING IS WHEN I SCREAM.
THE ONLY THING THAT FEELS REAL IS DEATH.
"WHY DID YOU LET ME GO?"
"BECAUSE I WAS IN DENIAL, RAYMOND. I DIDN'T WANT TO BELIEVE I HAD BECOME WHAT I HAVE BECOME.
"I LIKED YOUR FACE. I THOUGHT LETTING YOU LIVE WAS MY DECISION TO MAKE."
I DIDN'T KNOW WHAT *YOU* WERE.
I DON'T KNOW HOW THIS HAPPENED TO ME. I DON'T KNOW WHY I'M NOT SIX FEET UNDER, ROTTING AWAY IN SOME GRAVE.
THERE ARE ANSWERS BUT I CAN'T GRASP THEM.

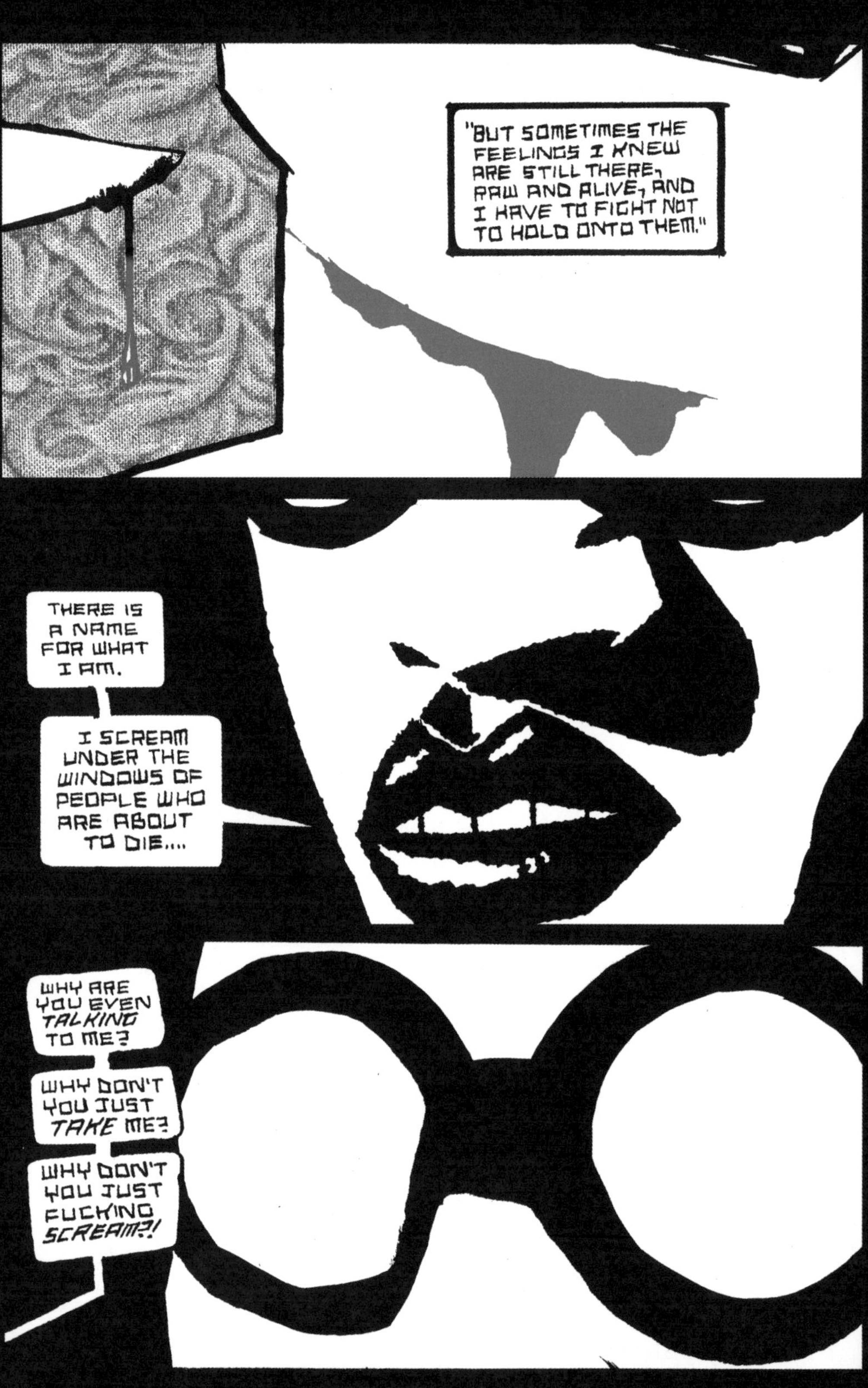
"BUT SOMETIMES THE FEELINGS I KNEW ARE STILL THERE, RAW AND ALIVE, AND I HAVE TO FIGHT NOT TO HOLD ONTO THEM."
THERE IS A NAME FOR WHAT I AM.
I SCREAM UNDER THE *WINDOWS* OF PEOPLE WHO ARE ABOUT TO DIE....
WHY ARE YOU EVEN *TALKING* TO ME?
WHY DON'T YOU JUST *TAKE* ME?
WHY DON'T YOU JUST FUCKING *SCREAM?!*

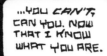

...YOU *CAN'T,* CAN YOU, NOW THAT I KNOW WHAT YOU ARE.

YOU NEED ME TO *AGREE* TO HEAR YOU—

RAYMOND, DO YOU THINK YOU'RE GOING TO LIVE FOREVER?

IF NOT ME, NEXT TIME IT WILL BE SOMEONE ELSE, AND I ASSURE YOU, SHE WON'T BE TOUCHING YOUR FACE.

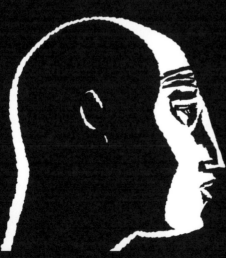

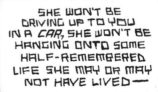

SHE WON'T BE DRIVING UP TO YOU IN A *CAR,* SHE WON'T BE HANGING ONTO SOME HALF-REMEMBERED LIFE SHE MAY OR MAY NOT HAVE LIVED—

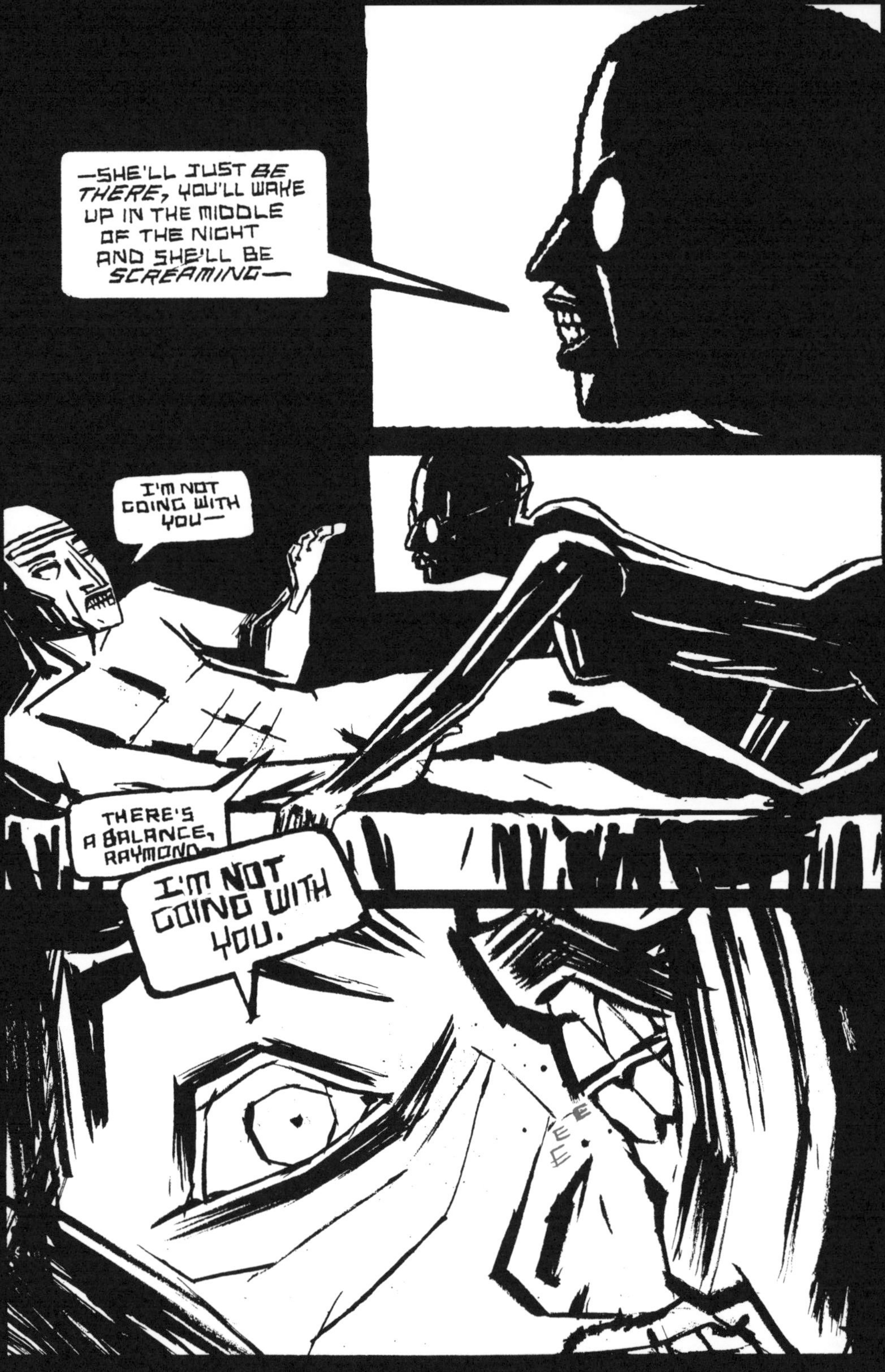
—SHE'LL JUST *BE THERE*, YOU'LL WAKE UP IN THE MIDDLE OF THE NIGHT AND SHE'LL BE *SCREAMING*—
I'M NOT GOING WITH YOU—
THERE'S A BALANCE, RAYMOND—
I'M NOT GOING WITH YOU.
EEE

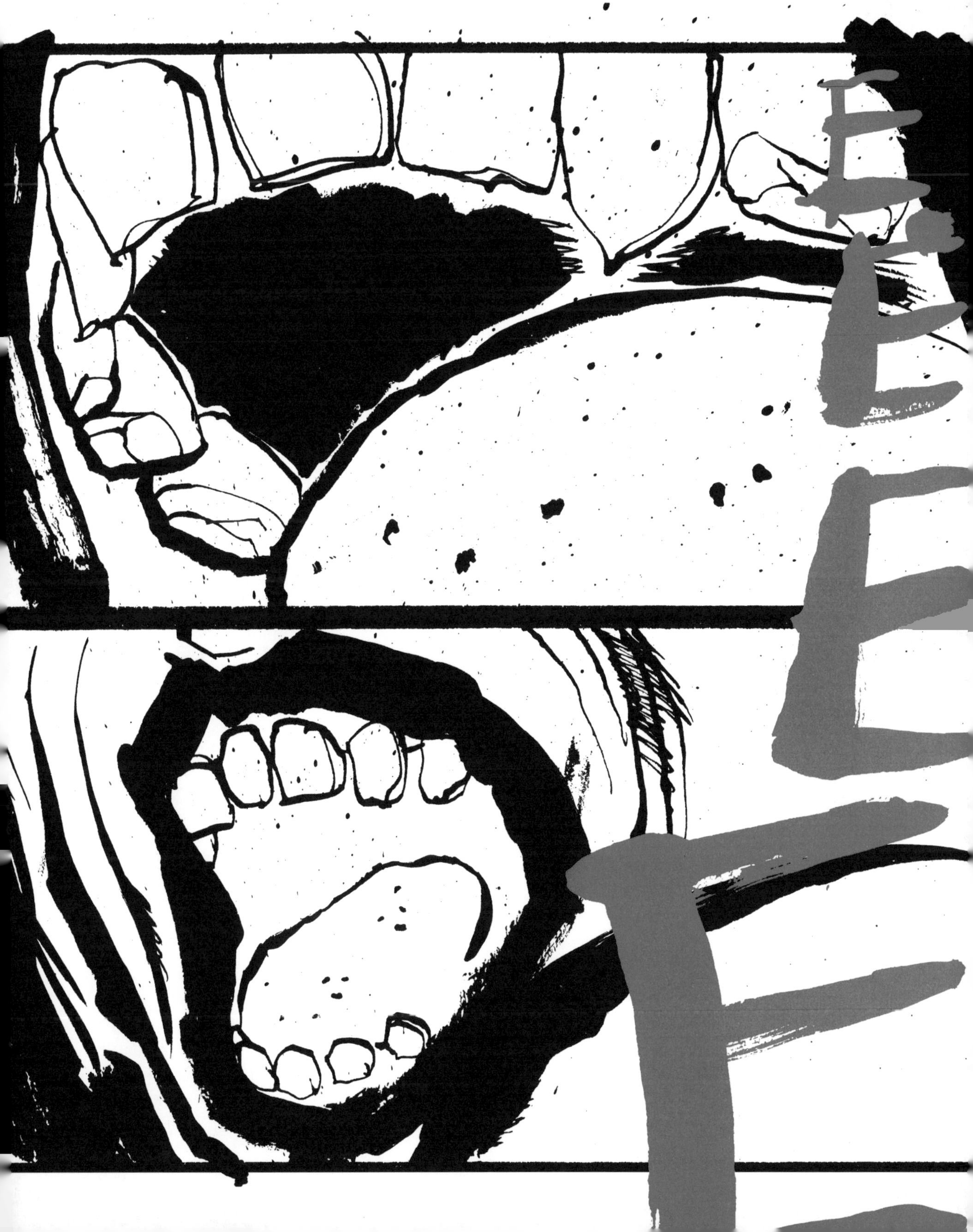
EEEEEE

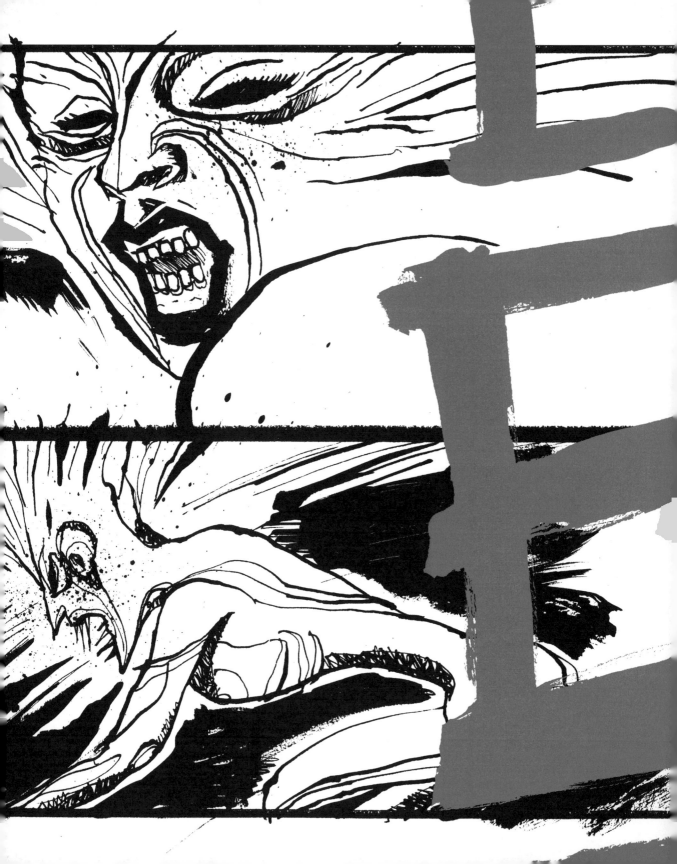

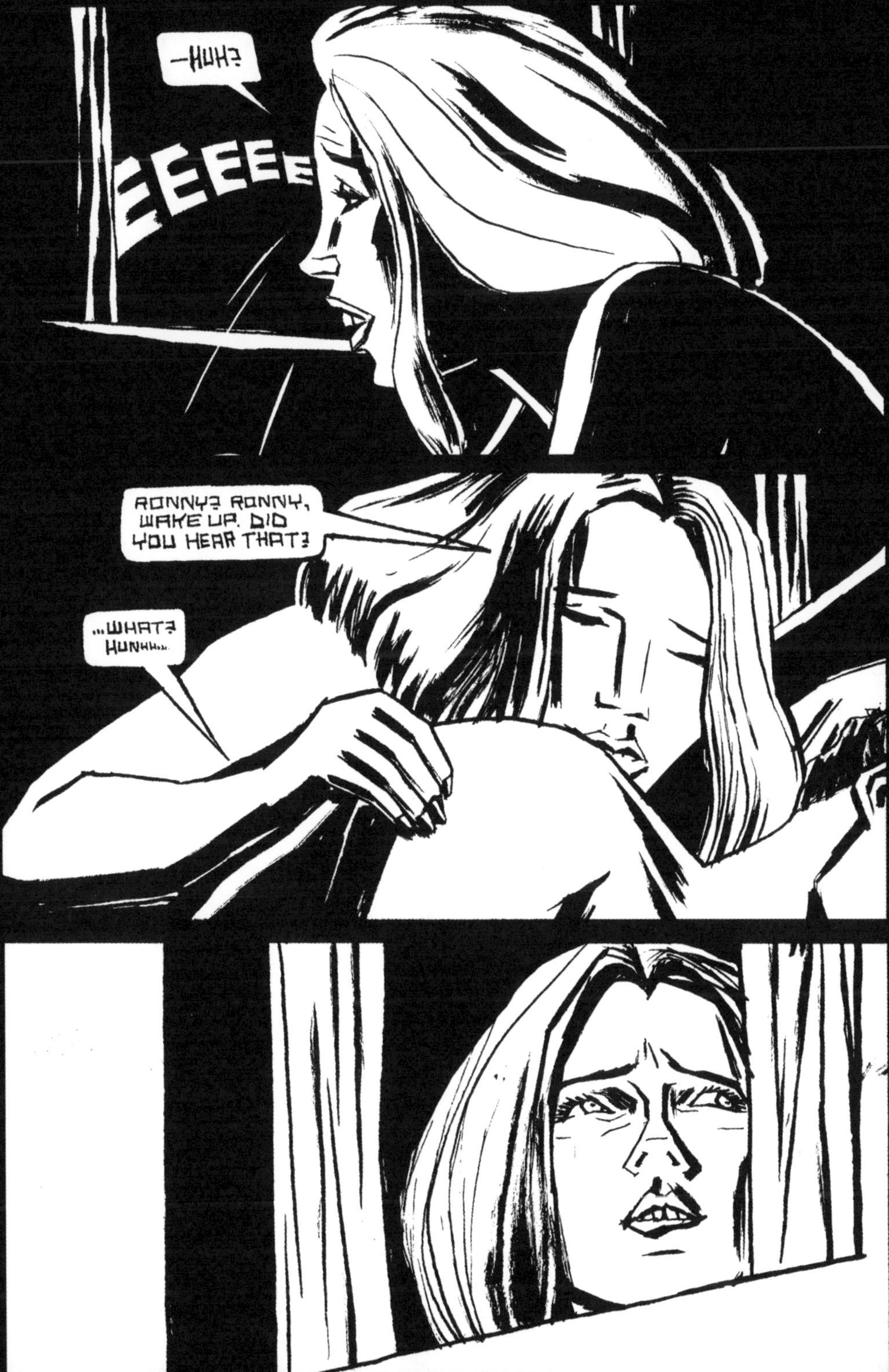
—HUH?
EEEEE
RONNY? RONNY, WAKE UP. DID YOU HEAR THAT?
...WHAT? HUNH...

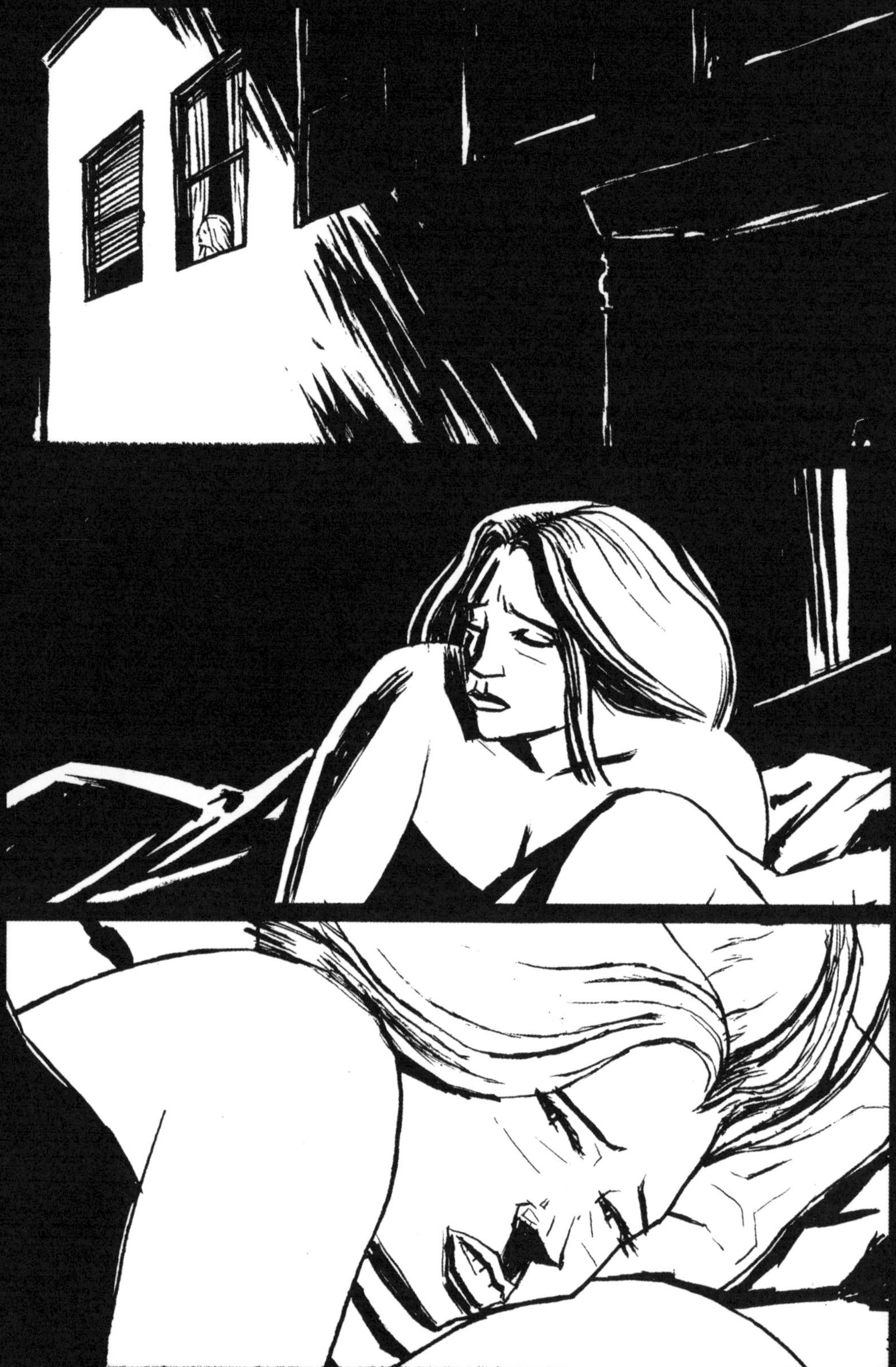

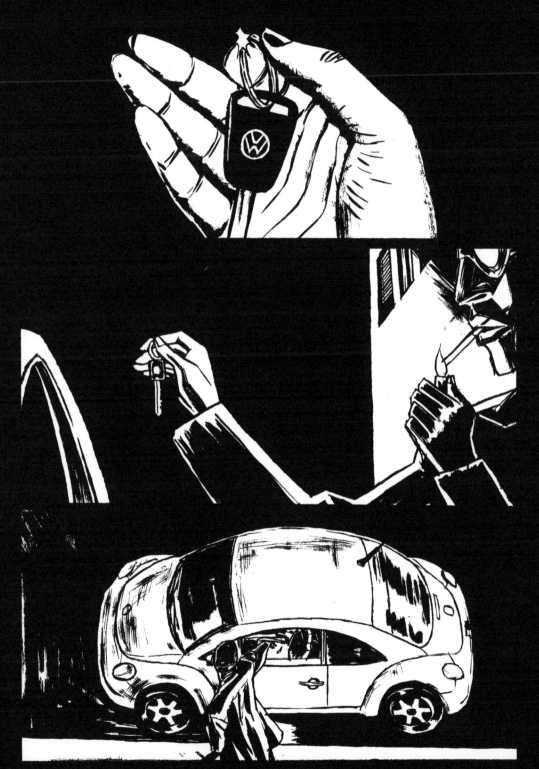

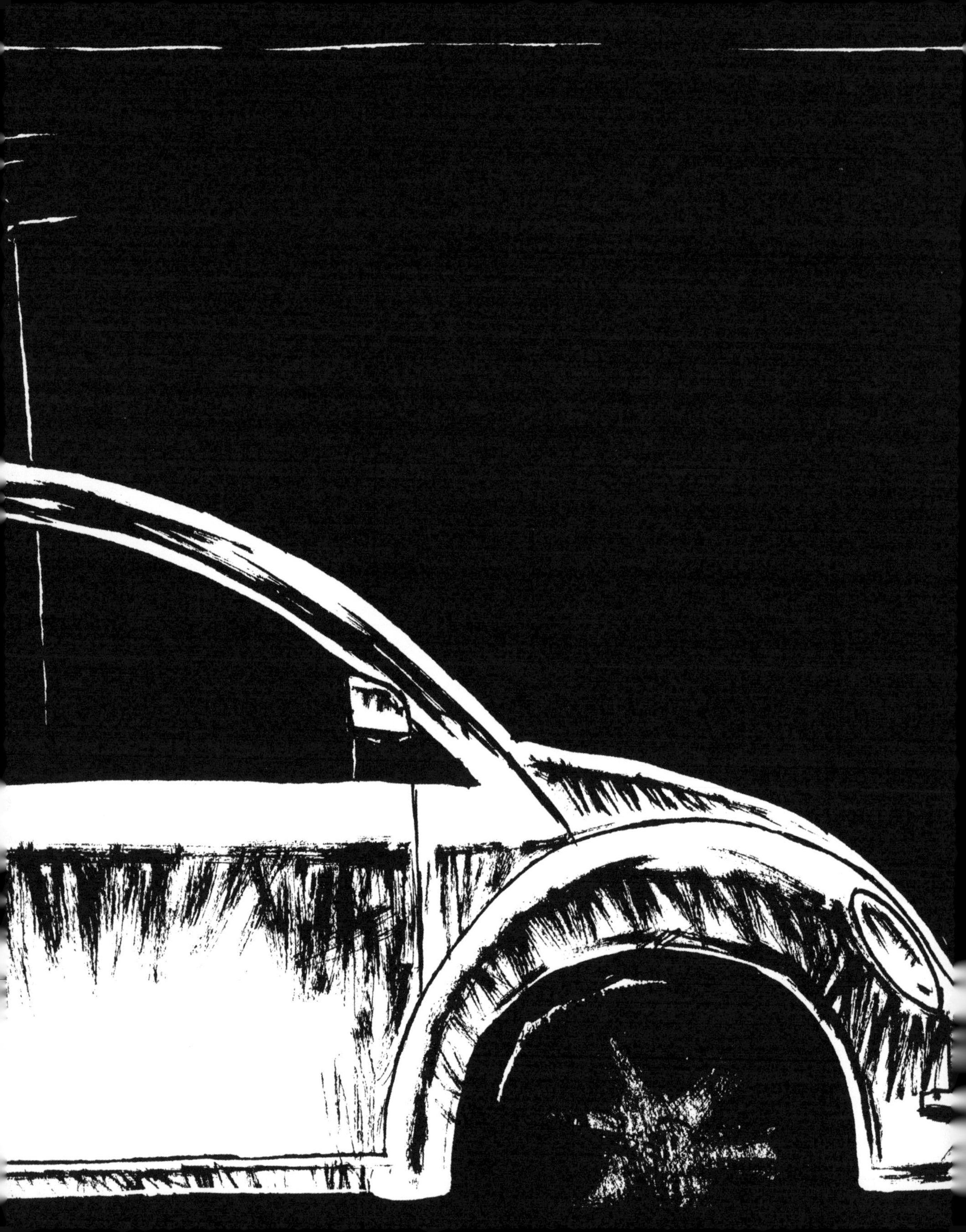

WHO AM I?
HOW DID
I COME TO BE?

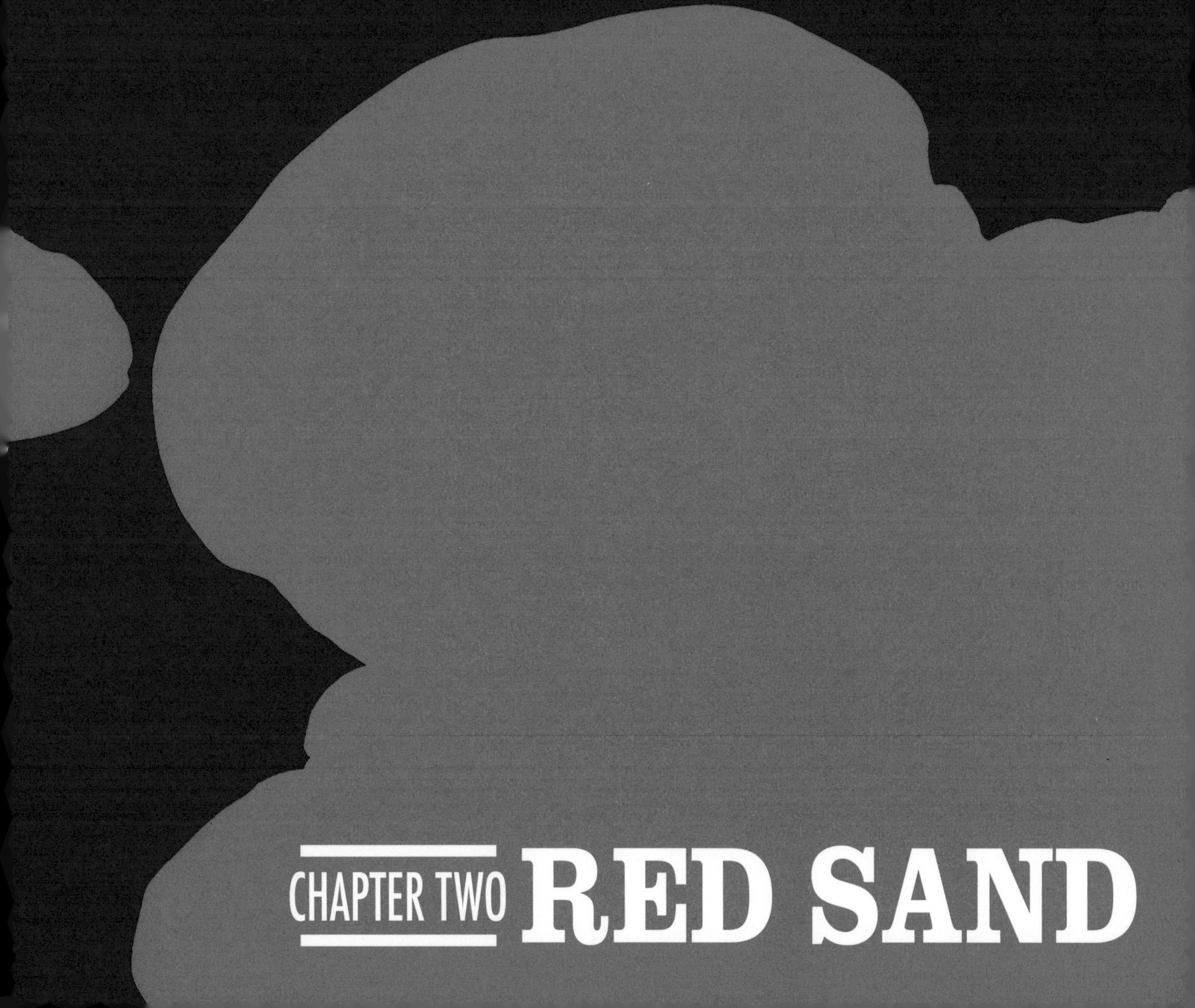

# CHAPTER TWO RED SAND

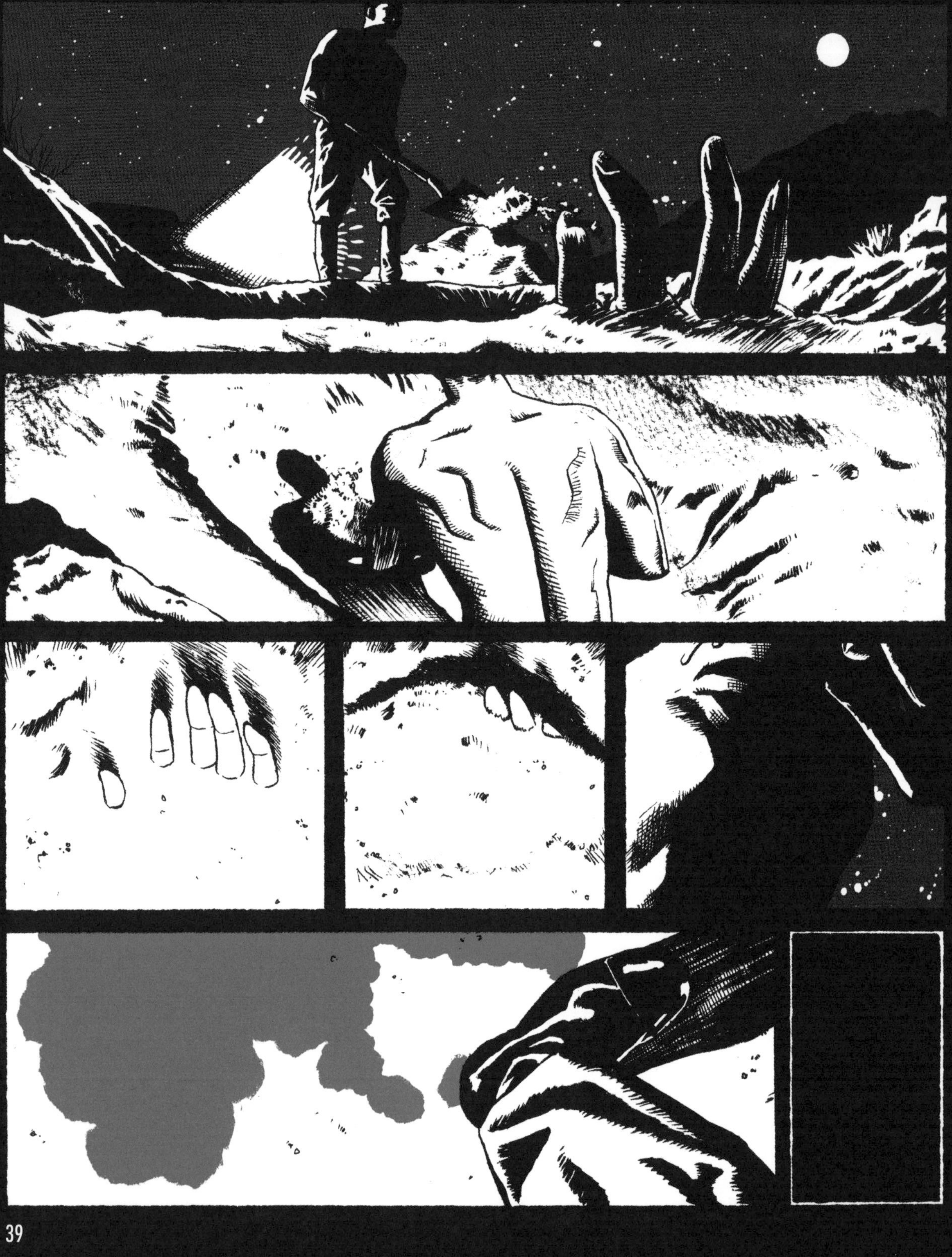

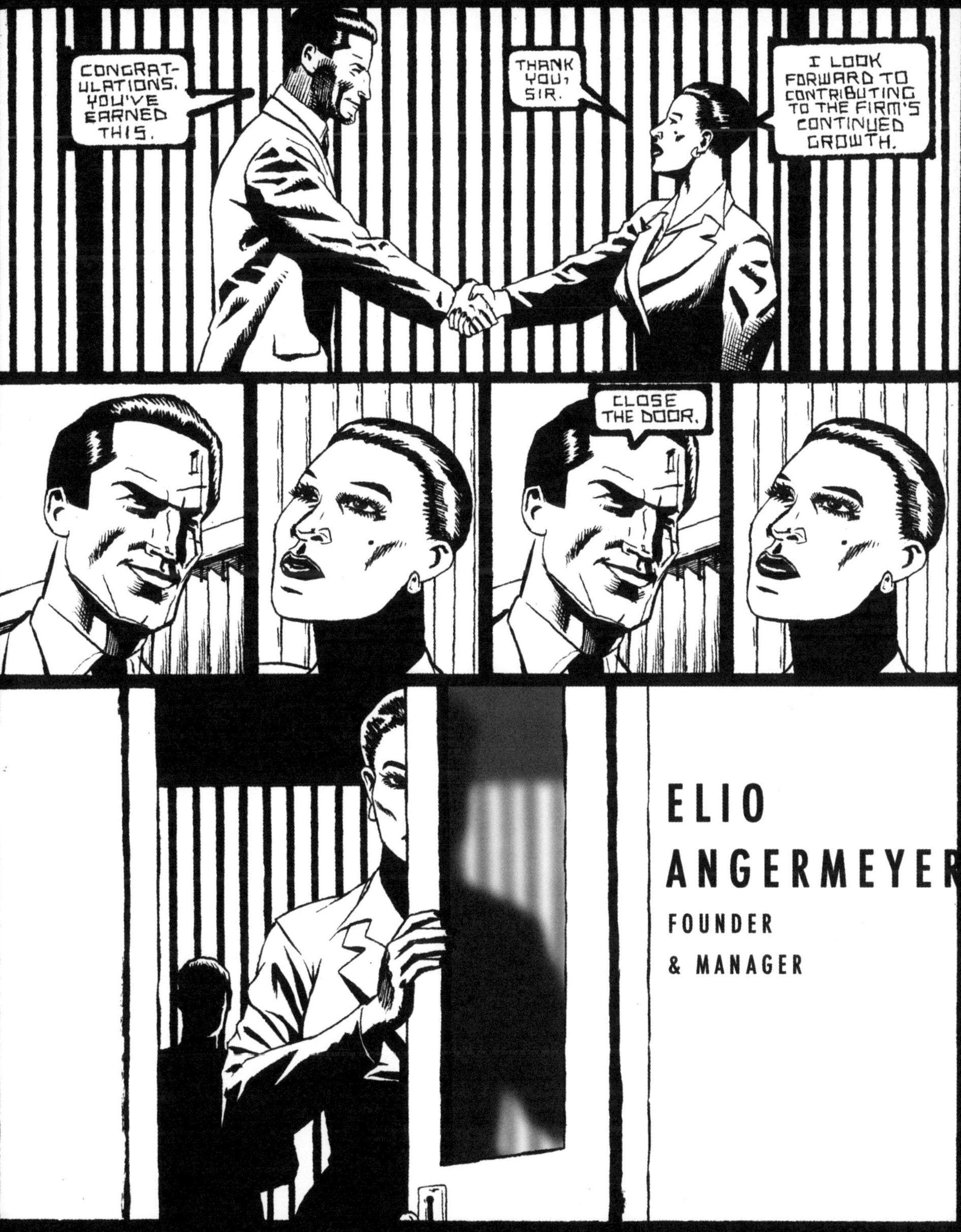
CONGRAT-ULATIONS. YOU'VE EARNED THIS.
THANK YOU, SIR.
I LOOK FORWARD TO CONTRIBUTING TO THE FIRM'S CONTINUED GROWTH.
CLOSE THE DOOR.
ELIO ANGERMEYER
FOUNDER
& MANAGER

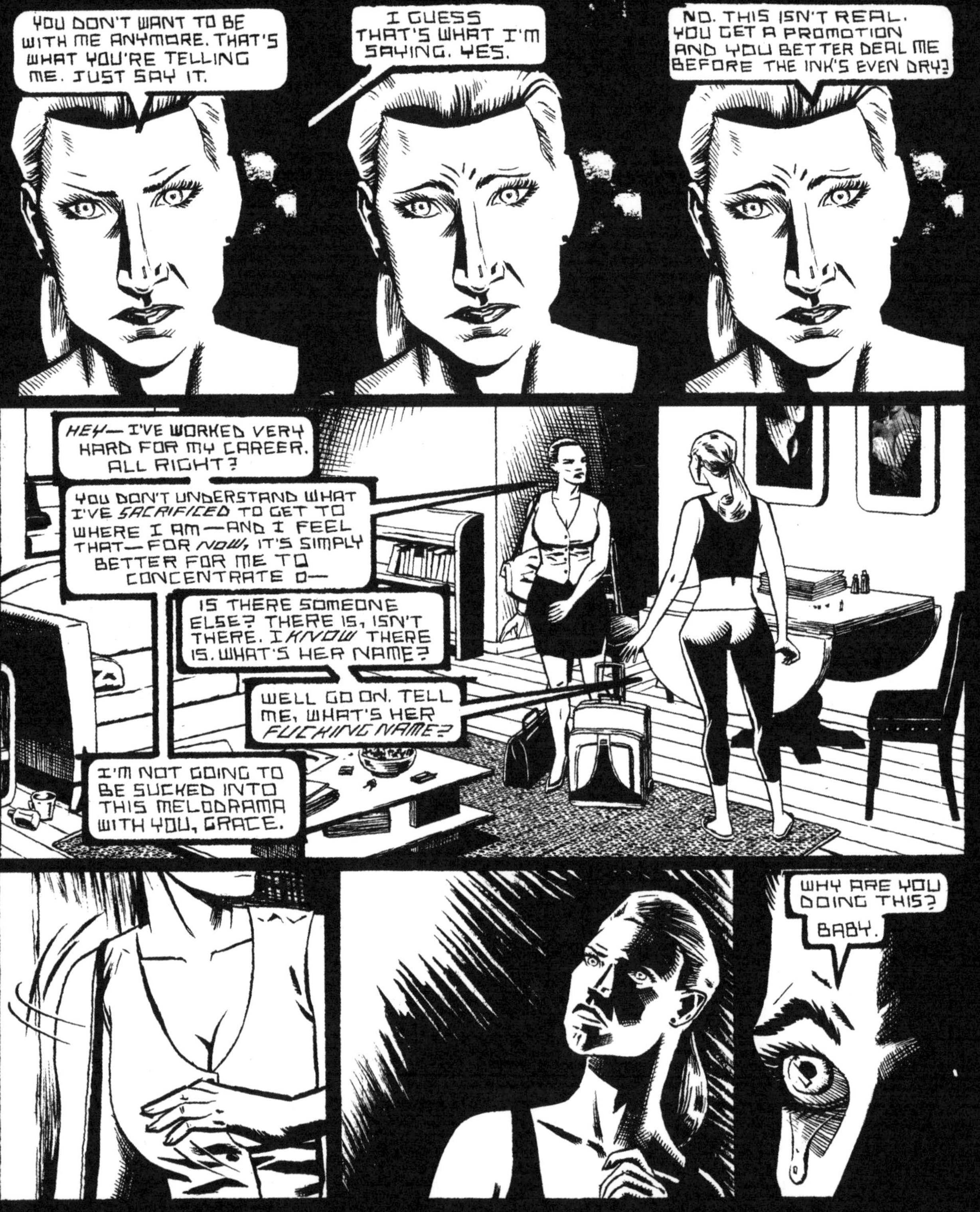
YOU DON'T WANT TO BE WITH ME ANYMORE. THAT'S WHAT YOU'RE TELLING ME. JUST SAY IT.
I GUESS THAT'S WHAT I'M SAYING. YES.
NO. THIS ISN'T REAL. YOU GET A PROMOTION AND YOU BETTER DEAL ME BEFORE THE INK'S EVEN DRY?
HEY— I'VE WORKED VERY HARD FOR MY CAREER. ALL RIGHT?
YOU DON'T UNDERSTAND WHAT I'VE SACRIFICED TO GET TO WHERE I AM —AND I FEEL THAT— FOR NOW, IT'S SIMPLY BETTER FOR ME TO CONCENTRATE O—
IS THERE SOMEONE ELSE? THERE IS, ISN'T THERE. I KNOW THERE IS. WHAT'S HER NAME?
WELL GO ON. TELL ME, WHAT'S HER FUCKING NAME?
I'M NOT GOING TO BE SUCKED INTO THIS MELODRAMA WITH YOU, GRACE.
WHY ARE YOU DOING THIS?
BABY.

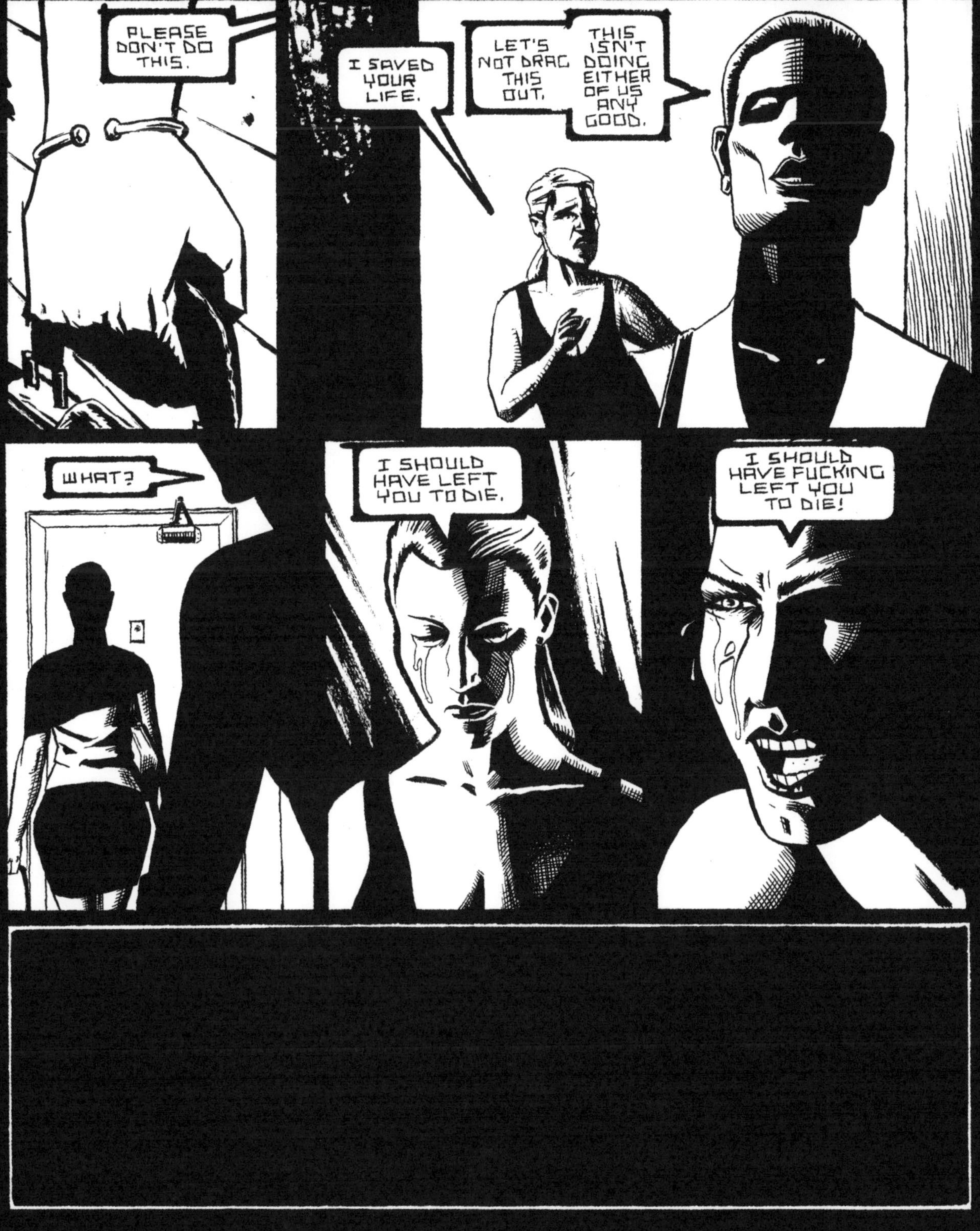
PLEASE DON'T DO THIS.
I SAVED YOUR LIFE.
LET'S NOT DRAG THIS OUT.
THIS ISN'T DOING EITHER OF US ANY GOOD.
WHAT?
I SHOULD HAVE LEFT YOU TO DIE.
I SHOULD HAVE FUCKING LEFT YOU TO DIE!

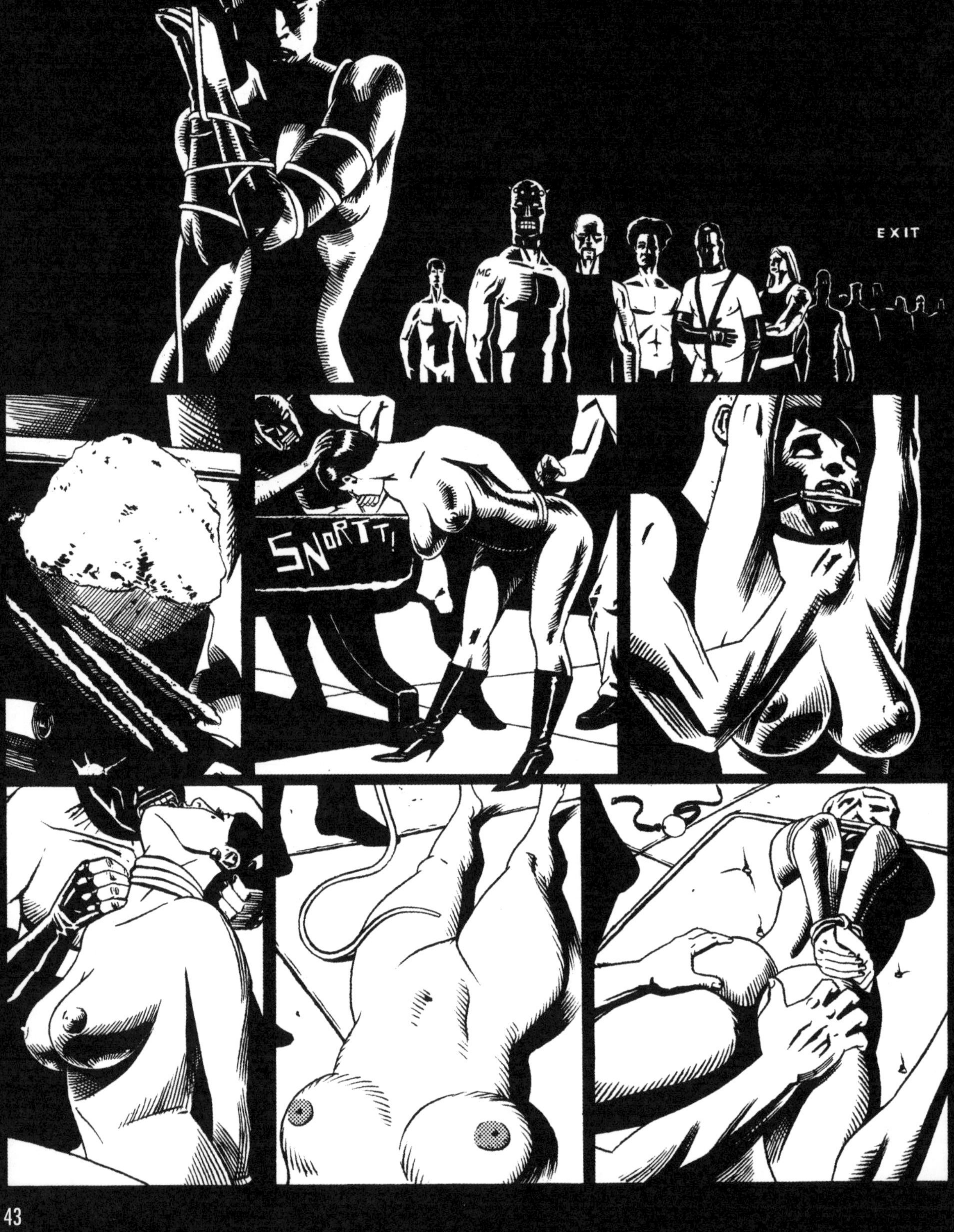
EXIT
SNORTT!

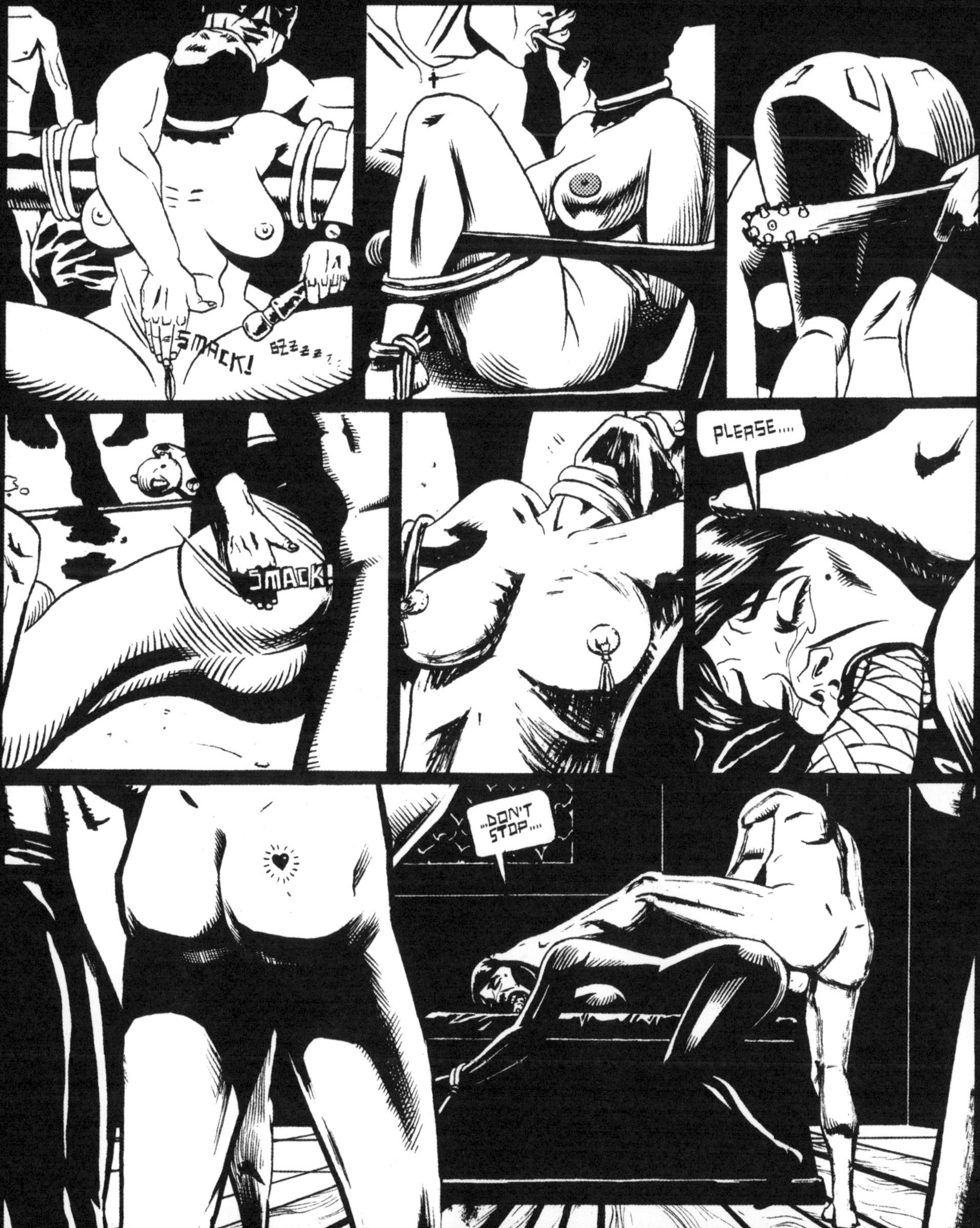
SMACK!
BZZzzz..
SMACK!
PLEASE....
...DON'T STOP....

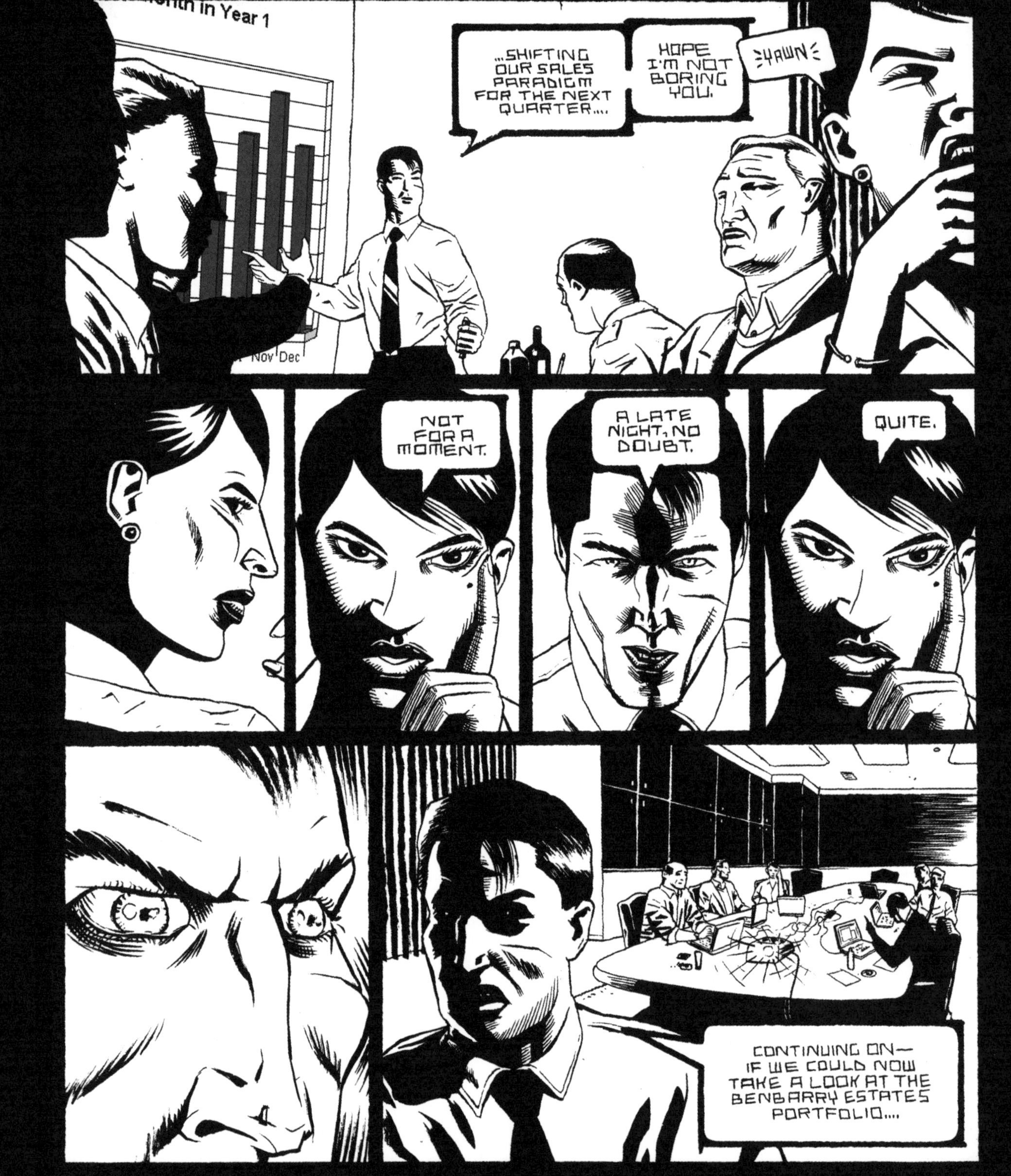

...onth in Year 1
Nov Dec
...SHIFTING OUR SALES PARADIGM FOR THE NEXT QUARTER....
HOPE I'M NOT BORING YOU.
YAWN
NOT FOR A MOMENT.
A LATE NIGHT, NO DOUBT.
QUITE.
CONTINUING ON— IF WE COULD NOW TAKE A LOOK AT THE BENBARRY ESTATES PORTFOLIO....

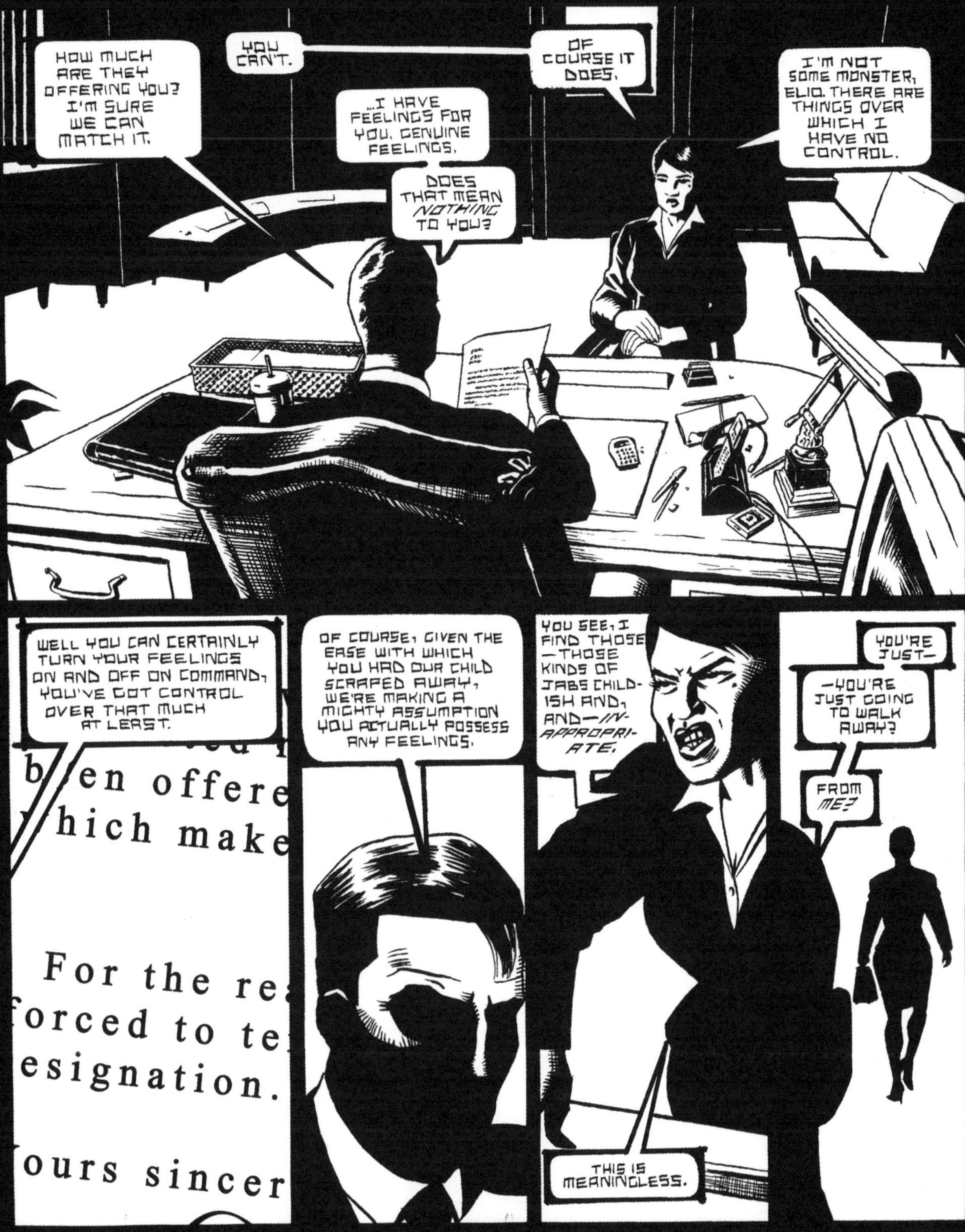
HOW MUCH ARE THEY OFFERING YOU? I'M SURE WE CAN MATCH IT.
YOU CAN'T.
...I HAVE FEELINGS FOR YOU, GENUINE FEELINGS.
DOES THAT MEAN *NOTHING* TO YOU?
OF COURSE IT DOES.
I'M NOT SOME MONSTER, ELIO. THERE ARE THINGS OVER WHICH I HAVE NO CONTROL.
WELL YOU CAN CERTAINLY TURN YOUR FEELINGS ON AND OFF ON COMMAND, YOU'VE GOT CONTROL OVER THAT MUCH AT LEAST.
b/en offere
/hich make
For the re
forced to te
esignation.
ours sincer
OF COURSE, GIVEN THE EASE WITH WHICH YOU HAD OUR CHILD SCRAPED AWAY, WE'RE MAKING A MIGHTY ASSUMPTION YOU ACTUALLY POSSESS ANY FEELINGS.
YOU SEE, I FIND THOSE —THOSE KINDS OF JABS CHILDISH AND, AND—*INAPPROPRIATE.*
THIS IS MEANINGLESS.
YOU'RE JUST—
—YOU'RE JUST GOING TO WALK AWAY?
FROM *ME?*

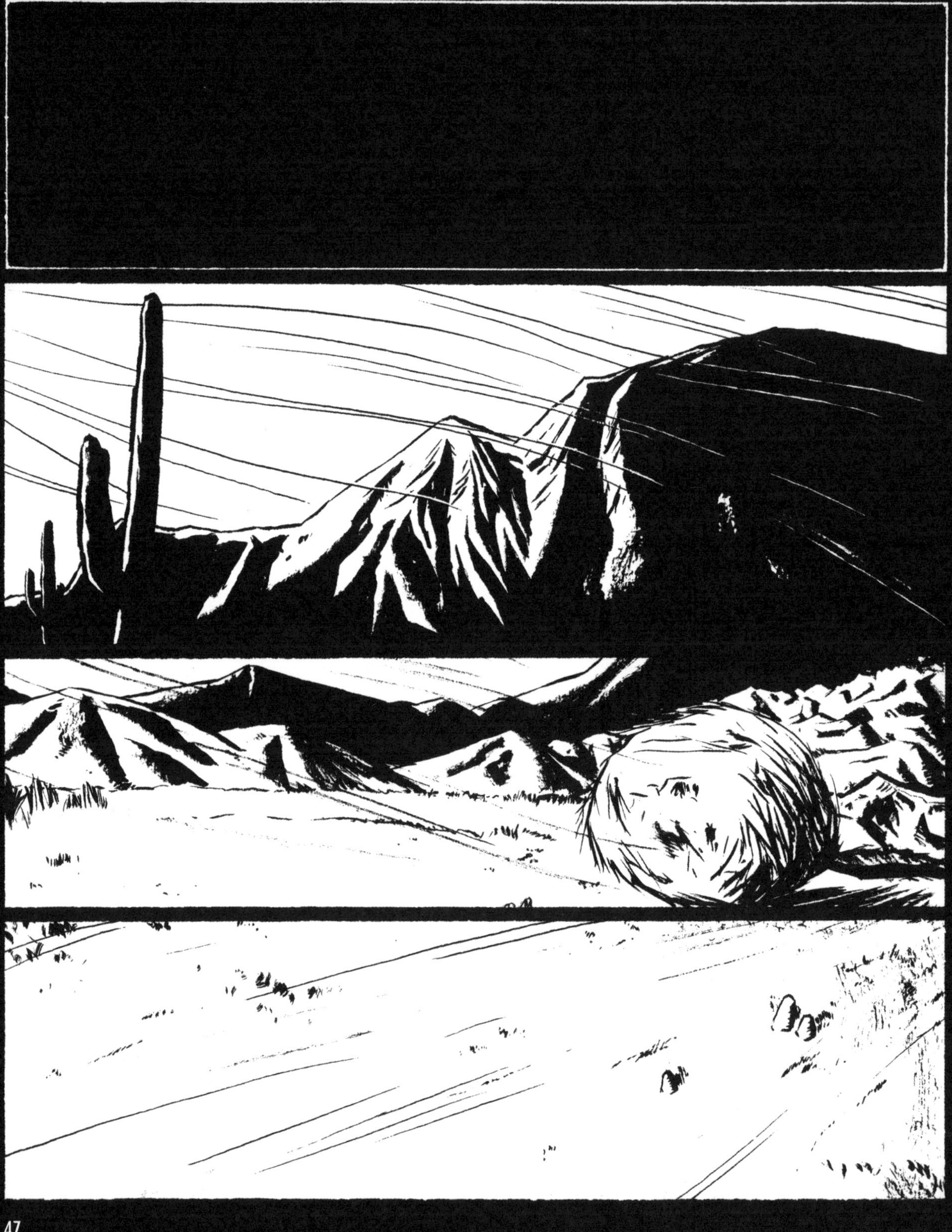

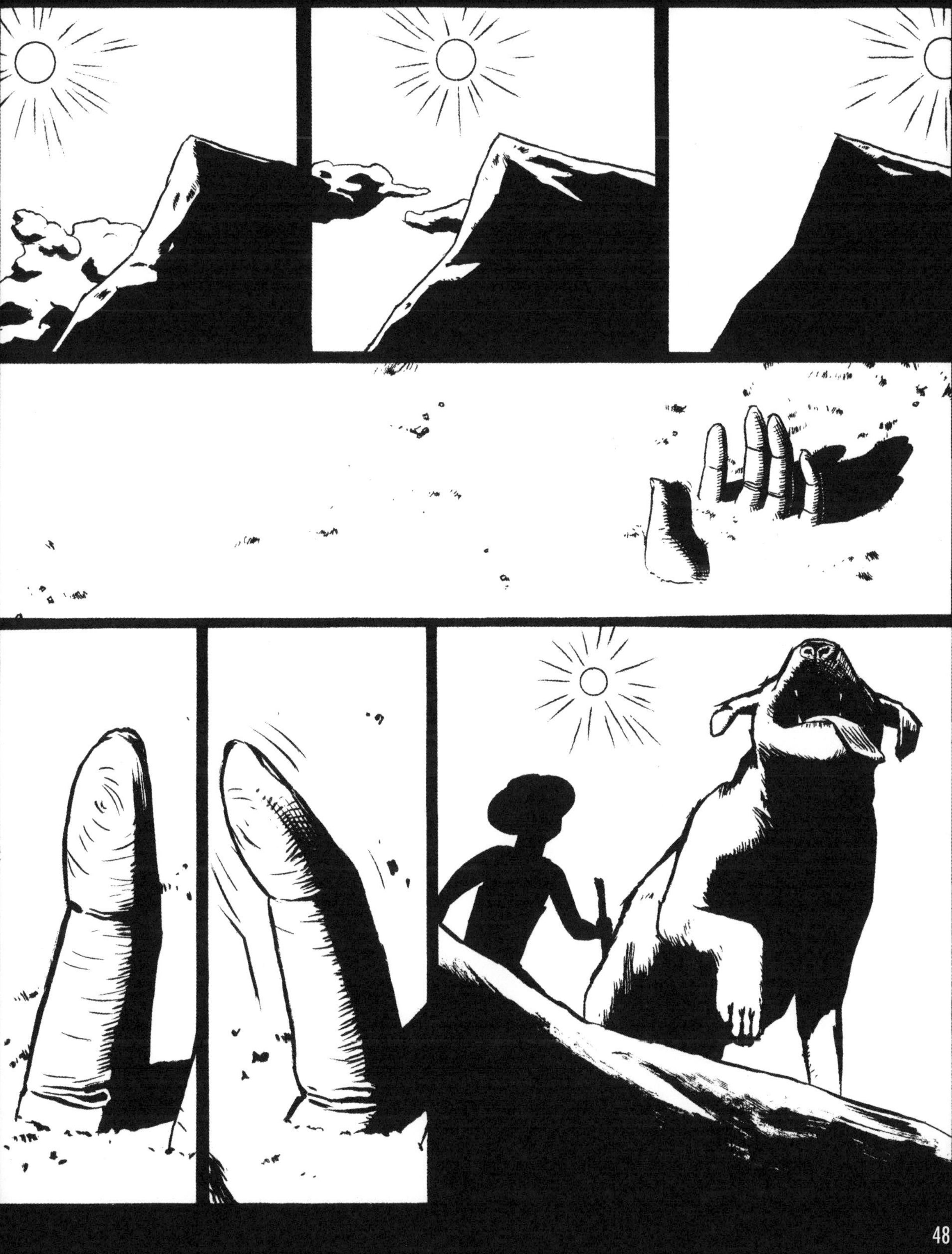

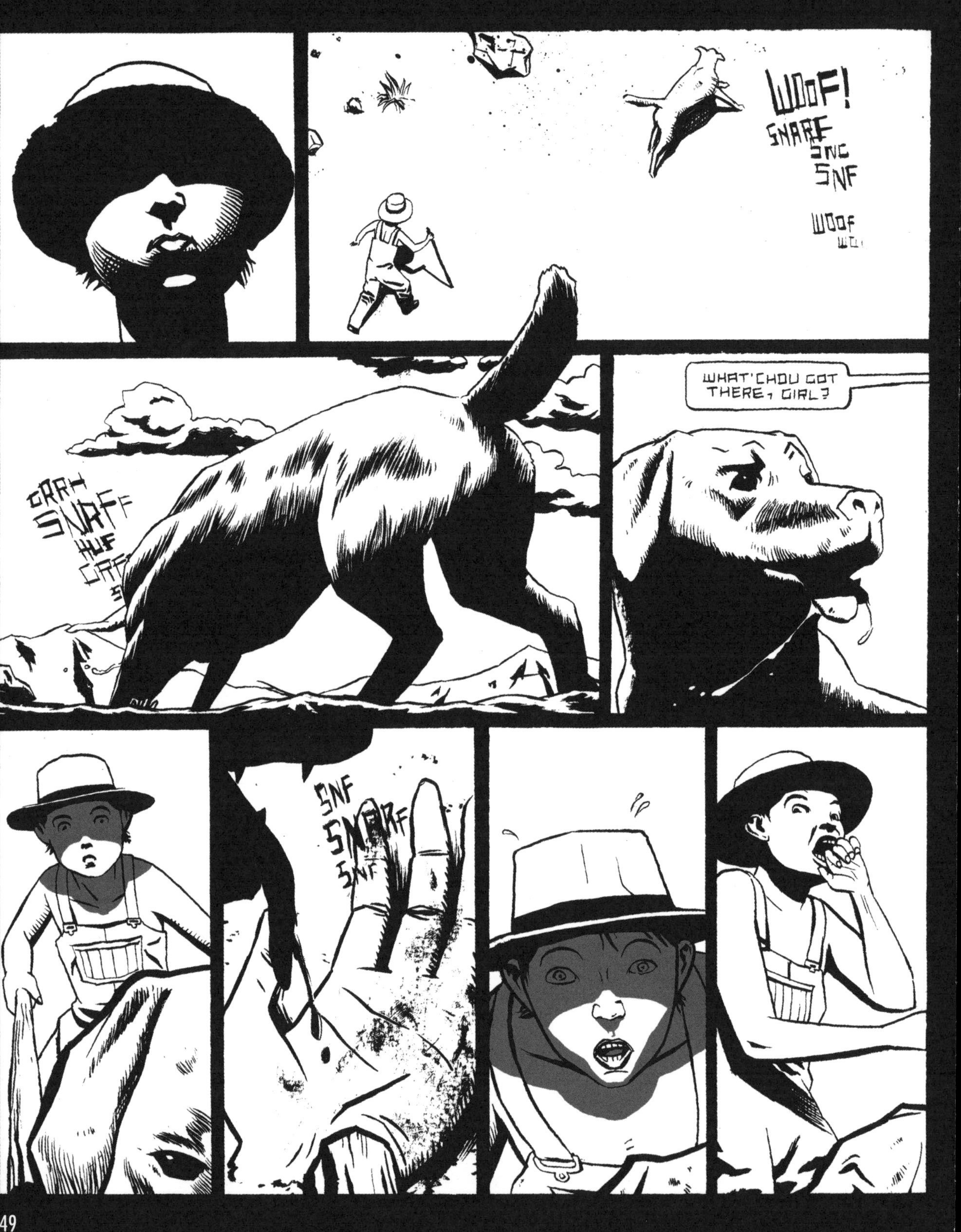
WOOF!
SNARF
SNG
SNF
WOOF
WHAT'CHOU GOT THERE, GIRL?
GRRH
SNARFF
HUF
SNF
SNARF
SNF

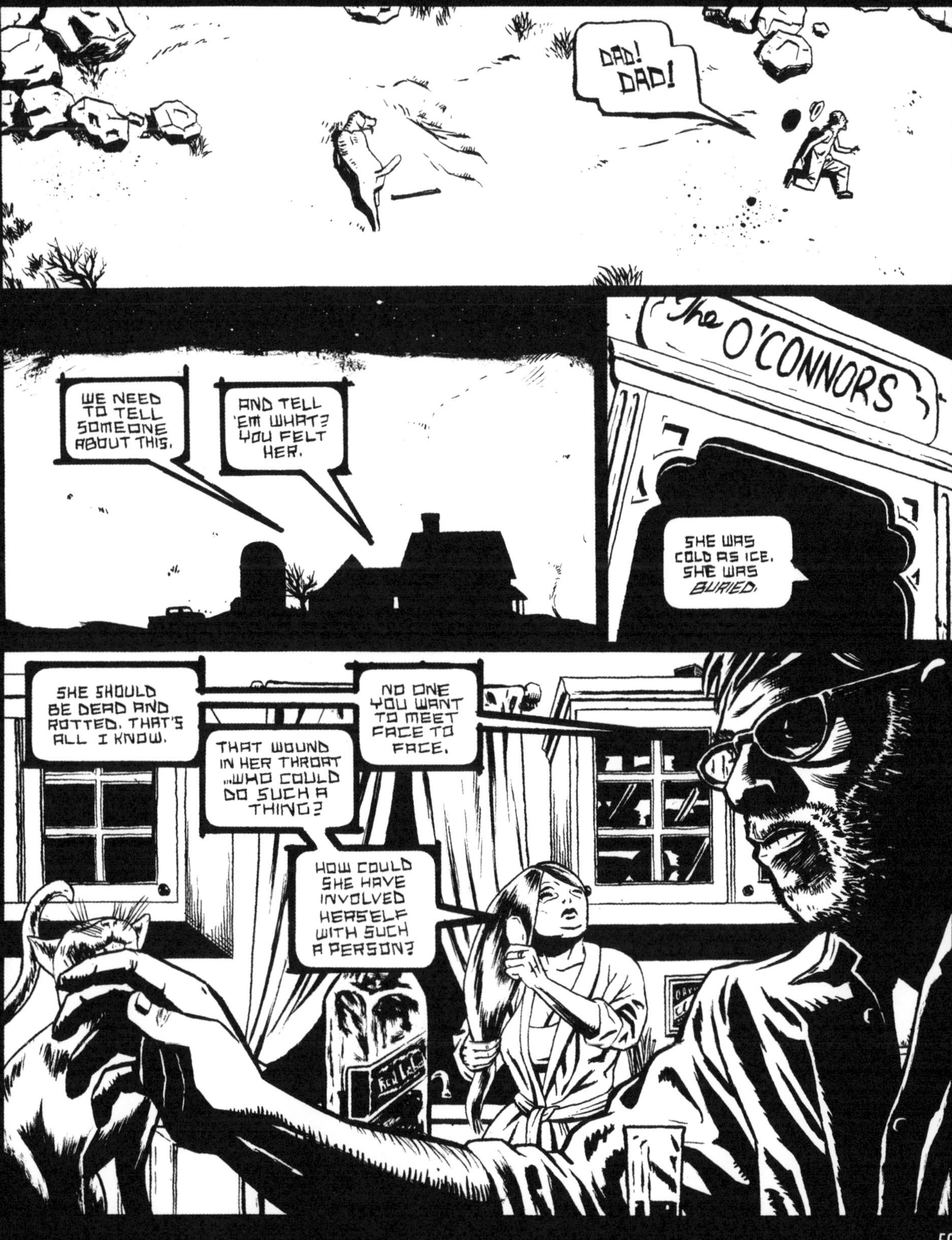
DAD! DAD!
WE NEED TO TELL SOMEONE ABOUT THIS.
AND TELL 'EM WHAT? YOU FELT HER.
The O'CONNORS
SHE WAS COLD AS ICE. SHE WAS BURIED.
SHE SHOULD BE DEAD AND ROTTED. THAT'S ALL I KNOW.
NO ONE YOU WANT TO MEET FACE TO FACE.
THAT WOUND IN HER THROAT ...WHO COULD DO SUCH A THING?
HOW COULD SHE HAVE INVOLVED HERSELF WITH SUCH A PERSON?

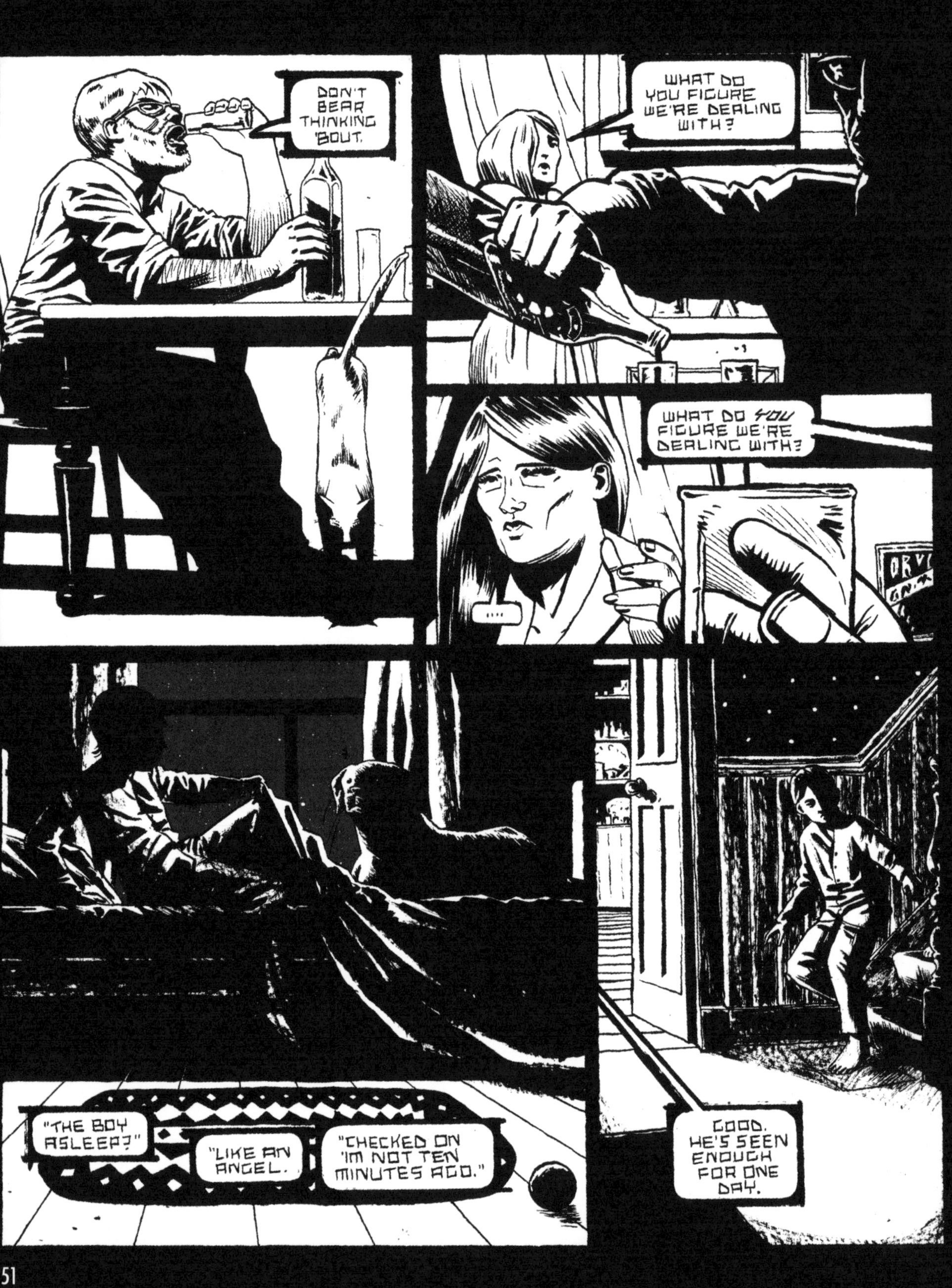
DON'T BEAR THINKING 'BOUT.
WHAT DO YOU FIGURE WE'RE DEALING WITH?
WHAT DO YOU FIGURE WE'RE DEALING WITH?
....
"THE BOY ASLEEP?"
"LIKE AN ANGEL.
"CHECKED ON 'IM NOT TEN MINUTES AGO."
GOOD. HE'S SEEN ENOUGH FOR ONE DAY.

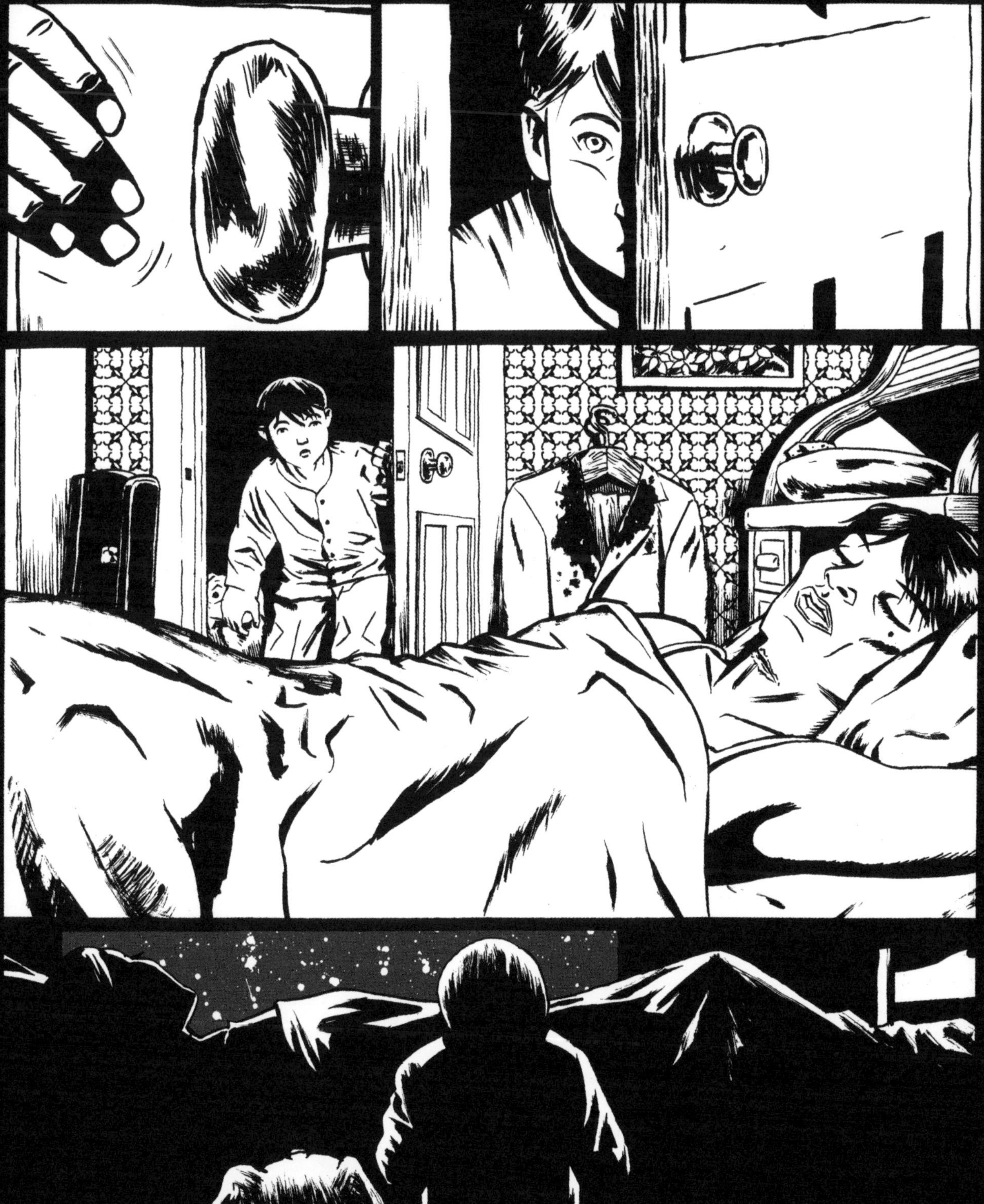

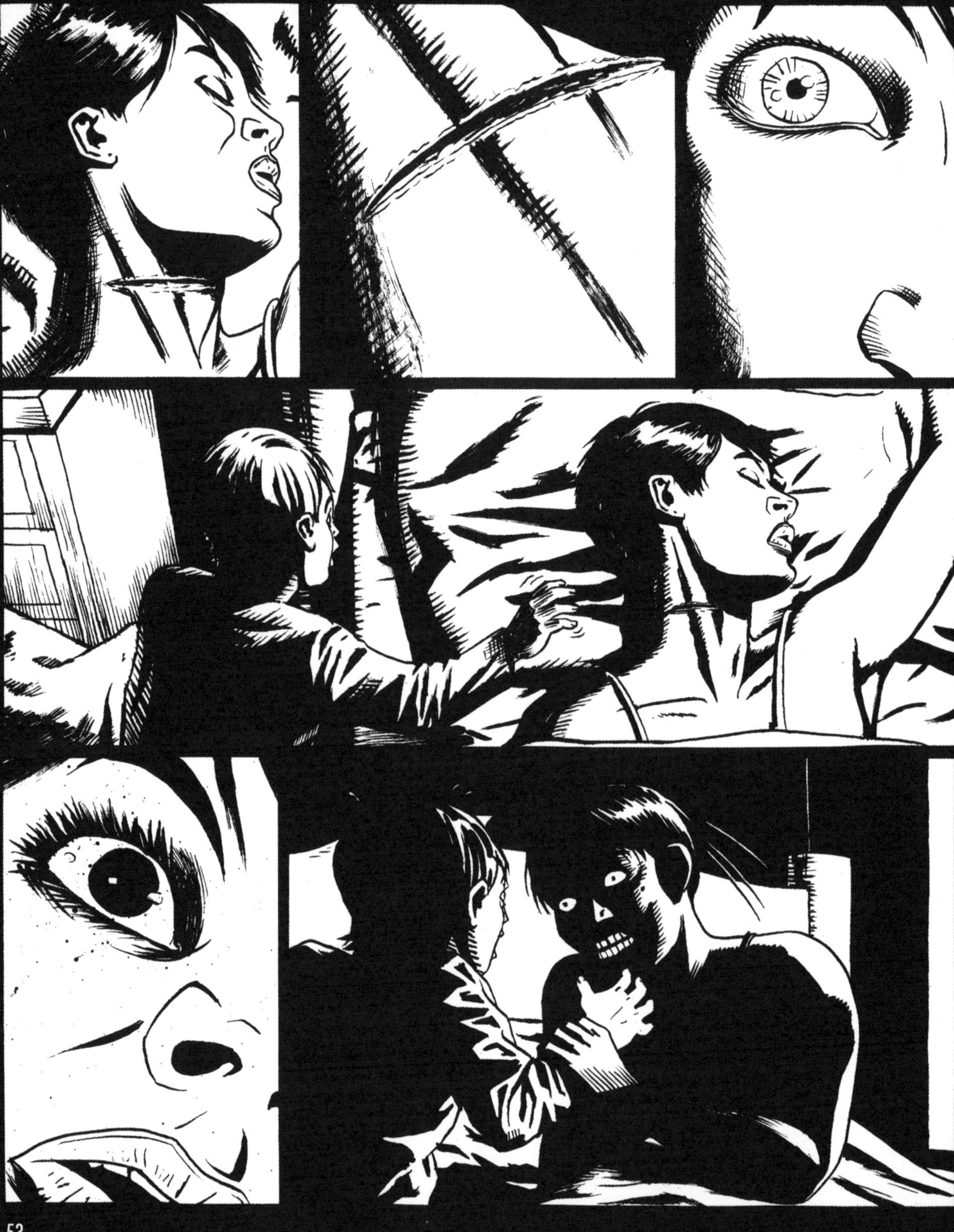

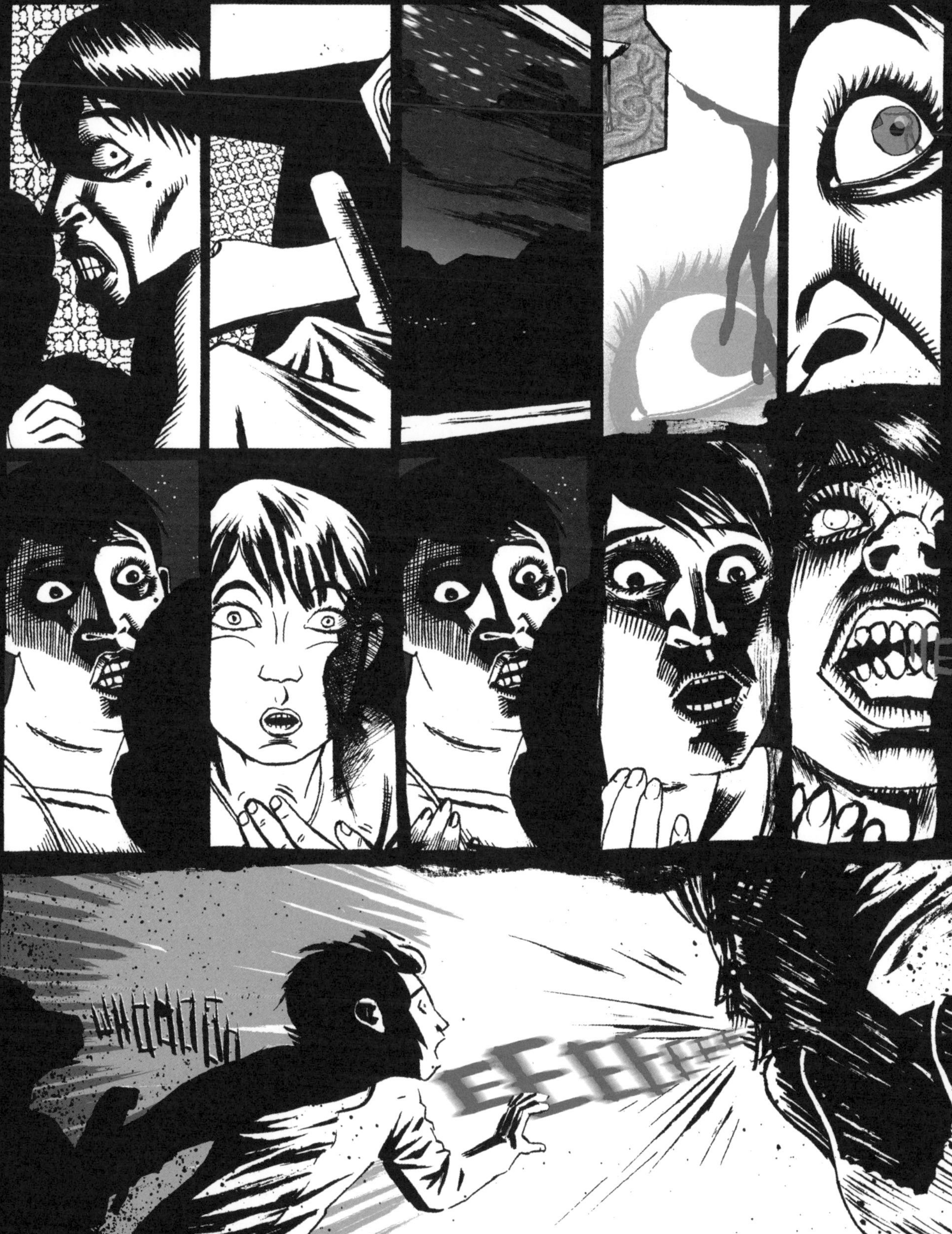
EEE

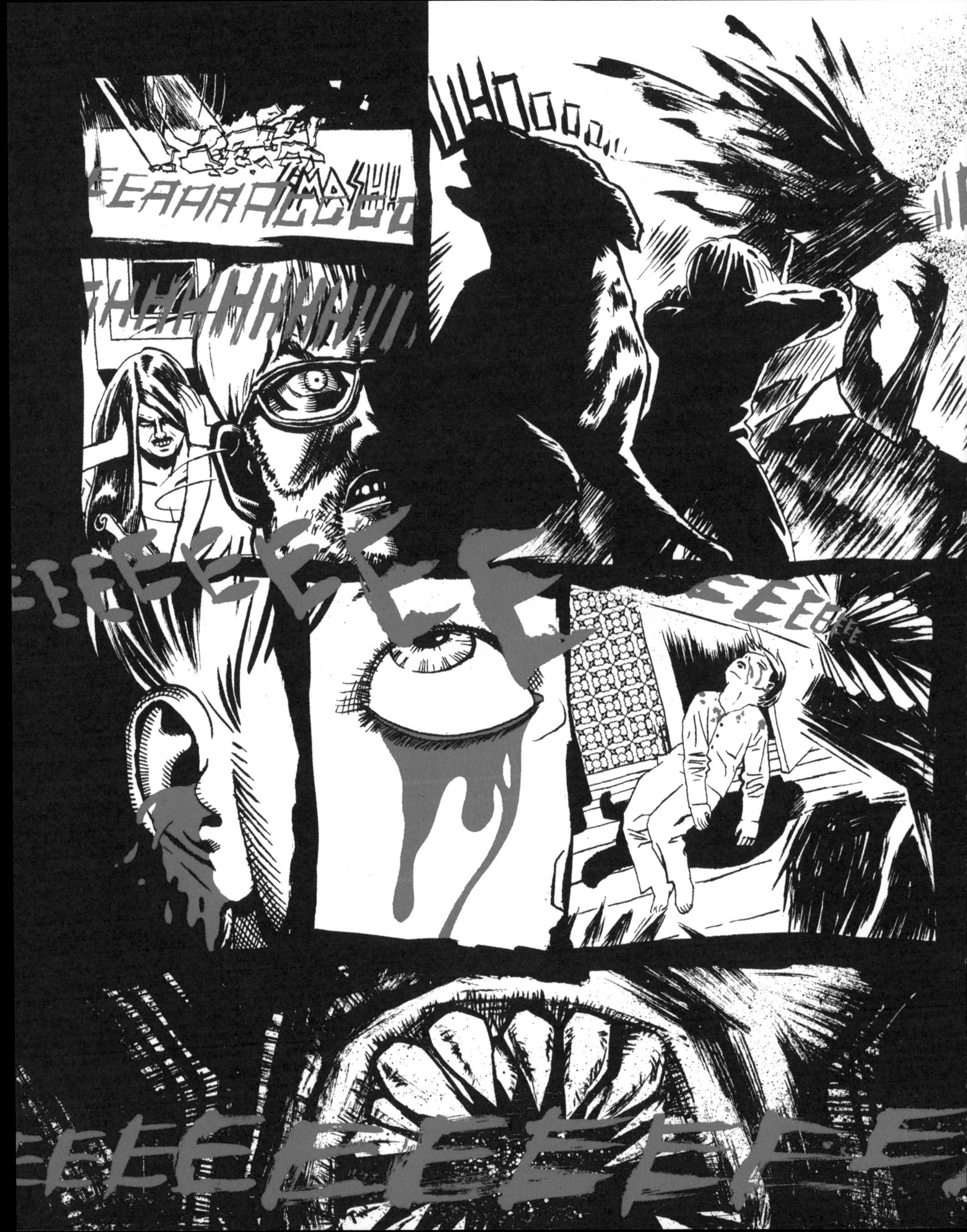
SMASH!!
EEAAARRGGGG
GHHHHHHHH!!!
WHOOOOO..!!
EEEEEEE
EEEEEE
EEEEEEEEEE

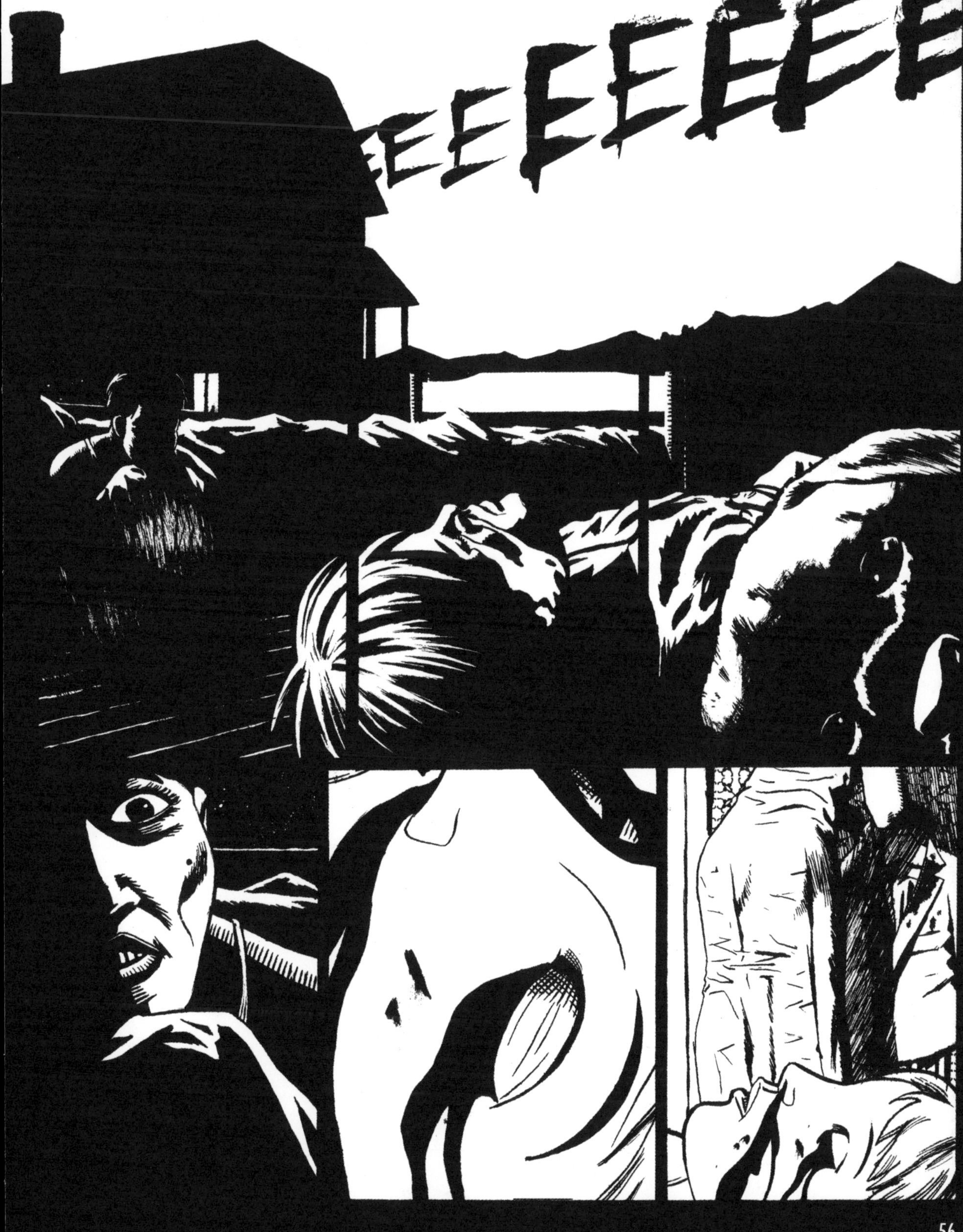
EEEEEEEEEEE

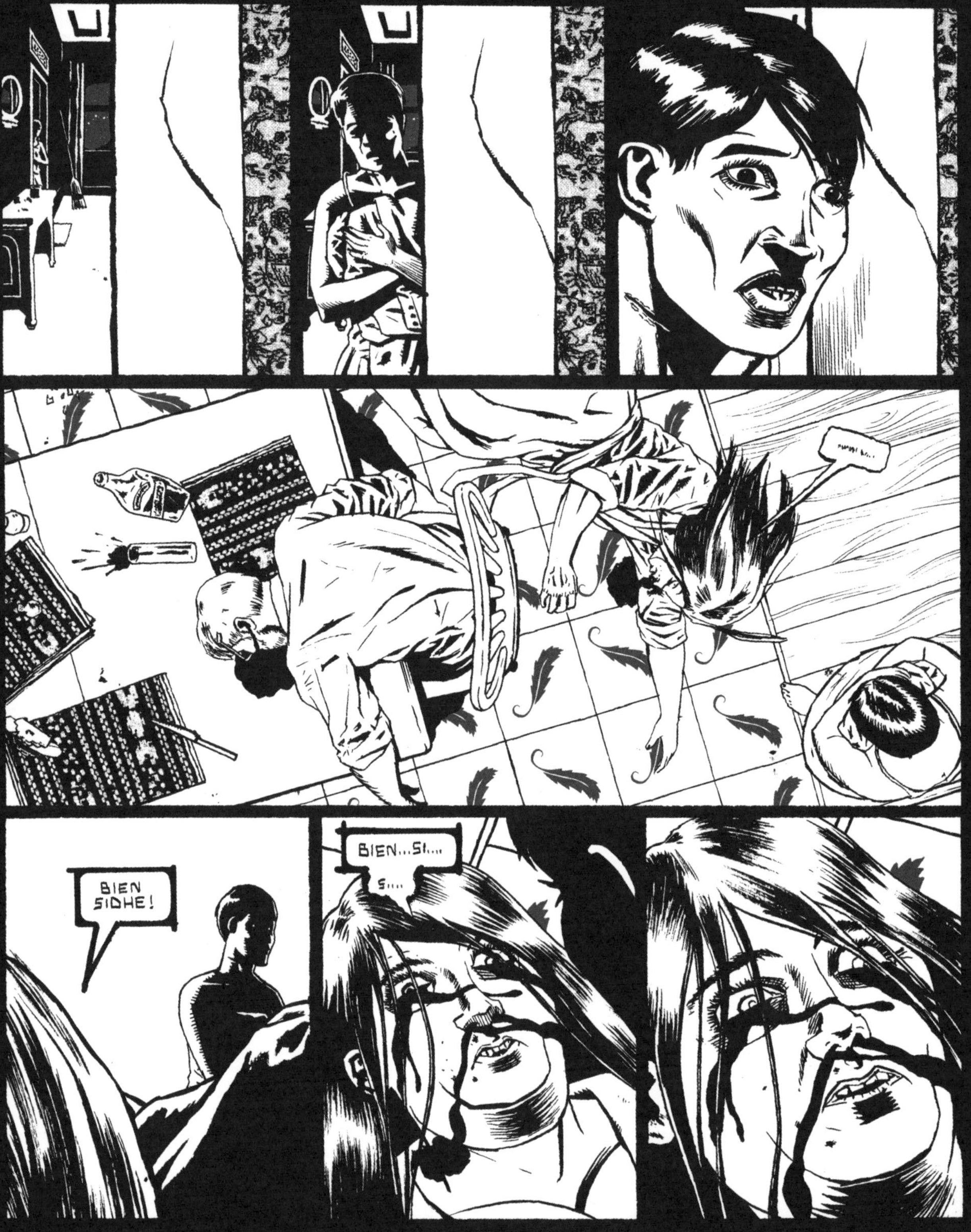
BIEN SIDHE!
BIEN...SI....
S....

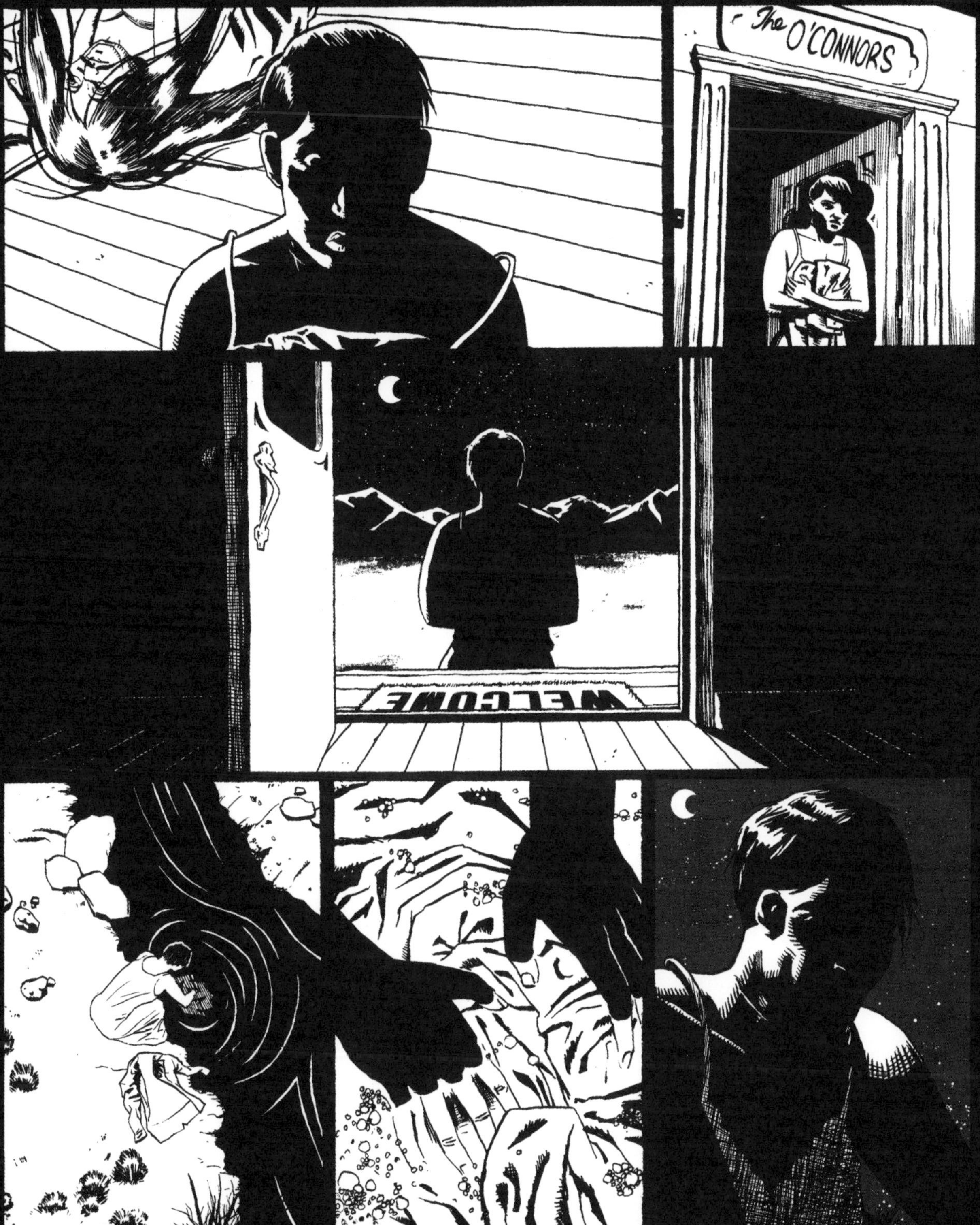
The O'CONNORS
WELCOME

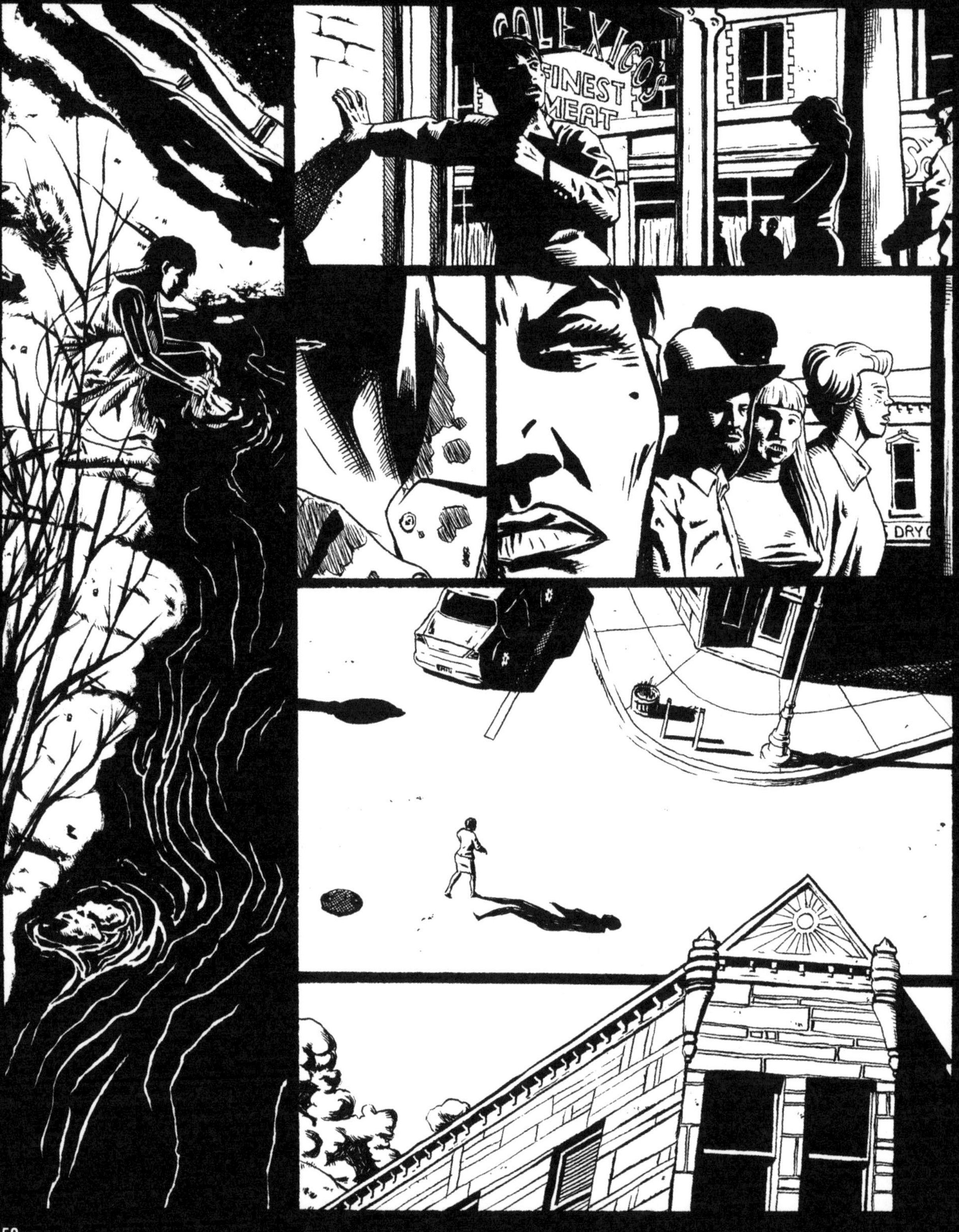
COLEXICO'S
FINEST
MEAT

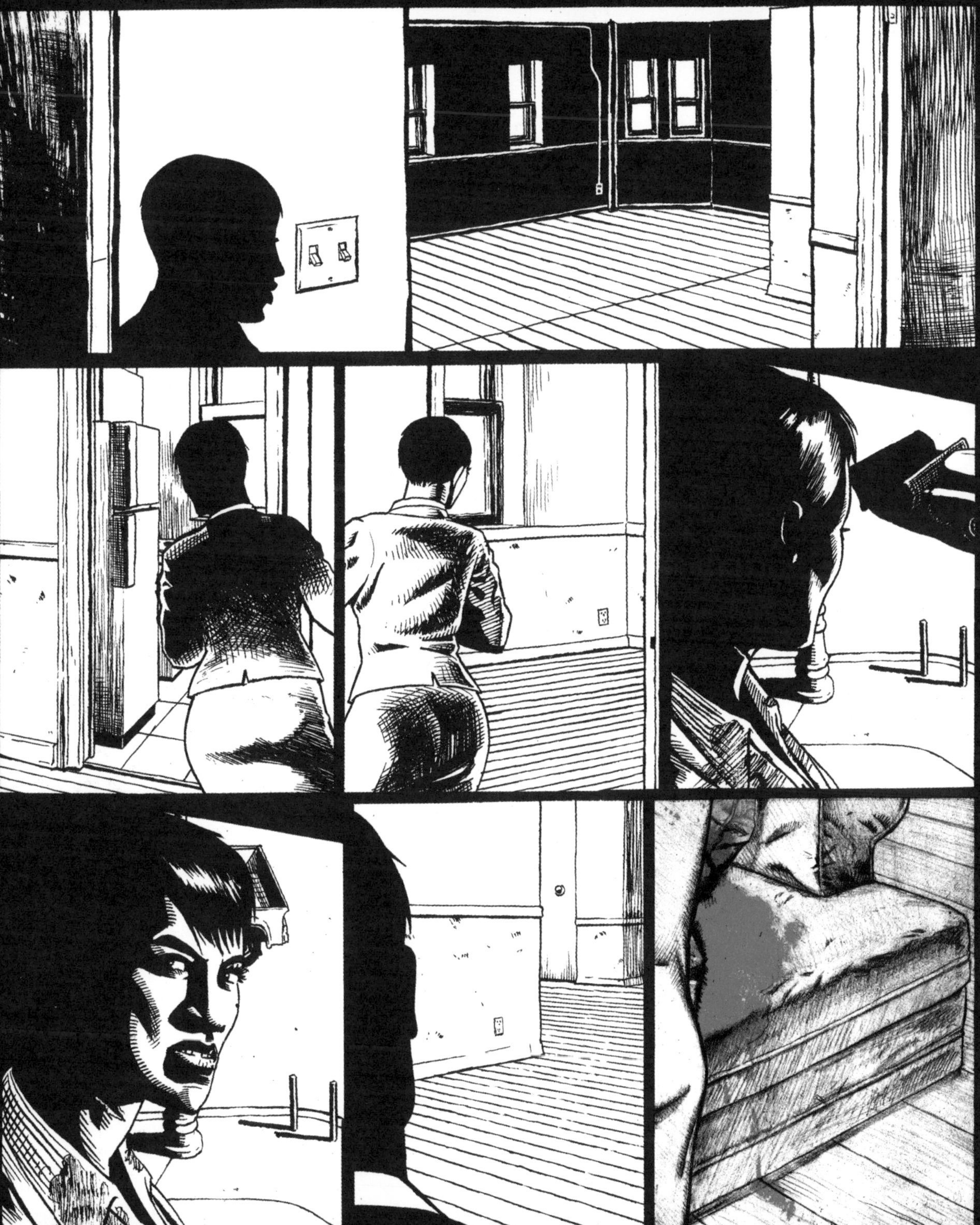

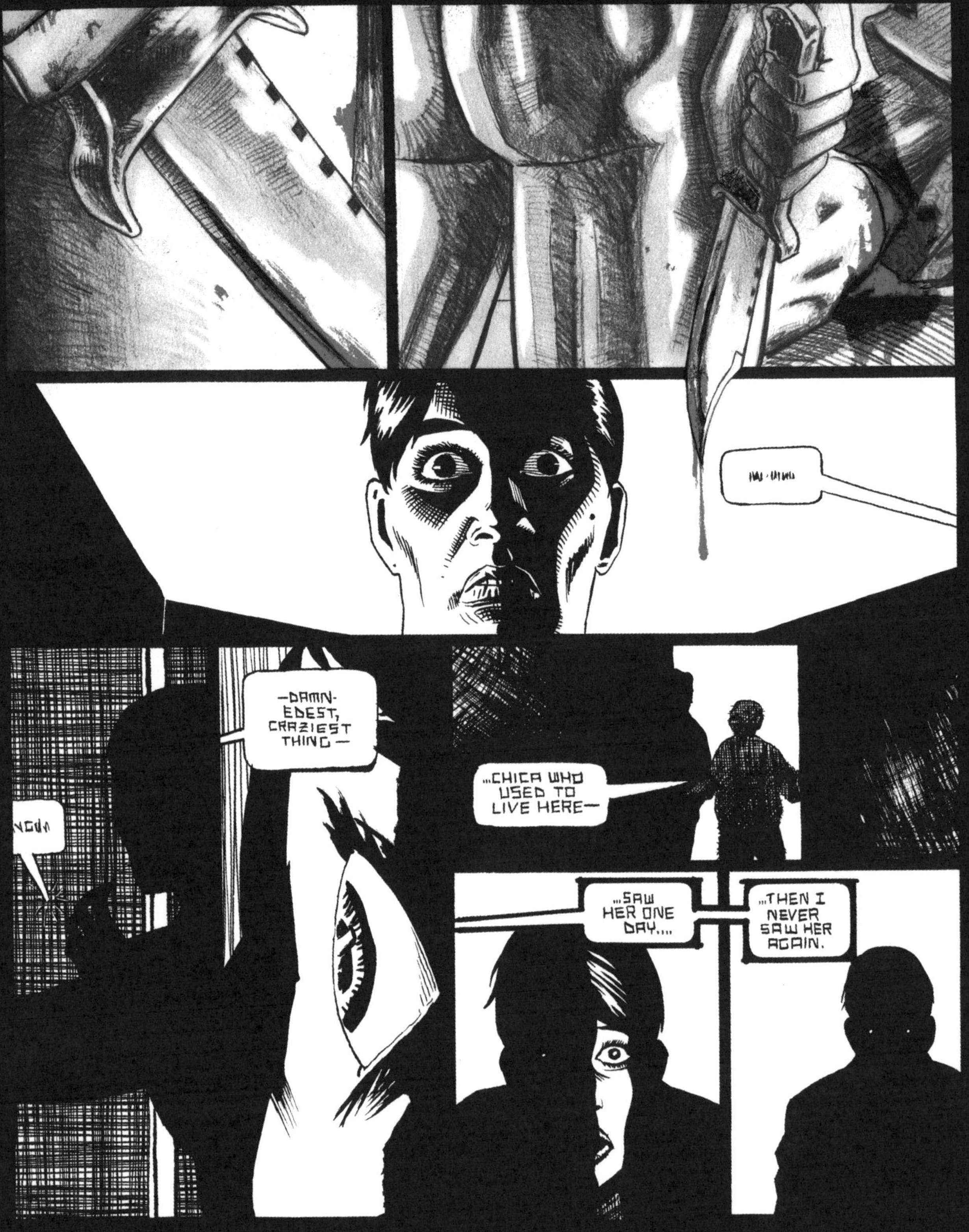

—DAMN-EDEST, CRAZIEST THING—
...CHICA WHO USED TO LIVE HERE—
...SAW HER ONE DAY....
...THEN I NEVER SAW HER AGAIN.

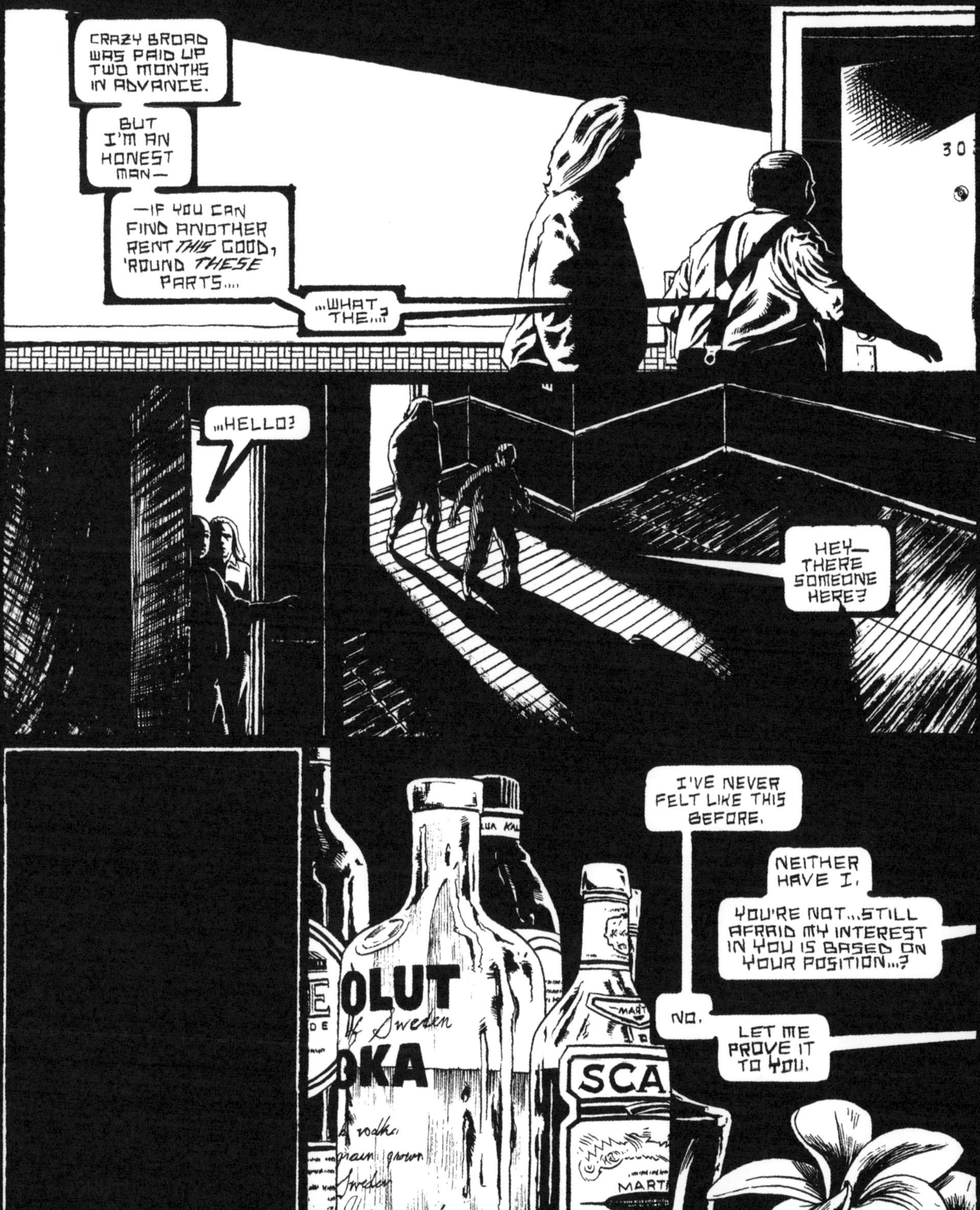
CRAZY BROAD WAS PAID UP TWO MONTHS IN ADVANCE.
BUT I'M AN HONEST MAN—
—IF YOU CAN FIND ANOTHER RENT *THIS* GOOD, 'ROUND *THESE* PARTS....
...WHAT THE...?
...HELLO?
HEY—THERE SOMEONE HERE?
I'VE NEVER FELT LIKE THIS BEFORE.
NEITHER HAVE I.
YOU'RE NOT...STILL AFRAID MY INTEREST IN YOU IS BASED ON YOUR POSITION...?
NO.
LET ME PROVE IT TO YOU.

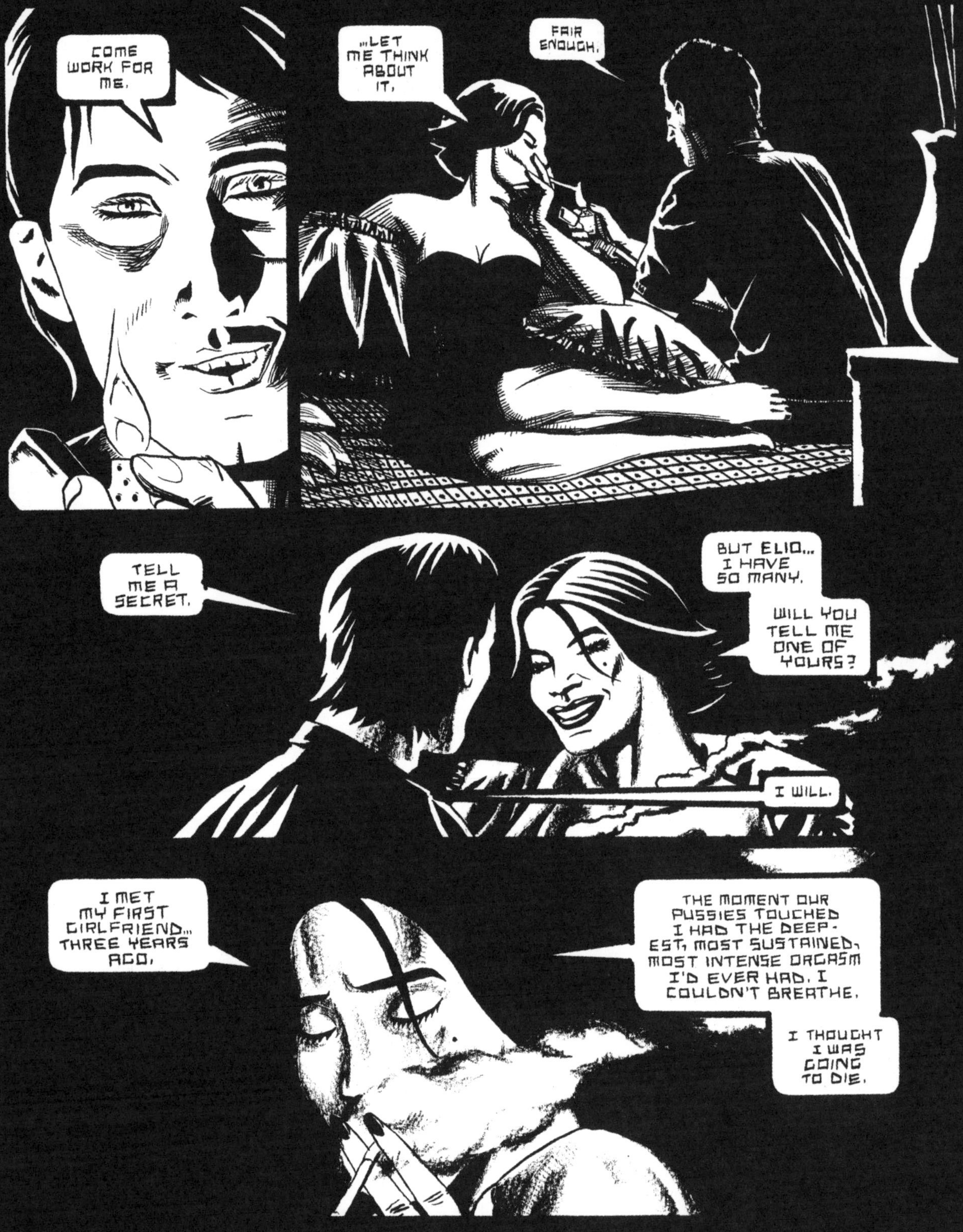
COME WORK FOR ME.
...LET ME THINK ABOUT IT.
FAIR ENOUGH.
TELL ME A SECRET.
BUT ELIO... I HAVE SO MANY.
WILL YOU TELL ME ONE OF YOURS?
I WILL.
I MET MY FIRST GIRLFRIEND... THREE YEARS AGO.
THE MOMENT OUR PUSSIES TOUCHED I HAD THE DEEP-EST, MOST SUSTAINED, MOST INTENSE ORGASM I'D EVER HAD. I COULDN'T BREATHE.
I THOUGHT I WAS GOING TO DIE.

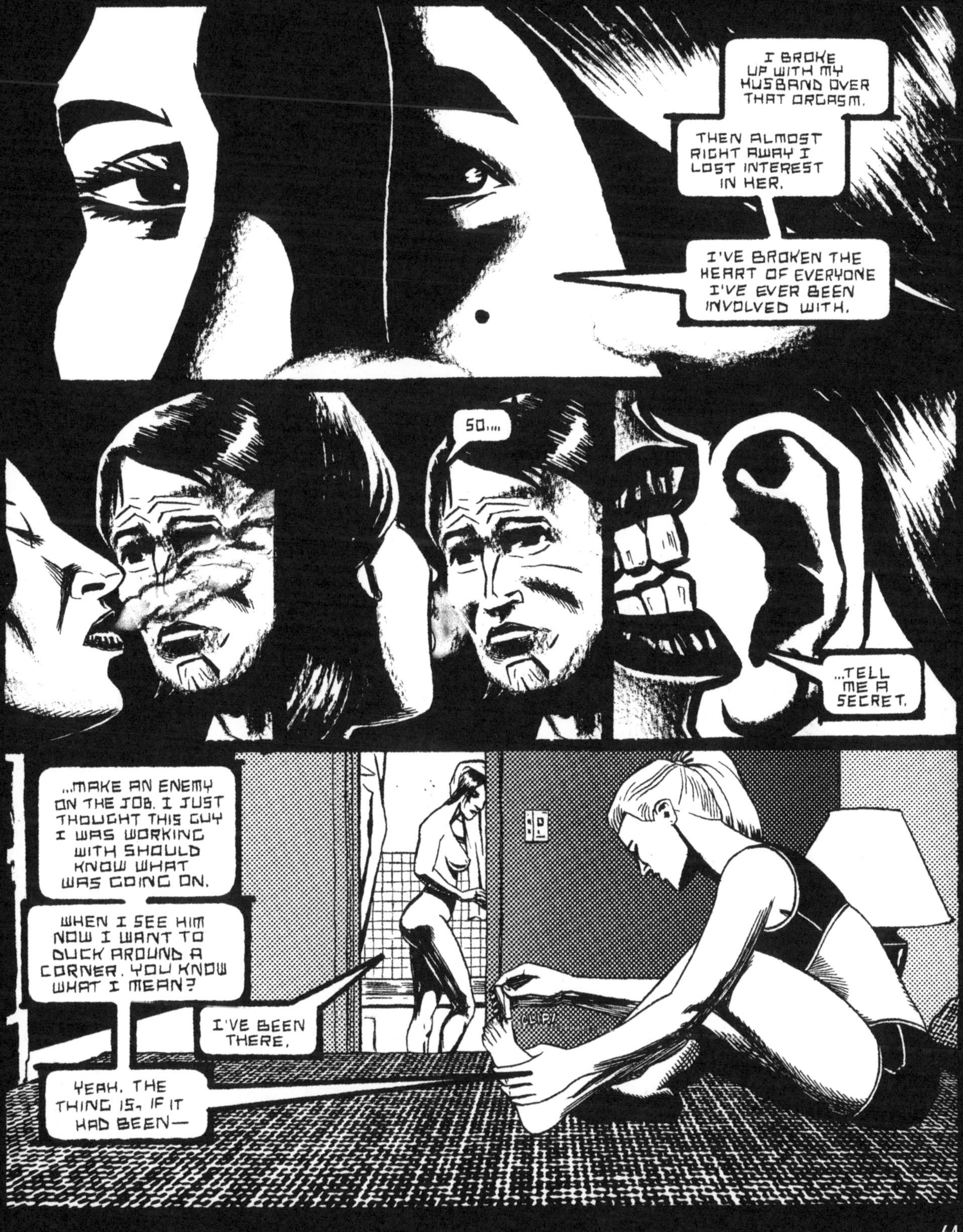
I BROKE UP WITH MY HUSBAND OVER THAT ORGASM.
THEN ALMOST RIGHT AWAY I LOST INTEREST IN HER.
I'VE BROKEN THE HEART OF EVERYONE I'VE EVER BEEN INVOLVED WITH.
SO....
...TELL ME A SECRET.
...MAKE AN ENEMY ON THE JOB. I JUST THOUGHT THIS GUY I WAS WORKING WITH SHOULD KNOW WHAT WAS GOING ON.
WHEN I SEE HIM NOW I WANT TO DUCK AROUND A CORNER. YOU KNOW WHAT I MEAN?
I'VE BEEN THERE.
YEAH. THE THING IS, IF IT HAD BEEN—
CLIP!

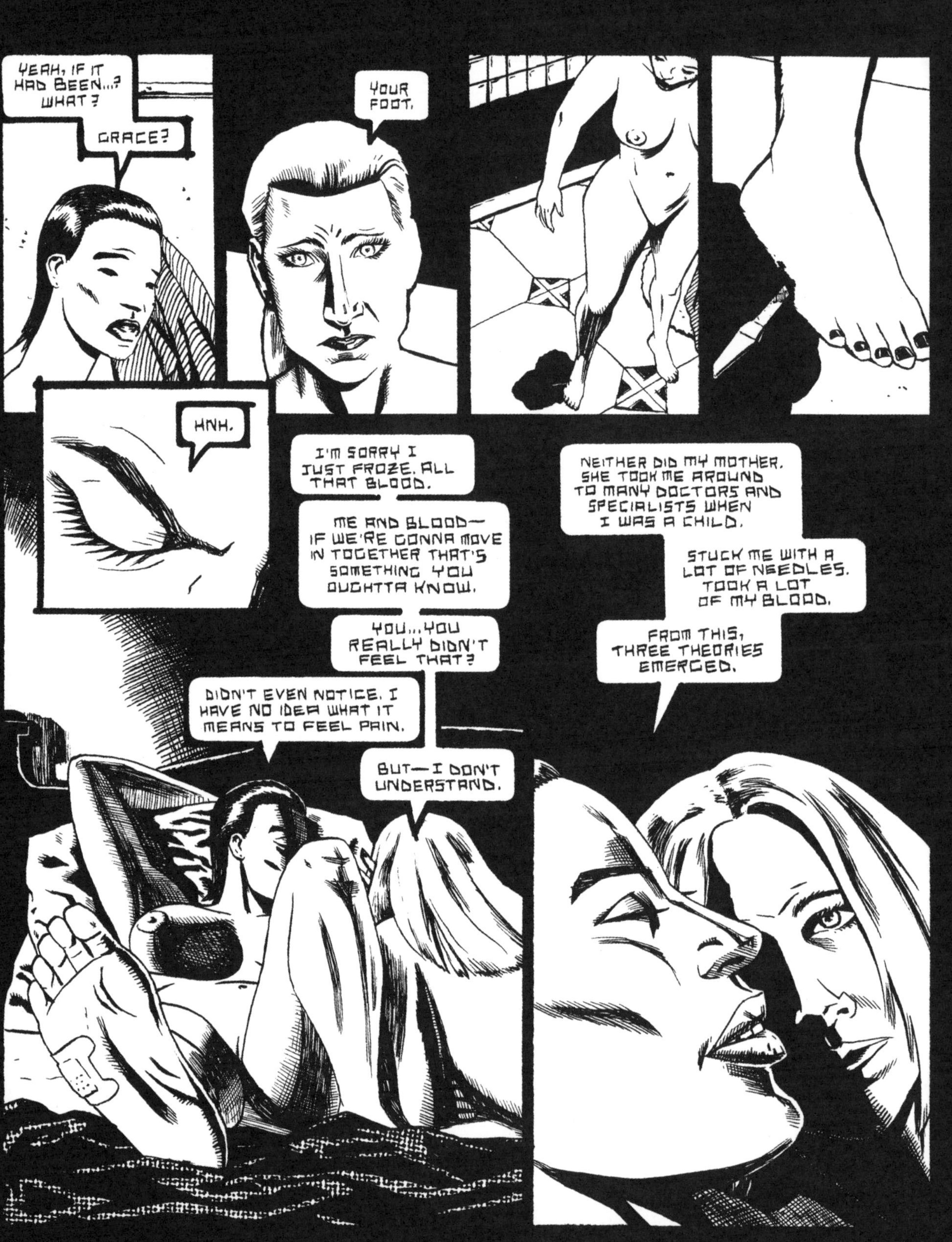
YEAH, IF IT HAD BEEN...? WHAT?
GRACE?
YOUR FOOT.
HNH.
I'M SORRY I JUST FROZE. ALL THAT BLOOD.
ME AND BLOOD— IF WE'RE GONNA MOVE IN TOGETHER THAT'S SOMETHING YOU OUGHTTA KNOW.
YOU...YOU REALLY DIDN'T FEEL THAT?
DIDN'T EVEN NOTICE. I HAVE NO IDEA WHAT IT MEANS TO FEEL PAIN.
BUT—I DON'T UNDERSTAND.
NEITHER DID MY MOTHER. SHE TOOK ME AROUND TO MANY DOCTORS AND SPECIALISTS WHEN I WAS A CHILD.
STUCK ME WITH A LOT OF NEEDLES. TOOK A LOT OF MY BLOOD.
FROM THIS, THREE THEORIES EMERGED.

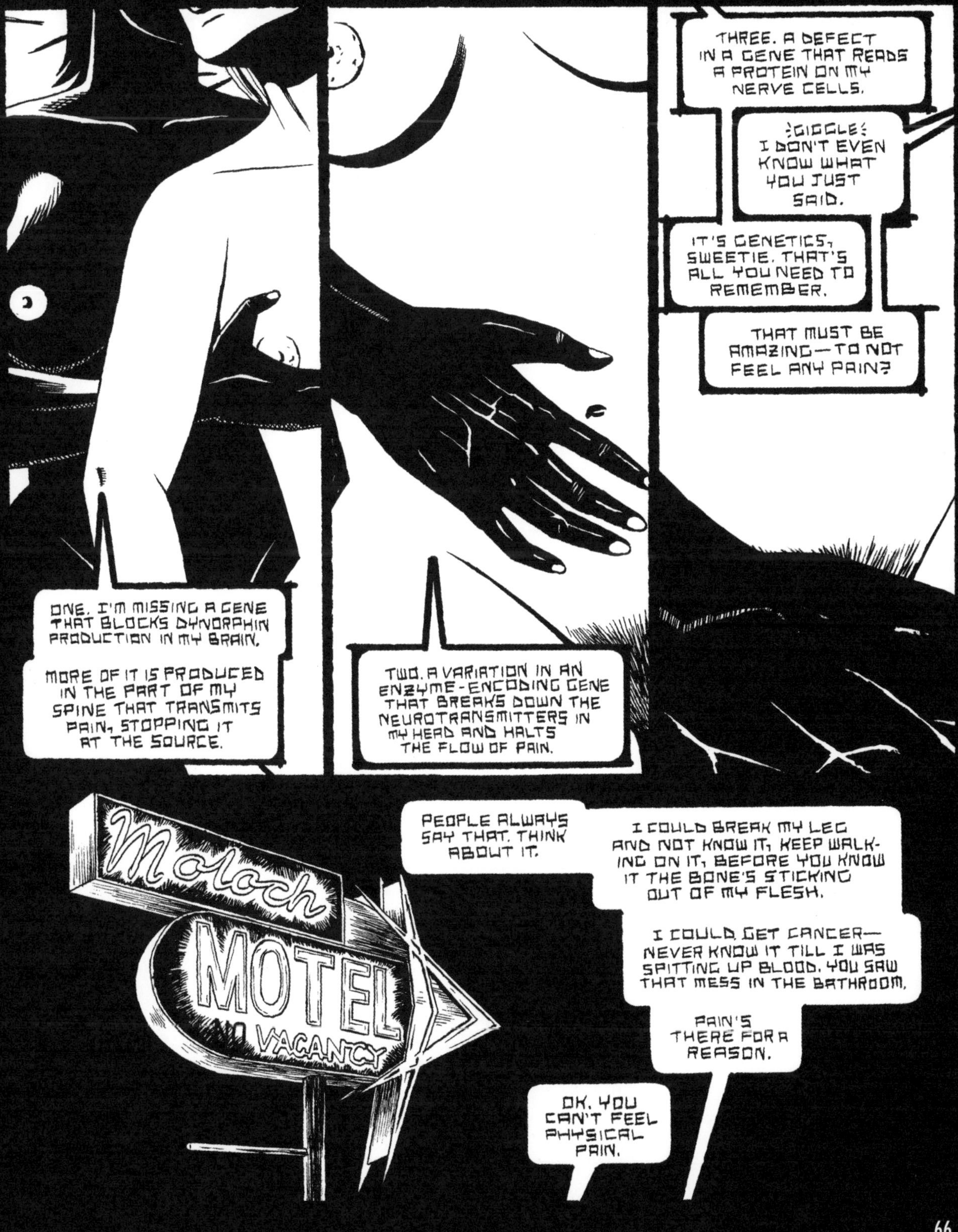
ONE. I'M MISSING A GENE THAT BLOCKS DYNORPHIN PRODUCTION IN MY BRAIN.
MORE OF IT IS PRODUCED IN THE PART OF MY SPINE THAT TRANSMITS PAIN, STOPPING IT AT THE SOURCE.
TWO. A VARIATION IN AN ENZYME-ENCODING GENE THAT BREAKS DOWN THE NEUROTRANSMITTERS IN MY HEAD AND HALTS THE FLOW OF PAIN.
THREE. A DEFECT IN A GENE THAT READS A PROTEIN ON MY NERVE CELLS.
GIGGLE I DON'T EVEN KNOW WHAT YOU JUST SAID.
IT'S GENETICS, SWEETIE. THAT'S ALL YOU NEED TO REMEMBER.
THAT MUST BE AMAZING—TO NOT FEEL ANY PAIN?
Moloch
MOTEL
NO VACANCY
PEOPLE ALWAYS SAY THAT. THINK ABOUT IT.
I COULD BREAK MY LEG AND NOT KNOW IT, KEEP WALKING ON IT, BEFORE YOU KNOW IT THE BONE'S STICKING OUT OF MY FLESH.
I COULD GET CANCER—NEVER KNOW IT TILL I WAS SPITTING UP BLOOD. YOU SAW THAT MESS IN THE BATHROOM.
PAIN'S THERE FOR A REASON.
OK. YOU CAN'T FEEL PHYSICAL PAIN.

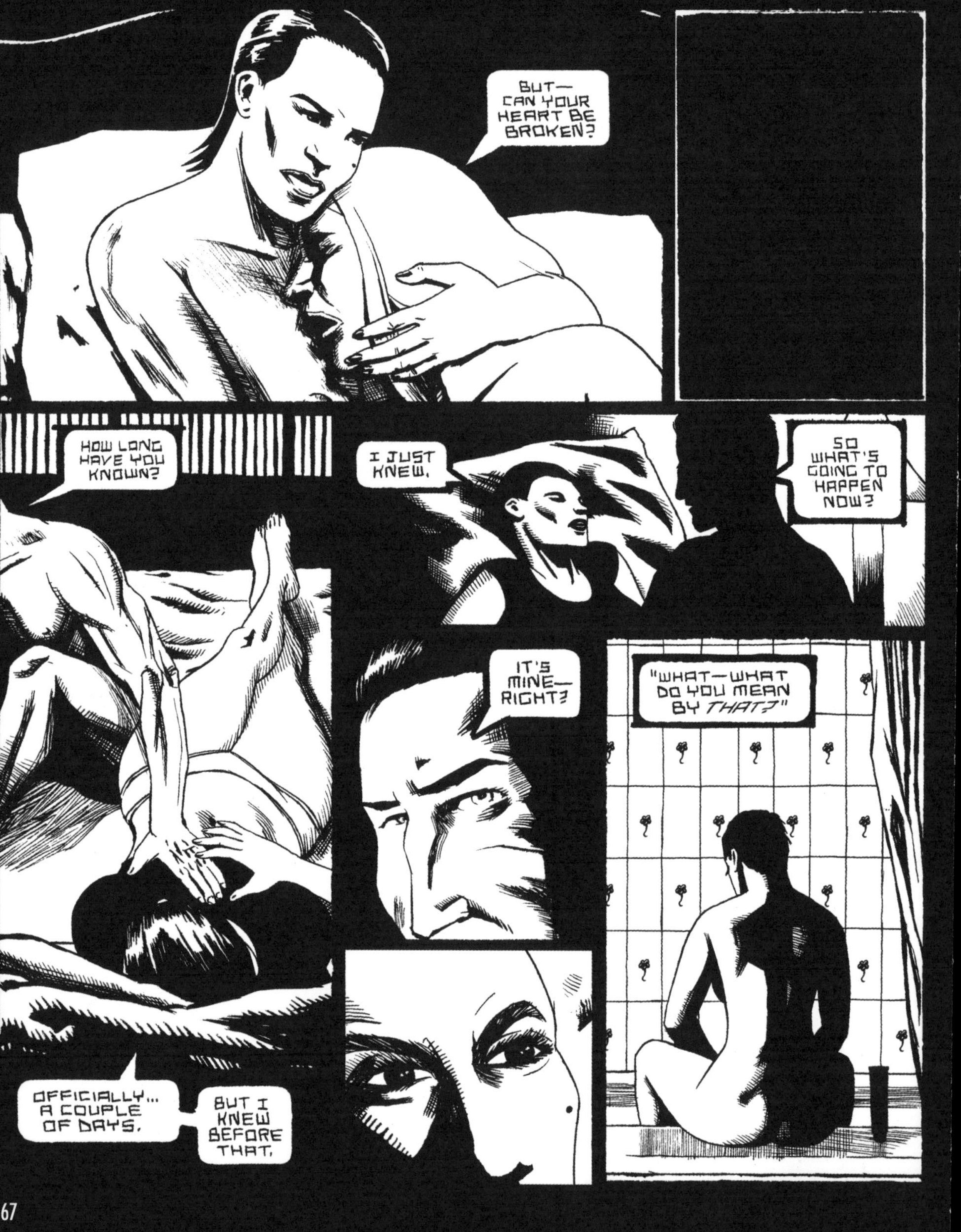
BUT—
CAN YOUR
HEART BE
BROKEN?
HOW LONG
HAVE YOU
KNOWN?
I JUST
KNEW.
SO
WHAT'S
GOING TO
HAPPEN
NOW?
IT'S
MINE—
RIGHT?
"WHAT—WHAT
DO YOU MEAN
BY *THAT?*"
OFFICIALLY...
A COUPLE
OF DAYS.
BUT I
KNEW
BEFORE
THAT.

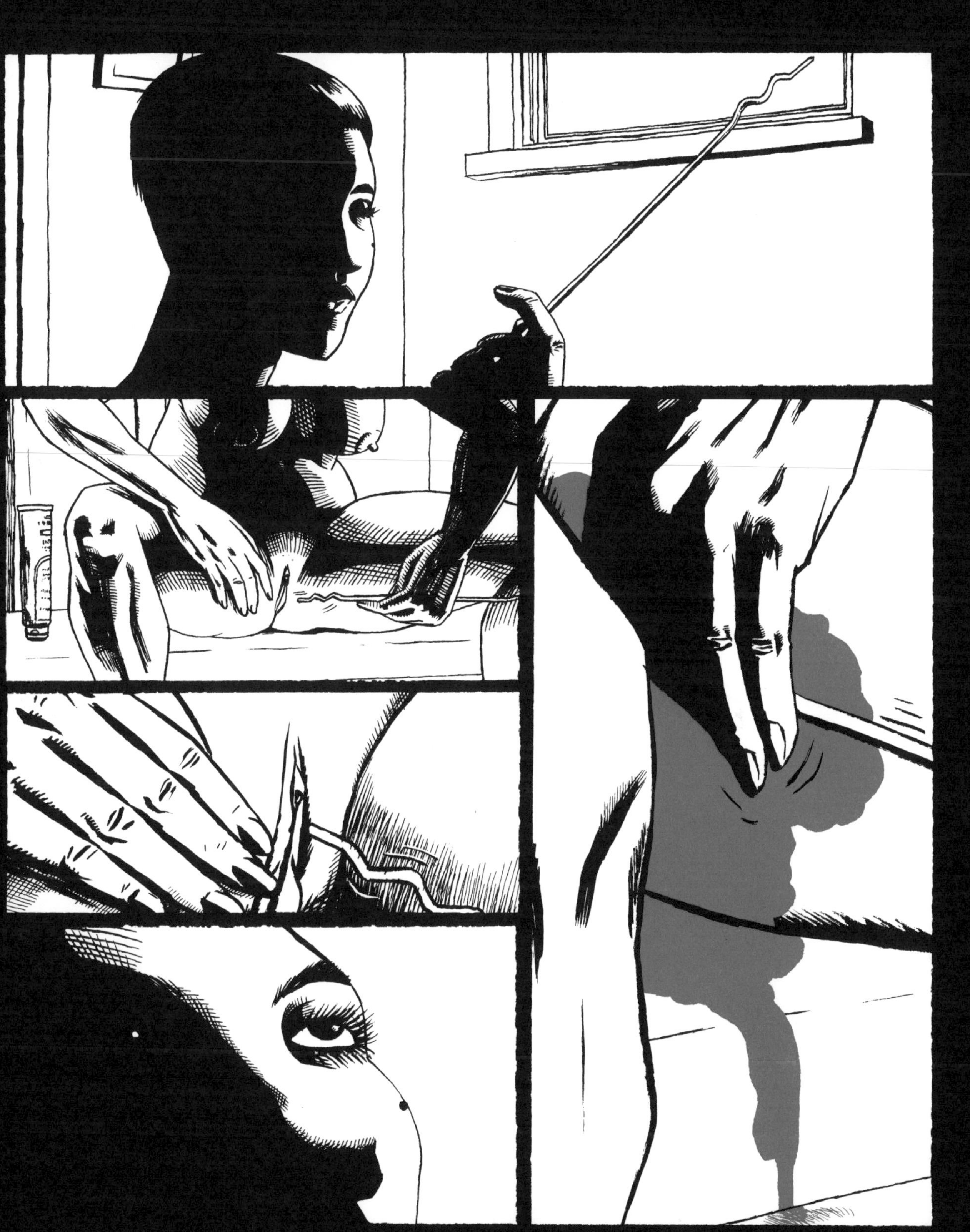

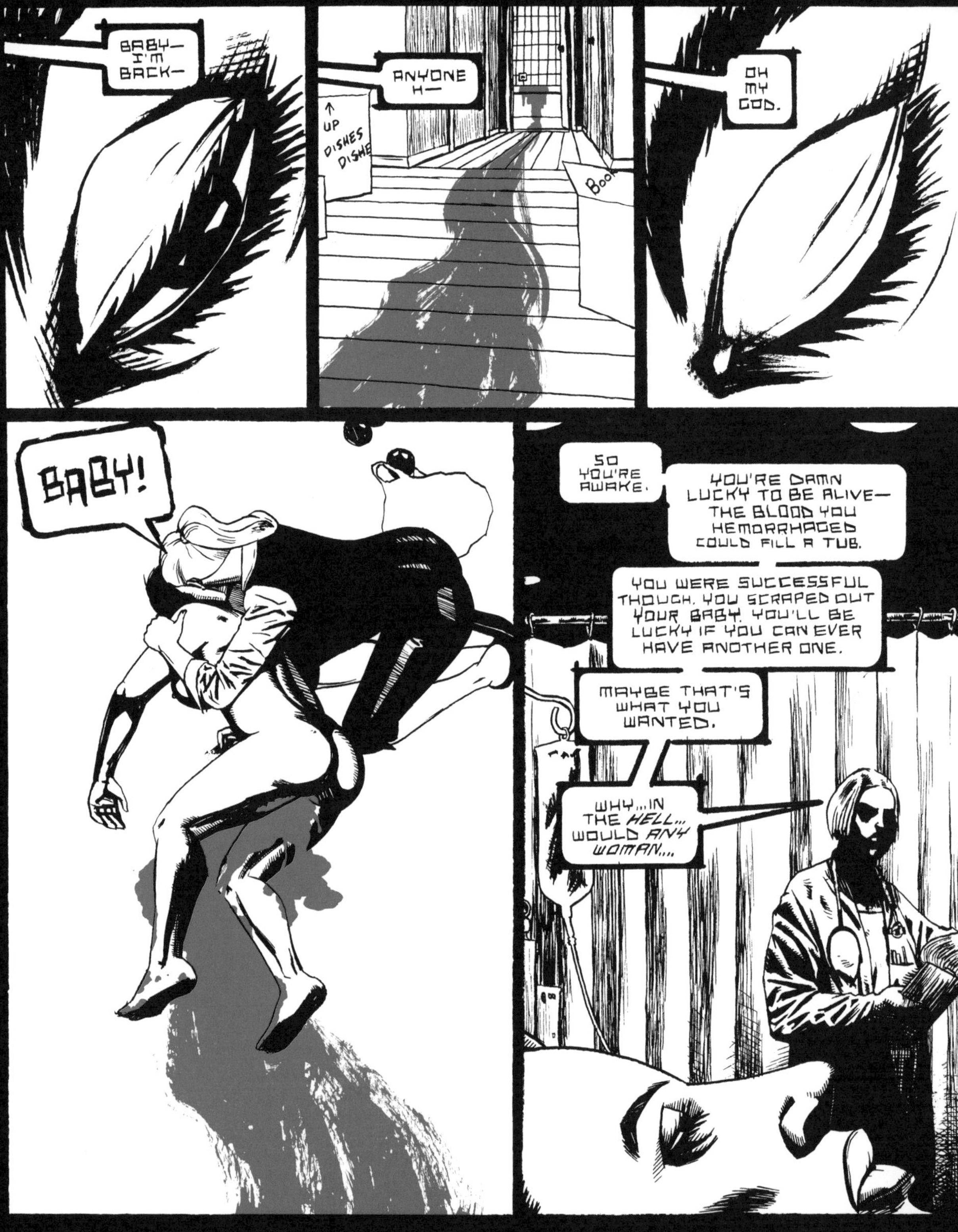
BABY— I'M BACK—
ANYONE H—
↑ UP
DISHES DISHE
Boo
OH MY GOD.
BABY!
SO YOU'RE AWAKE.
YOU'RE DAMN LUCKY TO BE ALIVE— THE BLOOD YOU HEMORRHAGED COULD FILL A TUB.
YOU WERE SUCCESSFUL THOUGH. YOU SCRAPED OUT YOUR BABY. YOU'LL BE LUCKY IF YOU CAN EVER HAVE ANOTHER ONE.
MAYBE THAT'S WHAT YOU WANTED.
WHY...IN THE *HELL*... WOULD *ANY WOMAN*....

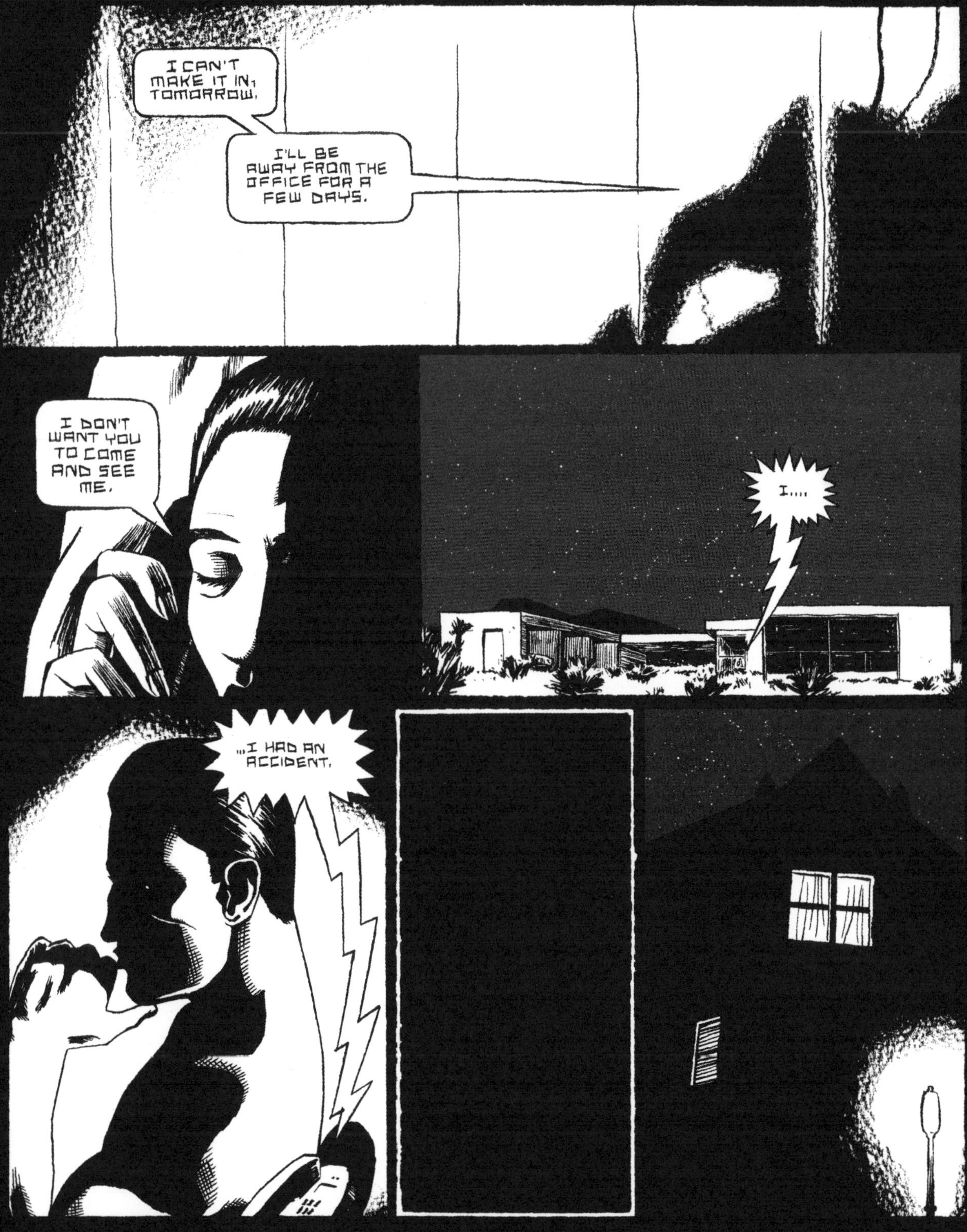
I CAN'T MAKE IT IN, TOMORROW.
I'LL BE AWAY FROM THE OFFICE FOR A FEW DAYS.
I DON'T WANT YOU TO COME AND SEE ME.
I....
...I HAD AN ACCIDENT.

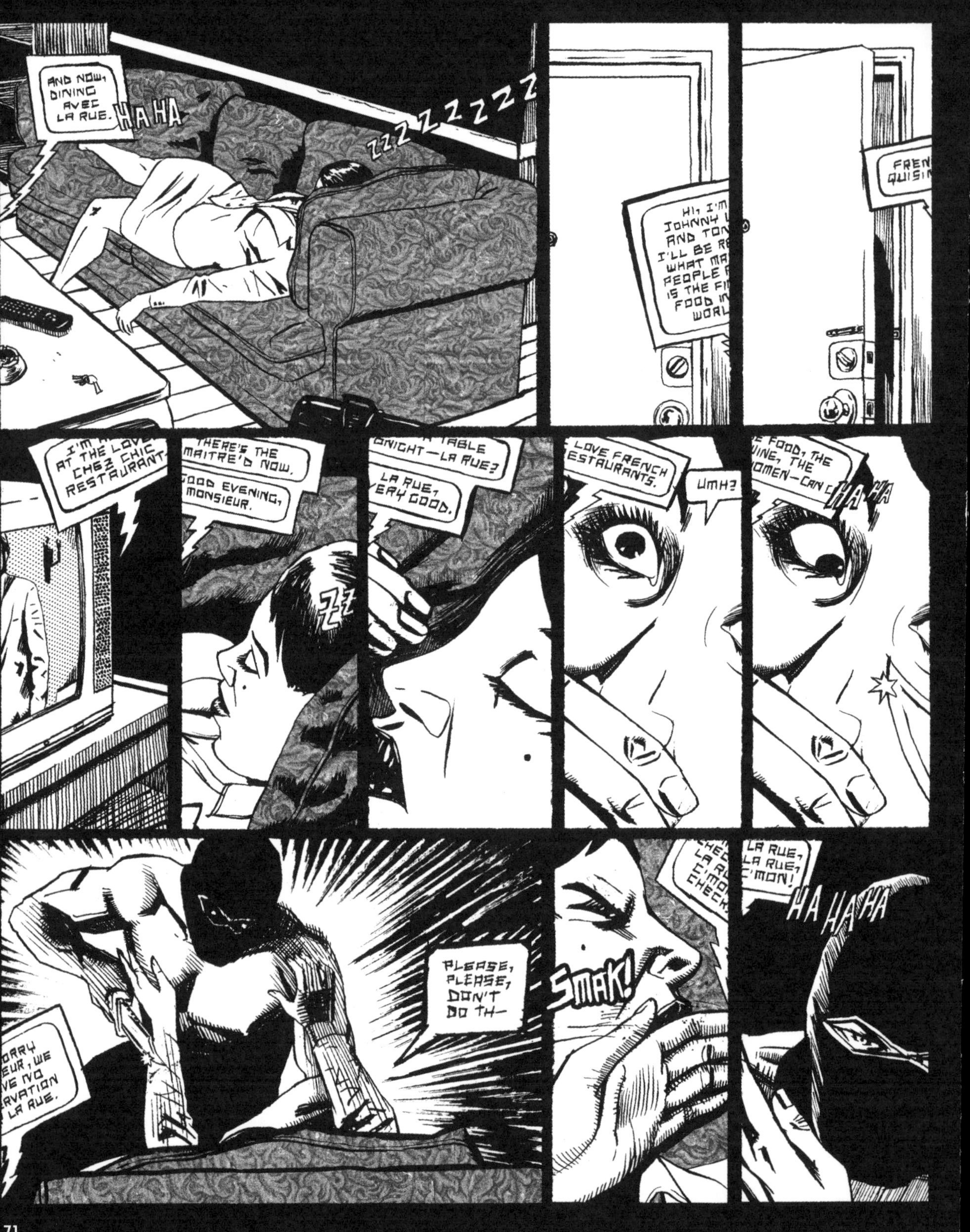

AND NOW, DINING AVEC LA RUE.
HA HA
ZZZZZZZZZZ
HI, I'M JOHNNY L AND TON I'LL BE RE WHAT MA PEOPLE IS THE FI FOOD IN WORL
FREN QUISIN
I'M AT THE LOVE CHEZ CHIC RESTAURANT
THERE'S THE MAITRE'D NOW.
GOOD EVENING, MONSIEUR.
TABLE ONIGHT—LA RUE?
LA RUE, VERY GOOD.
ZZ
LOVE FRENCH ESTAURANTS.
UMH?
E FOOD, THE UINE, THE OMEN—CAN
HA HA
ORRY EUR, WE VE NO RVATION LA RUE.
PLEASE, PLEASE, DON'T DO TH—
SMAK!
LA RUE, LA RUE, C'MON!
HA HA HA

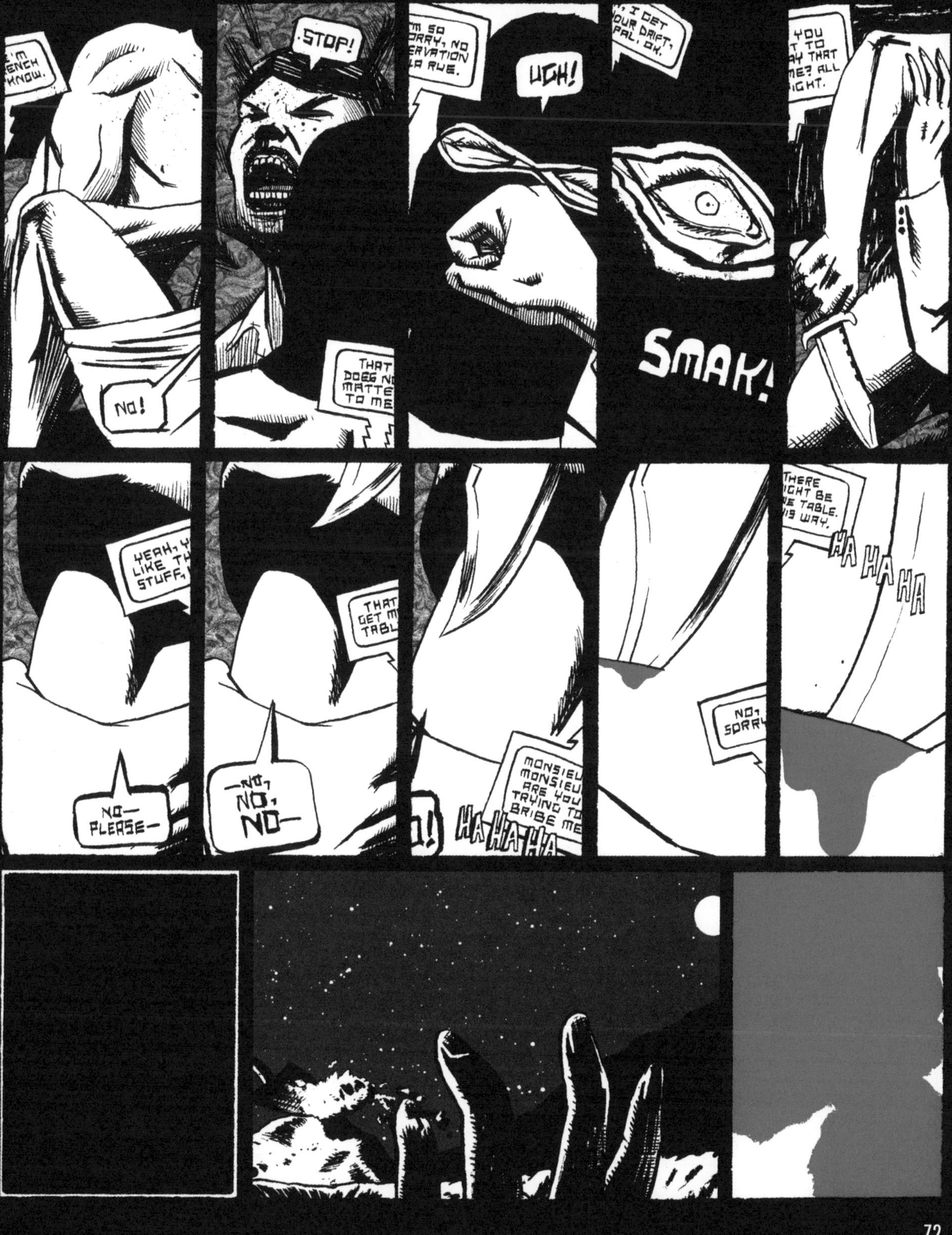
NO!
STOP!
THAT DOES NO MATTE TO ME
UGH!
I GET OUR DRIFT, PAL, OK.
SMAK!
YOU
YEAH, Y LIKE TH STUFF,
NO— PLEASE—
THAT GET M TABL
—NO, NO, NO—
MONSIEU MONSIEU ARE YOU TRYING TO BRIBE ME
HA HA HA HA
NO, SORRY
THERE IGHT BE E TABLE. IS WAY.
HA HA HA HA

WHERE AM I GOING?
HOW WILL I GET THERE?

# CHAPTER THREE SOUND & FURY

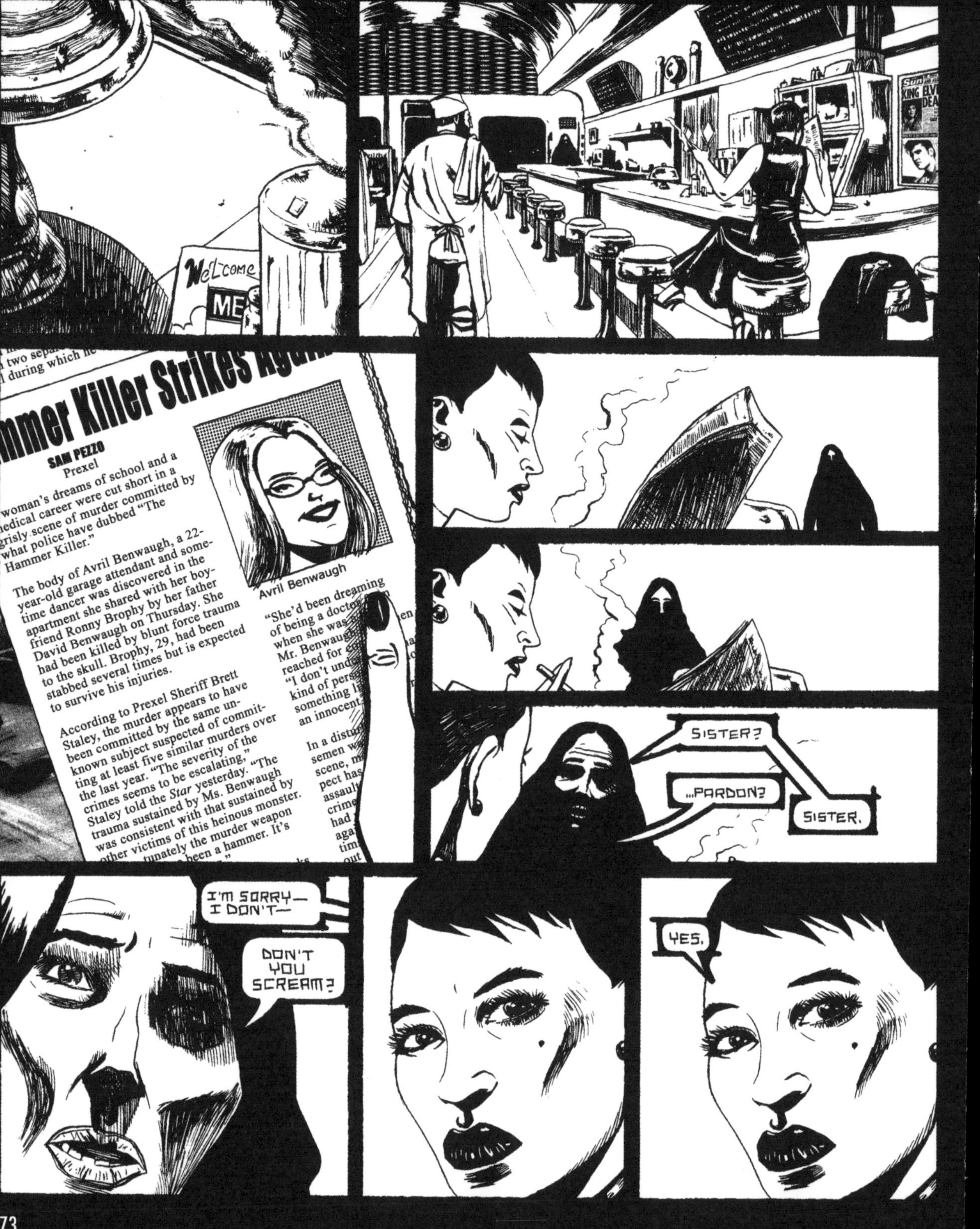
WELCOME
mmer Killer Strikes
SAM PEZZO
Prexel
woman's dreams of school and a
edical career were cut short in a
grisly scene of murder committed by
what police have dubbed "The
Hammer Killer."
The body of Avril Benwaugh, a 22-
year-old garage attendant and some-
time dancer was discovered in the
apartment she shared with her boyfriend Ronny Brophy by her father
David Benwaugh on Thursday. She
had been killed by blunt force trauma
to the skull. Brophy, 29, had been
stabbed several times but is expected
to survive his injuries.
According to Prexel Sheriff Brett
Staley, the murder appears to have
been committed by the same un-
known subject suspected of commit-
ting at least five similar murders over
the last year. "The severity of the
crimes seems to be escalating,"
Staley told the Star yesterday. "The
trauma sustained by Ms. Benwaugh
was consistent with that sustained by
other victims of this heinous monster.
Avril Benwaugh
"She'd been dreaming
SISTER?
...PARDON?
SISTER.
I'M SORRY— I DON'T—
DON'T YOU SCREAM?
YES.

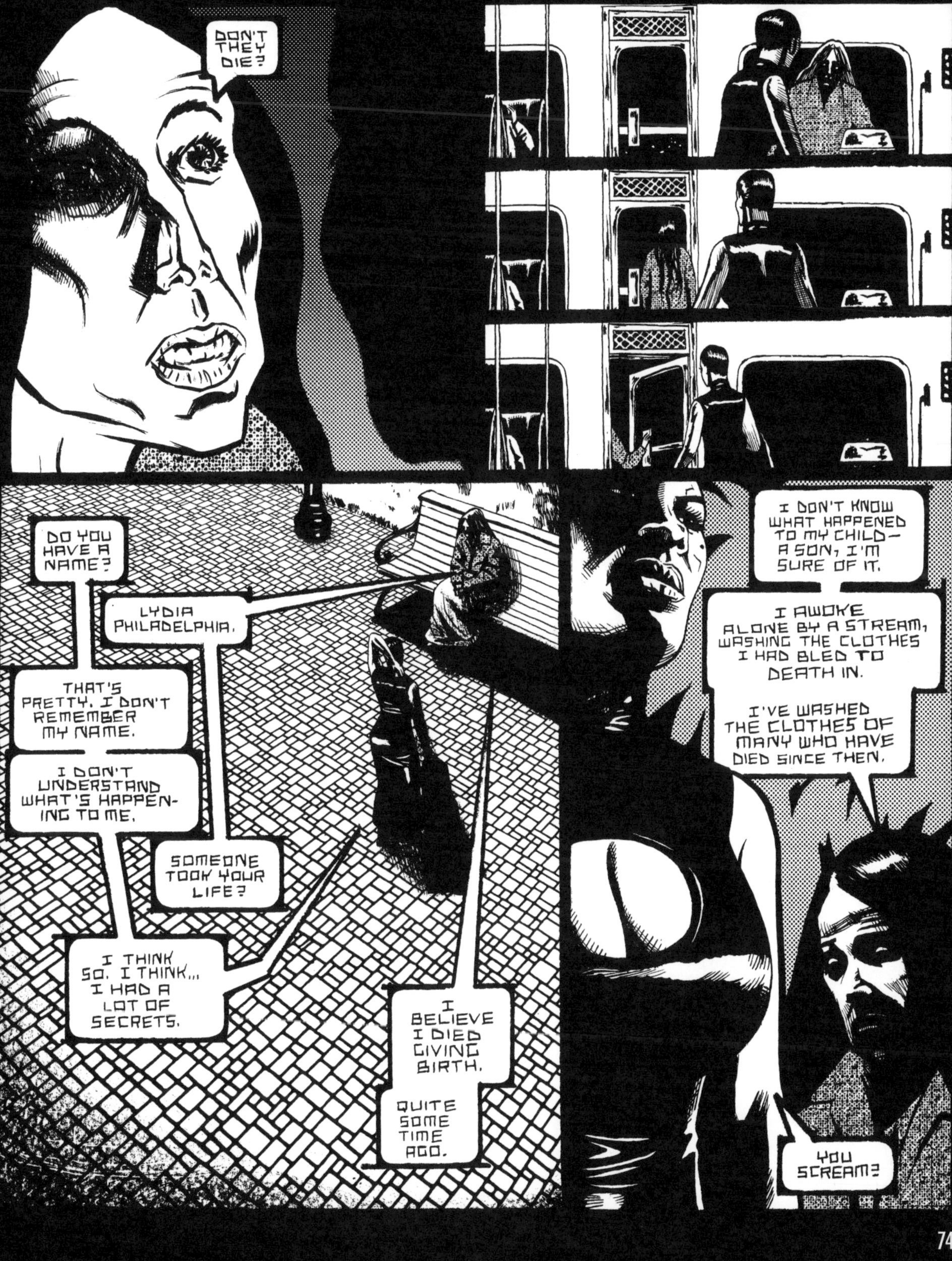
DON'T THEY DIE?
DO YOU HAVE A NAME?
LYDIA PHILADELPHIA.
THAT'S PRETTY. I DON'T REMEMBER MY NAME.
I DON'T UNDERSTAND WHAT'S HAPPENING TO ME.
SOMEONE TOOK YOUR LIFE?
I THINK SO. I THINK... I HAD A LOT OF SECRETS.
I BELIEVE I DIED GIVING BIRTH.
QUITE SOME TIME AGO.
I DON'T KNOW WHAT HAPPENED TO MY CHILD— A SON, I'M SURE OF IT.
I AWOKE ALONE BY A STREAM, WASHING THE CLOTHES I HAD BLED TO DEATH IN.
I'VE WASHED THE CLOTHES OF MANY WHO HAVE DIED SINCE THEN.
YOU SCREAM?

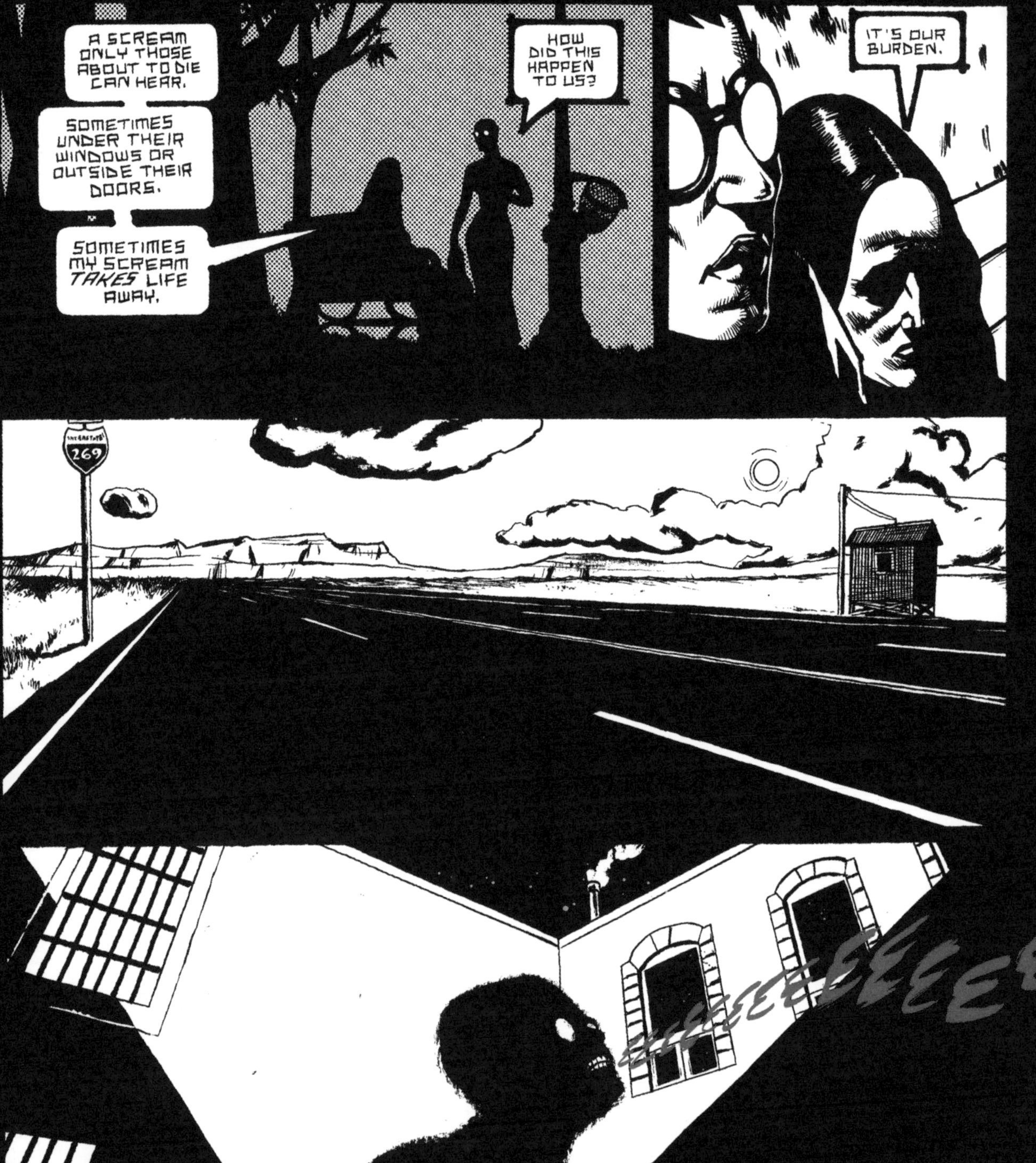
A SCREAM ONLY THOSE ABOUT TO DIE CAN HEAR.
SOMETIMES UNDER THEIR WINDOWS OR OUTSIDE THEIR DOORS.
SOMETIMES MY SCREAM *TAKES* LIFE AWAY.
HOW DID THIS HAPPEN TO US?
IT'S OUR BURDEN.
269

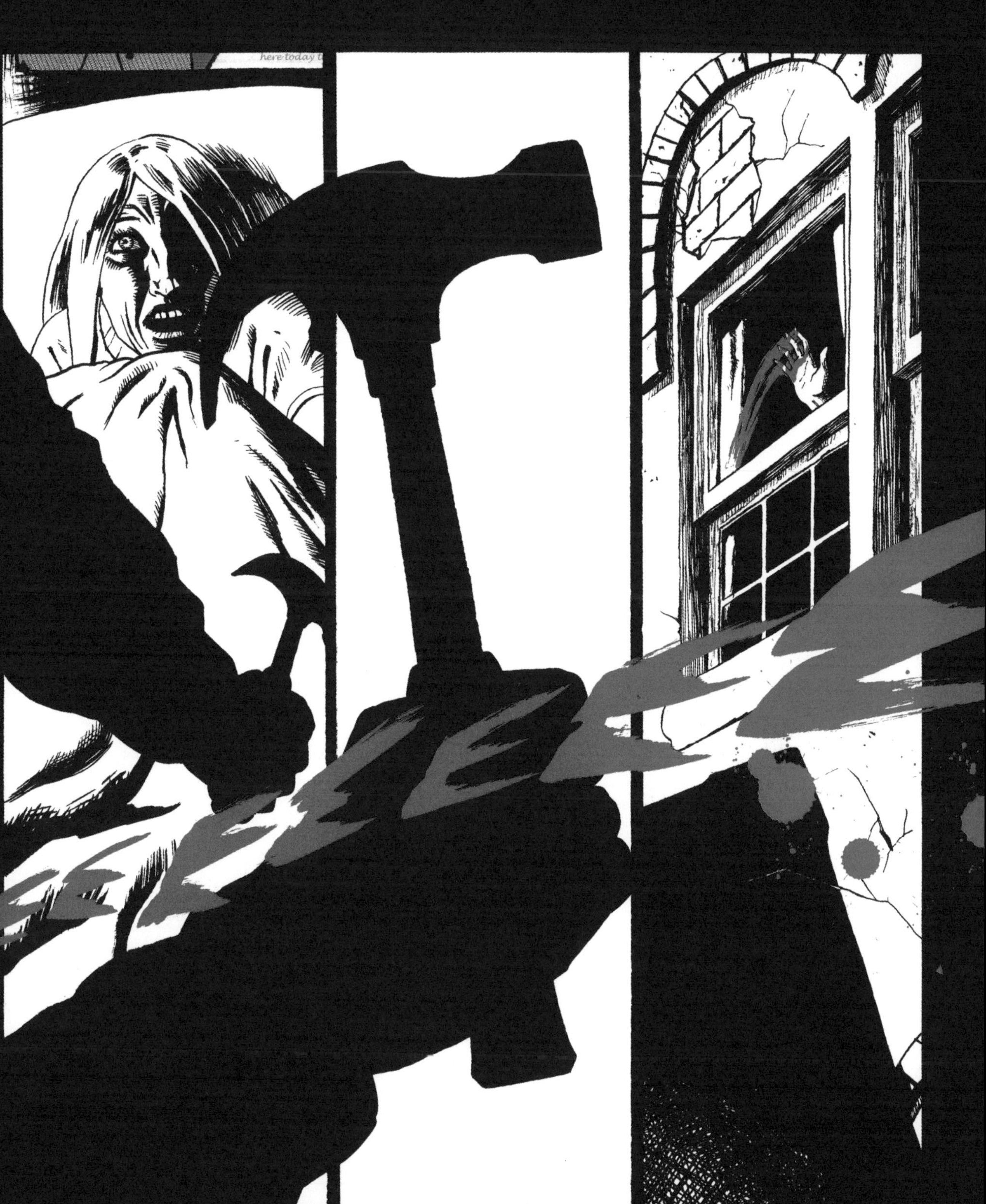
here today

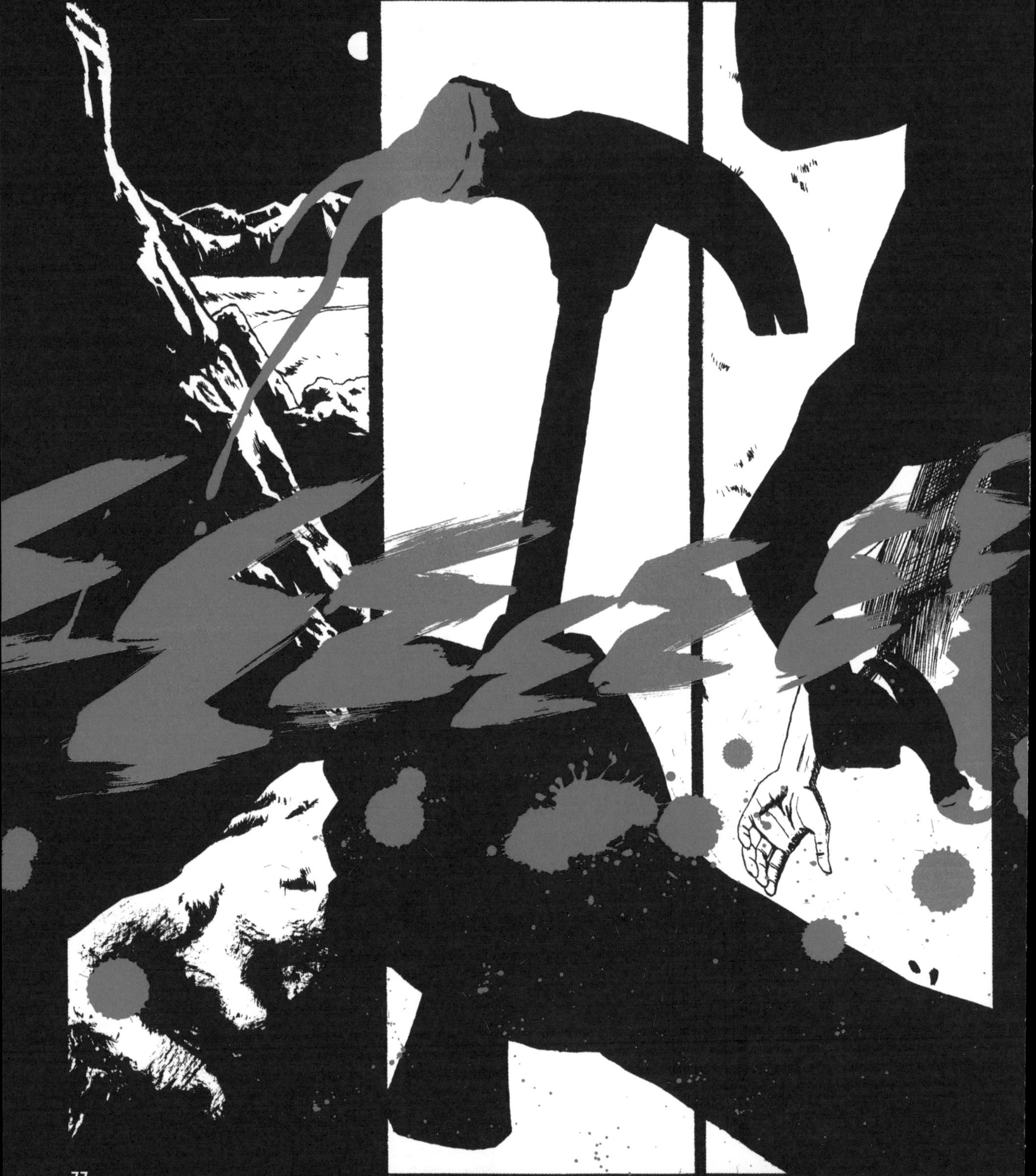

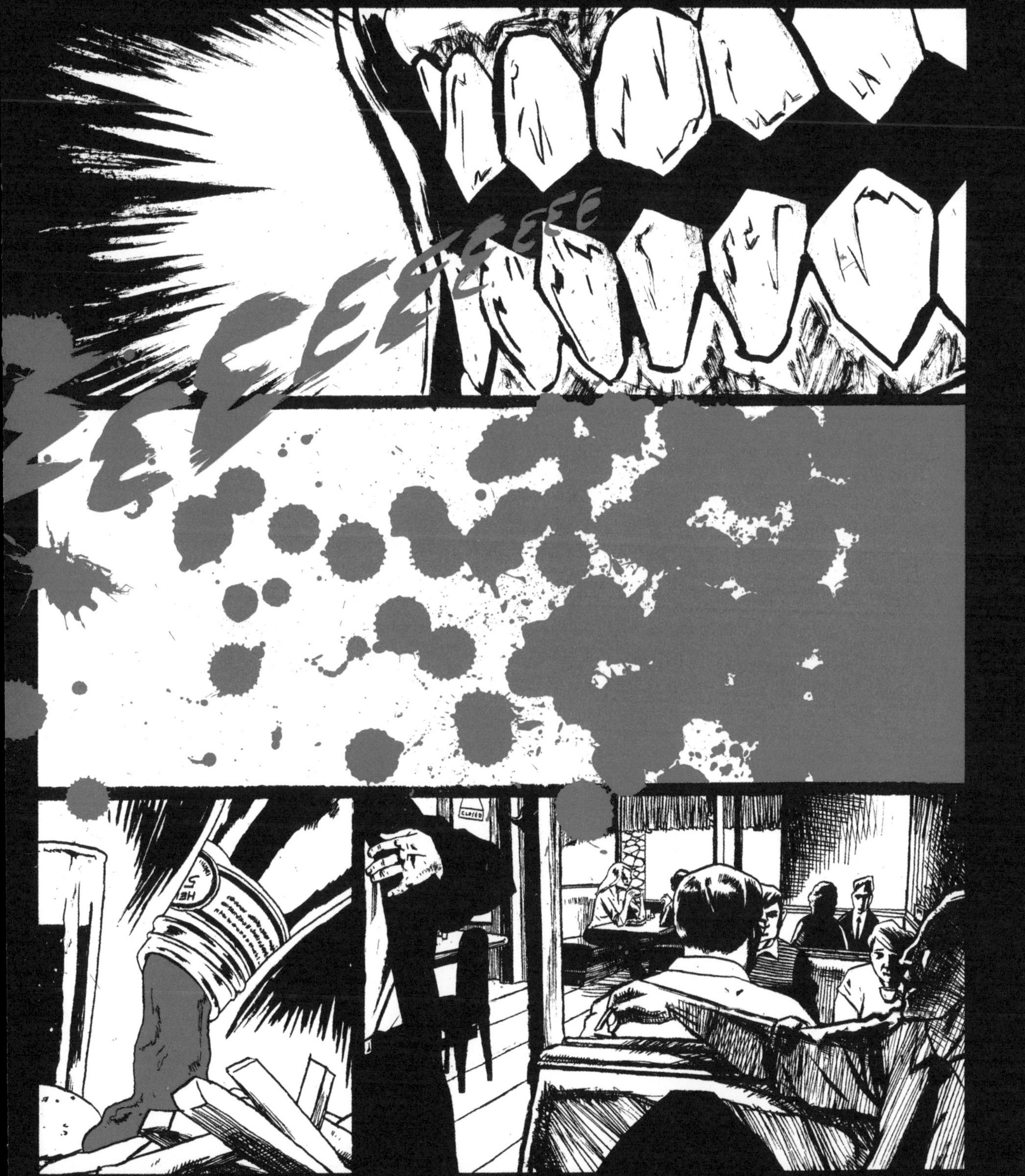

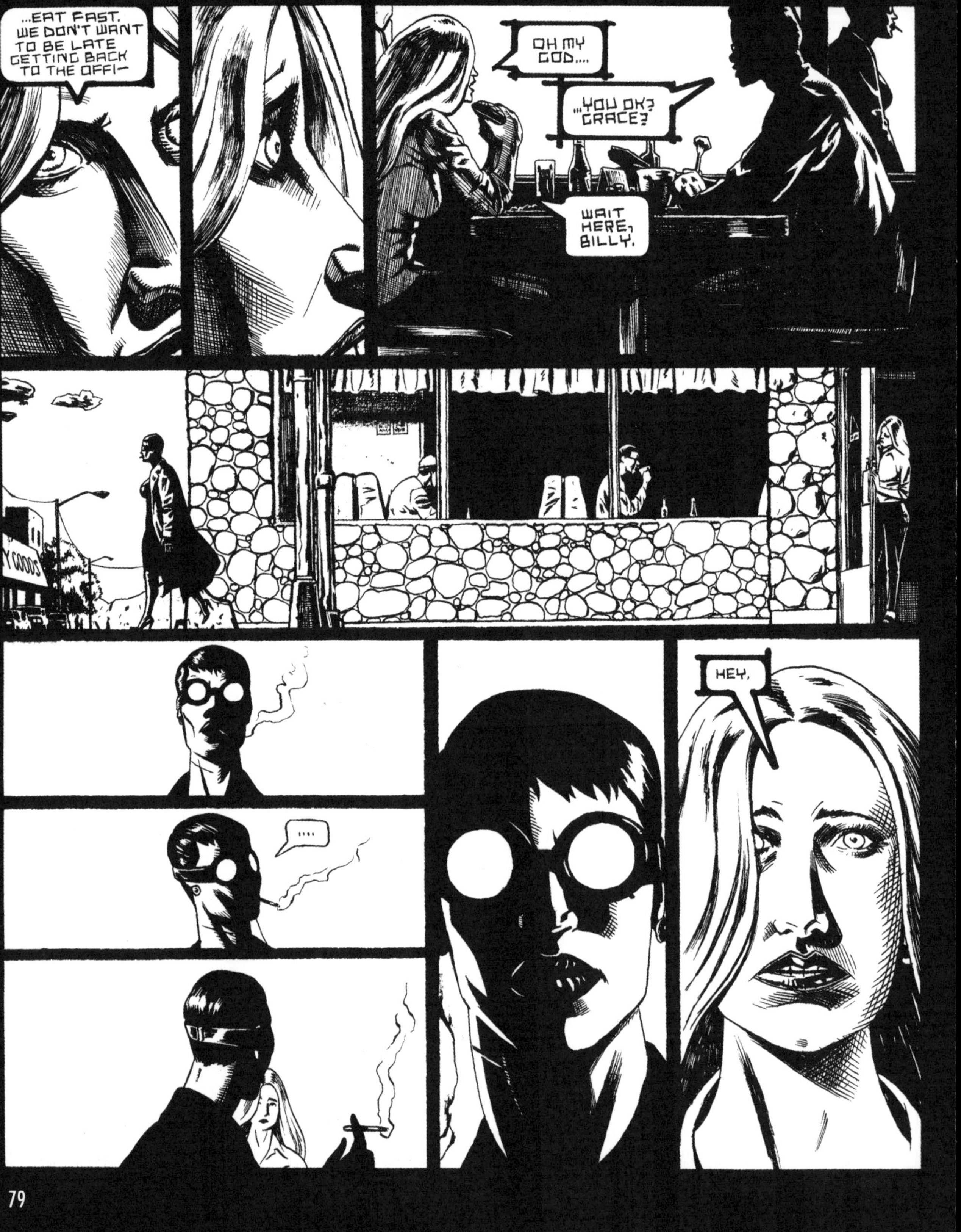
...EAT FAST. WE DON'T WANT TO BE LATE GETTING BACK TO THE OFFI—
OH MY GOD....
...YOU OK? GRACE?
WAIT HERE, BILLY.
Y GOODS
....
HEY.

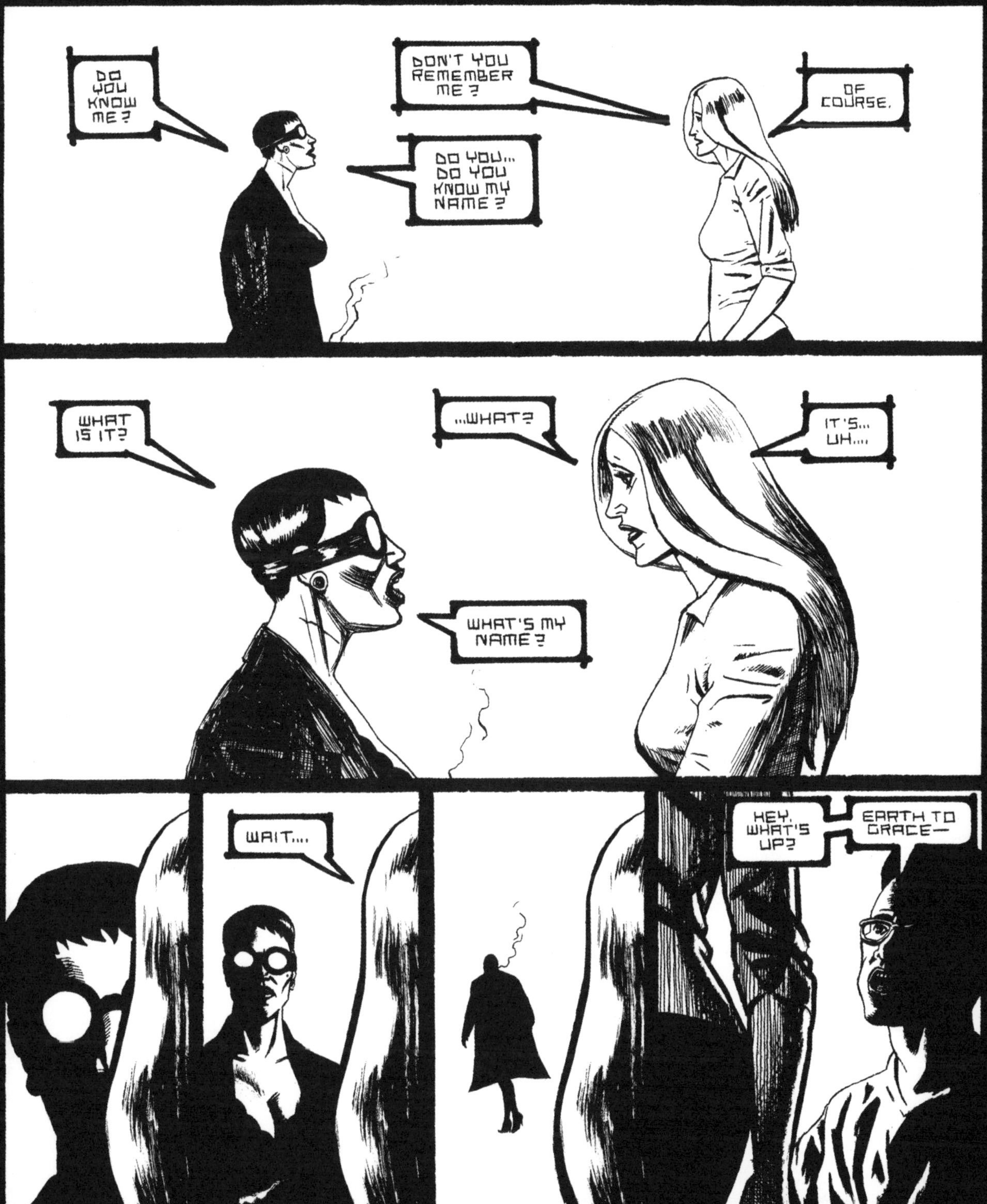
DO YOU KNOW ME?
DON'T YOU REMEMBER ME?
OF COURSE.
DO YOU... DO YOU KNOW MY NAME?
WHAT IS IT?
...WHAT?
IT'S... UH....
WHAT'S MY NAME?
WAIT....
HEY, WHAT'S UP?
EARTH TO GRACE—

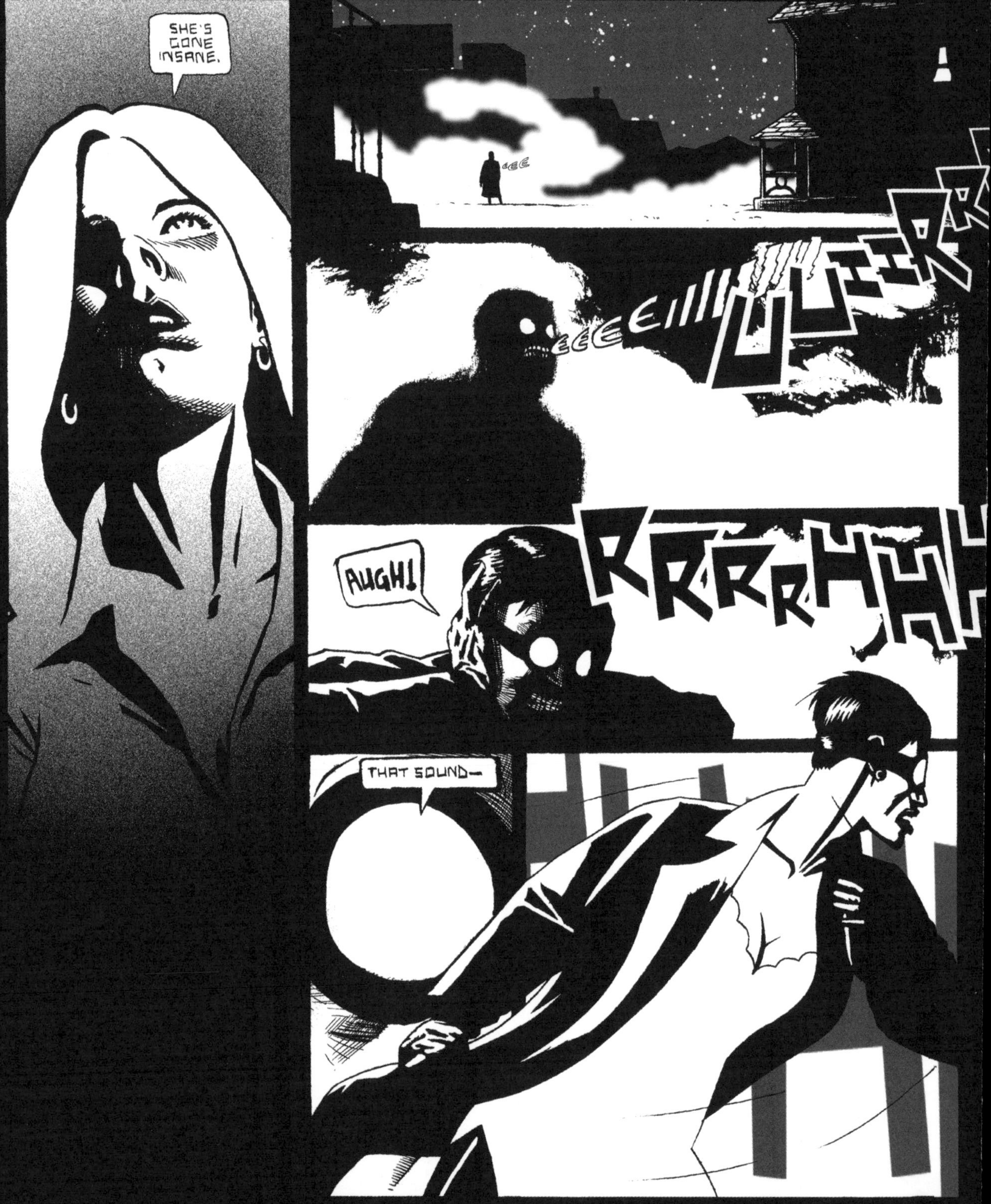

SHE'S GONE INSANE.
EEE
EEEE
AUGH!
RRRRHHH
THAT SOUND—

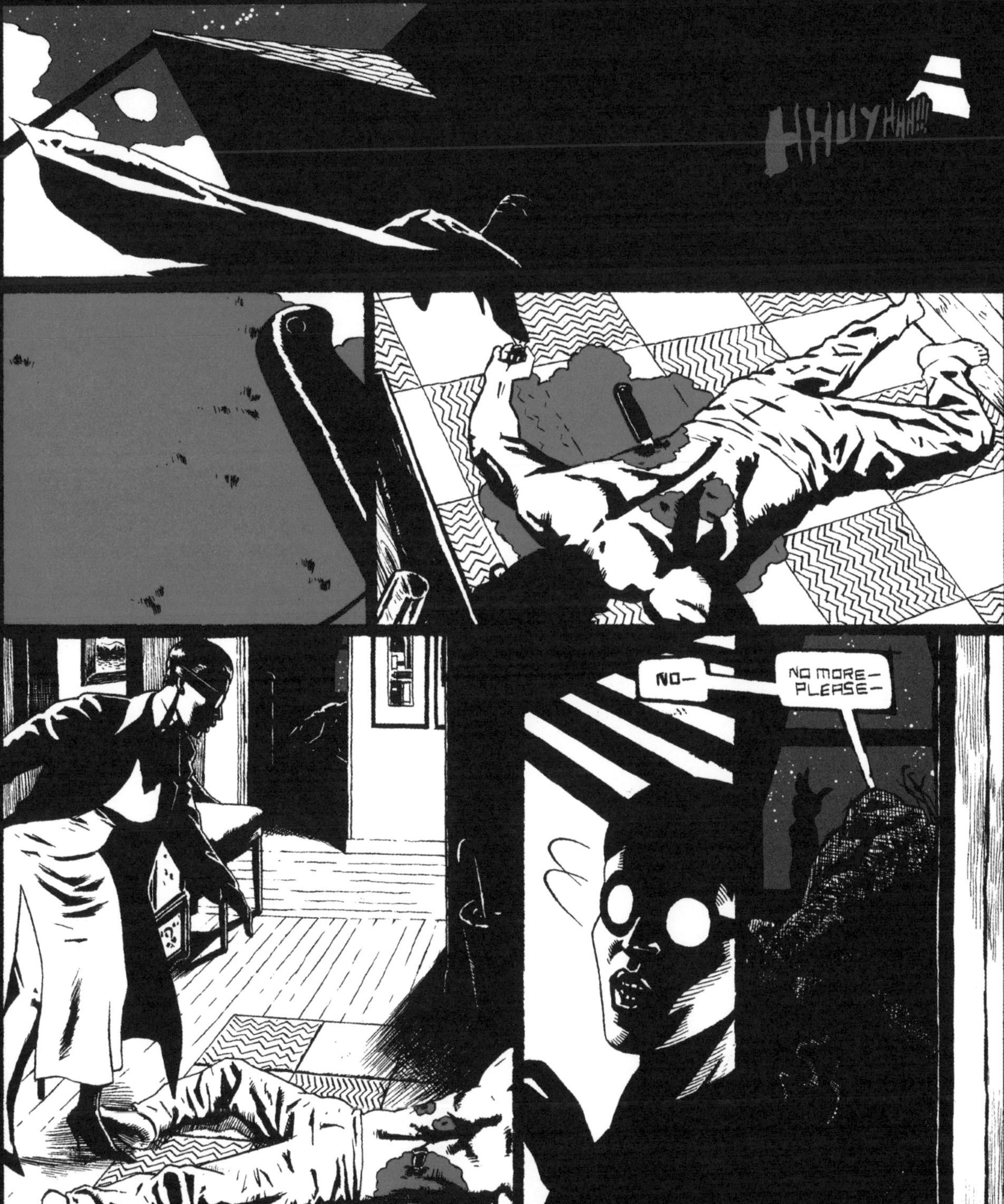
HHUYHHH!!
NO—
NO MORE—
PLEASE—

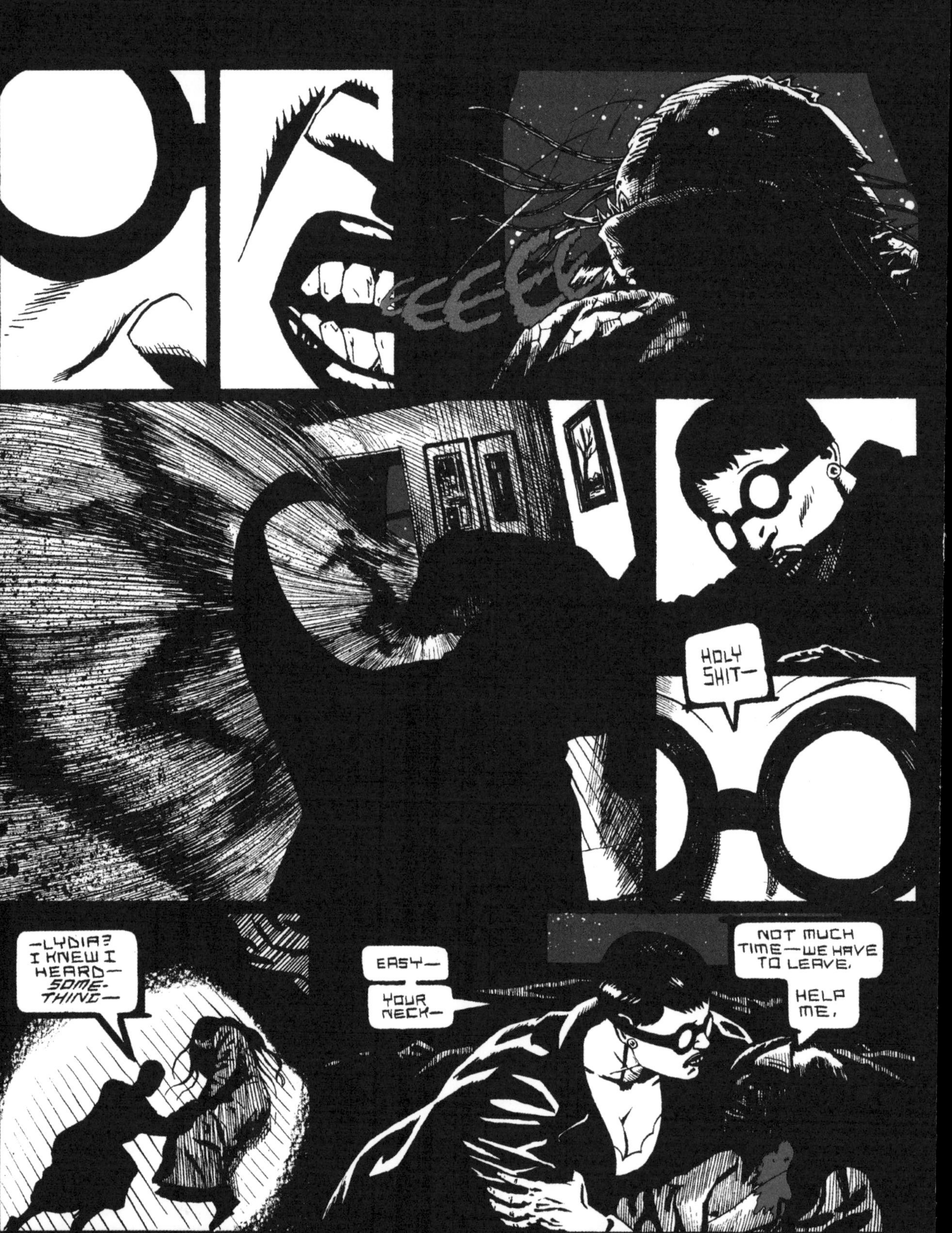
EEEEEE
HOLY SHIT—
—LYDIA? I KNEW I HEARD— SOME-THING—
EASY—
YOUR NECK—
NOT MUCH TIME—WE HAVE TO LEAVE.
HELP ME.

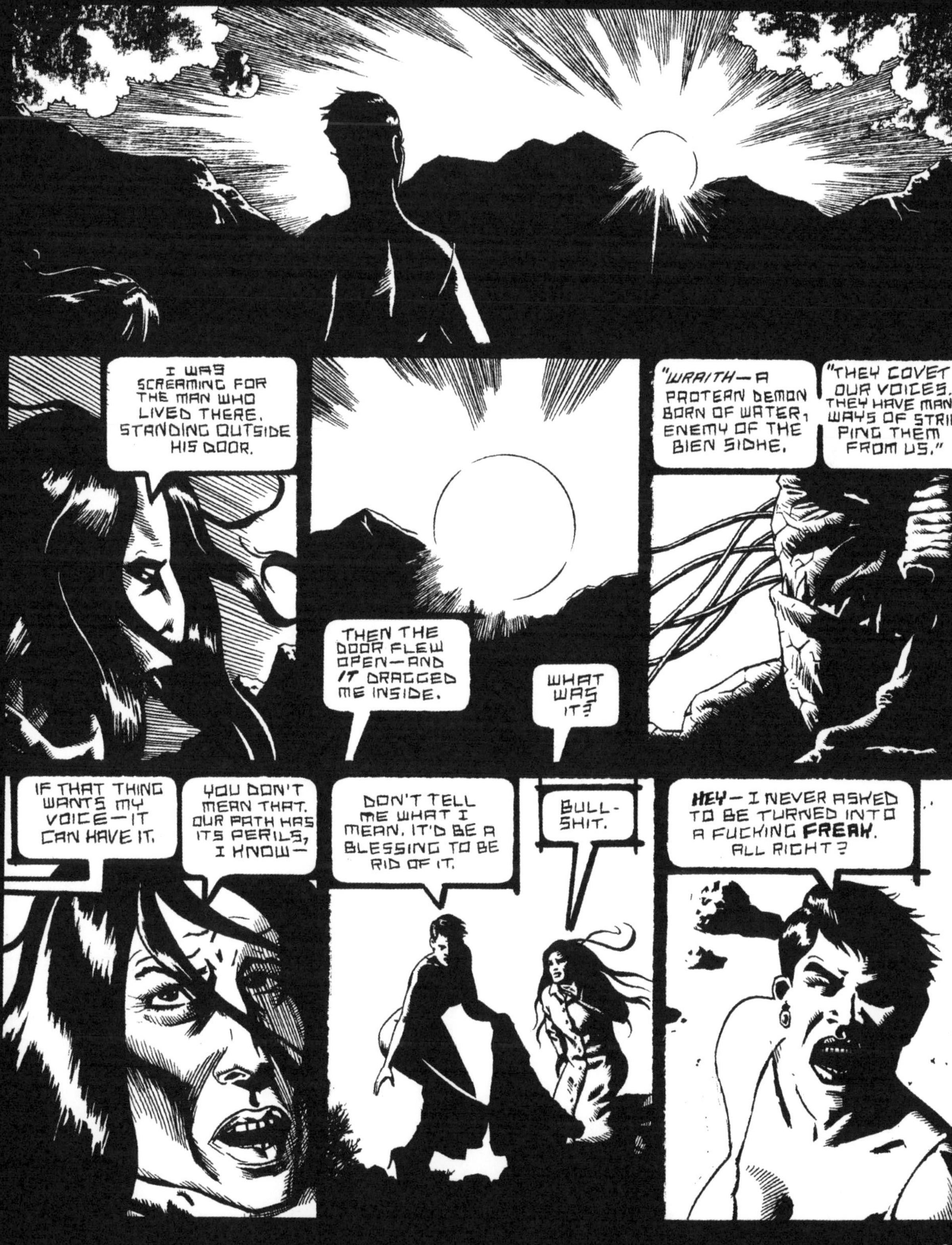
I WAS SCREAMING FOR THE MAN WHO LIVED THERE. STANDING OUTSIDE HIS DOOR.
THEN THE DOOR FLEW OPEN—AND *IT* DRAGGED ME INSIDE.
WHAT WAS IT?
"*WRAITH*—A PROTEAN DEMON BORN OF WATER, ENEMY OF THE BIEN SIDHE.
"THEY COVET OUR VOICES. THEY HAVE MANY WAYS OF STRIP-PING THEM FROM US."
IF THAT THING WANTS MY VOICE—IT CAN HAVE IT.
YOU DON'T MEAN THAT. OUR PATH HAS ITS PERILS, I KNOW—
DON'T TELL ME WHAT I MEAN. IT'D BE A BLESSING TO BE RID OF IT.
BULL-SHIT.
**HEY**—I NEVER ASKED TO BE TURNED INTO A FUCKING **FREAK**. ALL RIGHT?

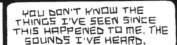 YOU DON'T KNOW THE THINGS I'VE SEEN SINCE THIS HAPPENED TO ME. THE SOUNDS I'VE HEARD.

THE SCREAMING IS LIKE SOME COMPULSION I CAN'T CONTROL.

WE ARE STEWARDS OF A TREMENDOUS RESPONSI- BILITY—

—OUR VOICES ARE A MIGHTY POWER—THE ONLY POWER WE HAVE LEFT IN THIS WORLD.

 OUR ONLY MEANS OF...OF....

 OF MAIN- TAINING THE BALANCE.

THERE'S A KILLER WORKING THE INTERSTATE. I KEEP SCREAM- ING FOR HIS VICTIMS.

 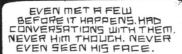 EVEN MET A FEW BEFORE IT HAPPENS. HAD CONVERSATIONS WITH THEM. NEVER HIM THOUGH. NEVER EVEN SEEN HIS FACE.

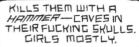 KILLS THEM WITH A *HAMMER*—CAVES IN THEIR FUCKING SKULLS. GIRLS MOSTLY.

 IN THEIR HOUSES...OTHER TIMES HE DRAGS THEM OUT TO THE DESERT. STICKS HIS COCK IN THEIR MOUTHS...THEIR VOICES ARE GONE BUT THE SOUNDS THEY MAKE....

 ...THE *SOUNDS*... I KEEP THINKING I SHOULD—*STOP* HIM—USE *MY* VOICE ON HIM.... I HAVE THAT POWER, BUT I DON'T USE IT.

 LYDIA, HOW CAN I LEARN WHO KILLED ME?

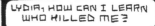 DO YOU HAVE AN IDEA WHO DID IT?

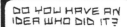 I HAVE A THEORY...BUT NO PROOF.

85

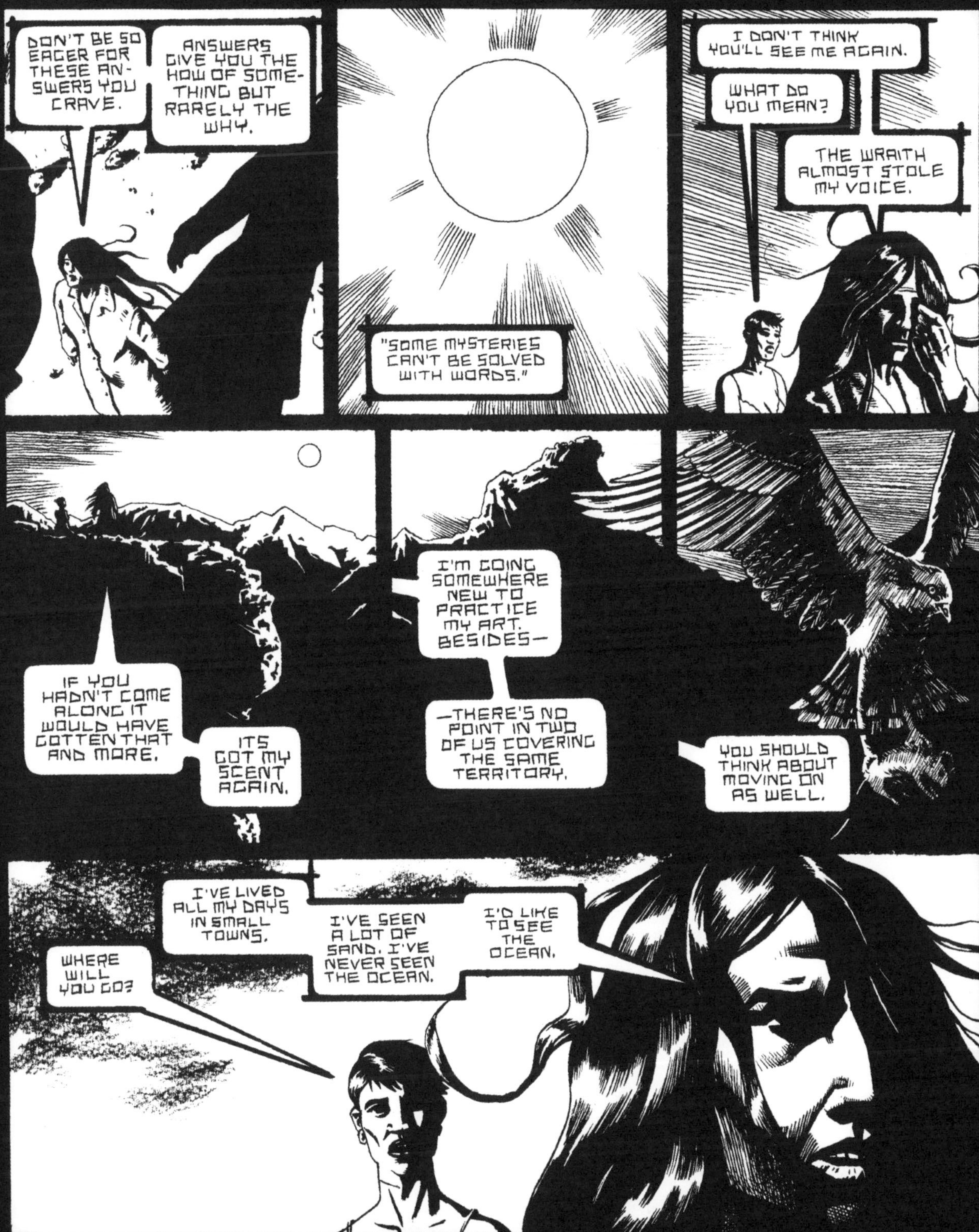
DON'T BE SO EAGER FOR THESE AN-SWERS YOU CRAVE.
ANSWERS GIVE YOU THE HOW OF SOME-THING BUT RARELY THE WHY.
"SOME MYSTERIES CAN'T BE SOLVED WITH WORDS."
I DON'T THINK YOU'LL SEE ME AGAIN.
WHAT DO YOU MEAN?
THE WRAITH ALMOST STOLE MY VOICE.
IF YOU HADN'T COME ALONG IT WOULD HAVE GOTTEN THAT AND MORE.
ITS GOT MY SCENT AGAIN.
I'M GOING SOMEWHERE NEW TO PRACTICE MY ART. BESIDES—
—THERE'S NO POINT IN TWO OF US COVERING THE SAME TERRITORY.
YOU SHOULD THINK ABOUT MOVING ON AS WELL.
WHERE WILL YOU GO?
I'VE LIVED ALL MY DAYS IN SMALL TOWNS.
I'VE SEEN A LOT OF SAND. I'VE NEVER SEEN THE OCEAN.
I'D LIKE TO SEE THE OCEAN.

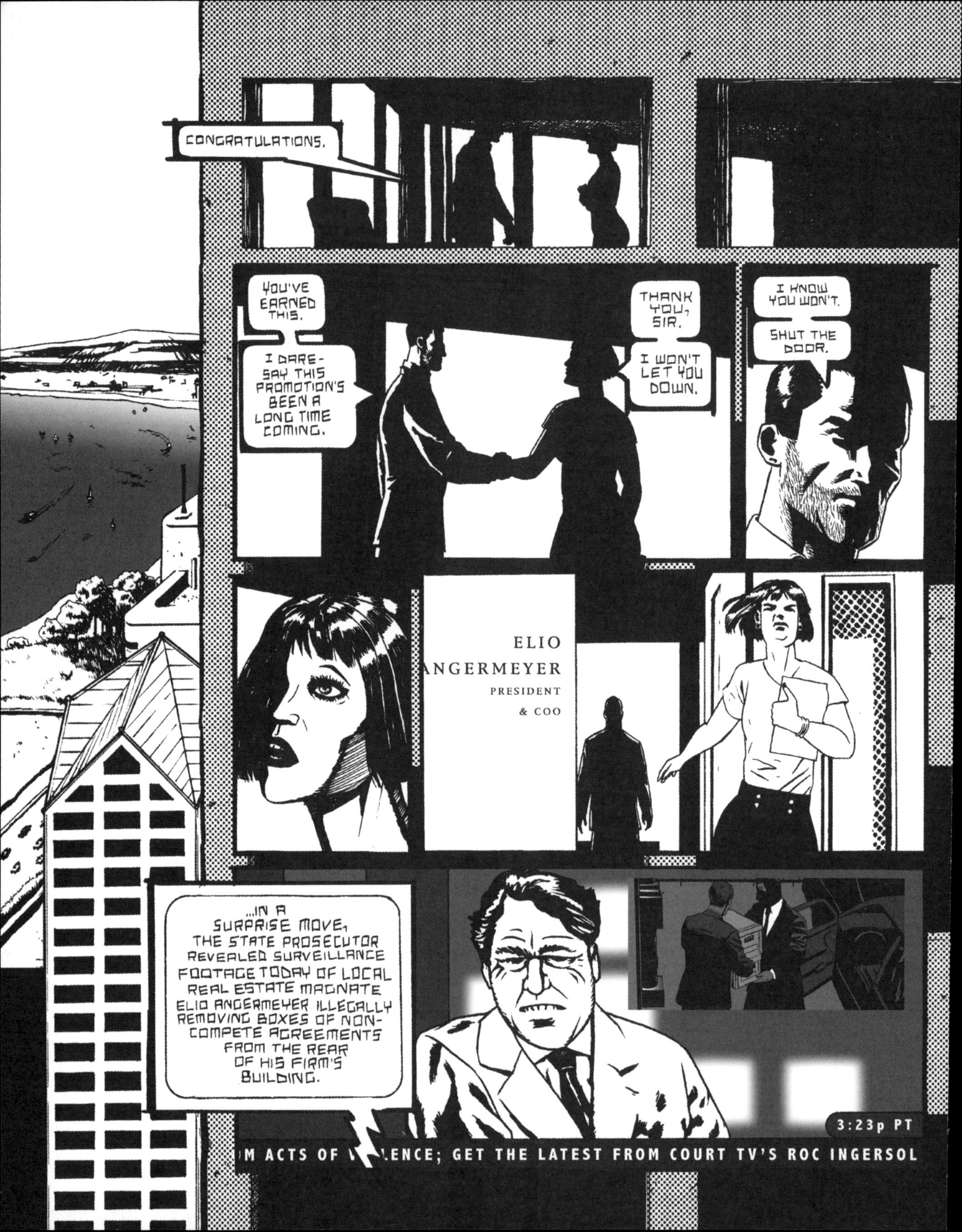
CONGRATULATIONS.
YOU'VE EARNED THIS.
I DARE-SAY THIS PROMOTION'S BEEN A LONG TIME COMING.
THANK YOU, SIR.
I WON'T LET YOU DOWN.
I KNOW YOU WON'T.
SHUT THE DOOR.
ELIO ANGERMEYER
PRESIDENT & COO
...IN A SURPRISE MOVE, THE STATE PROSECUTOR REVEALED SURVEILLANCE FOOTAGE TODAY OF LOCAL REAL ESTATE MAGNATE ELIO ANGERMEYER ILLEGALLY REMOVING BOXES OF NON-COMPETE AGREEMENTS FROM THE REAR OF HIS FIRM'S BUILDING.
3:23p PT
LENCE; GET THE LATEST FROM COURT TV'S ROC INGERSOL

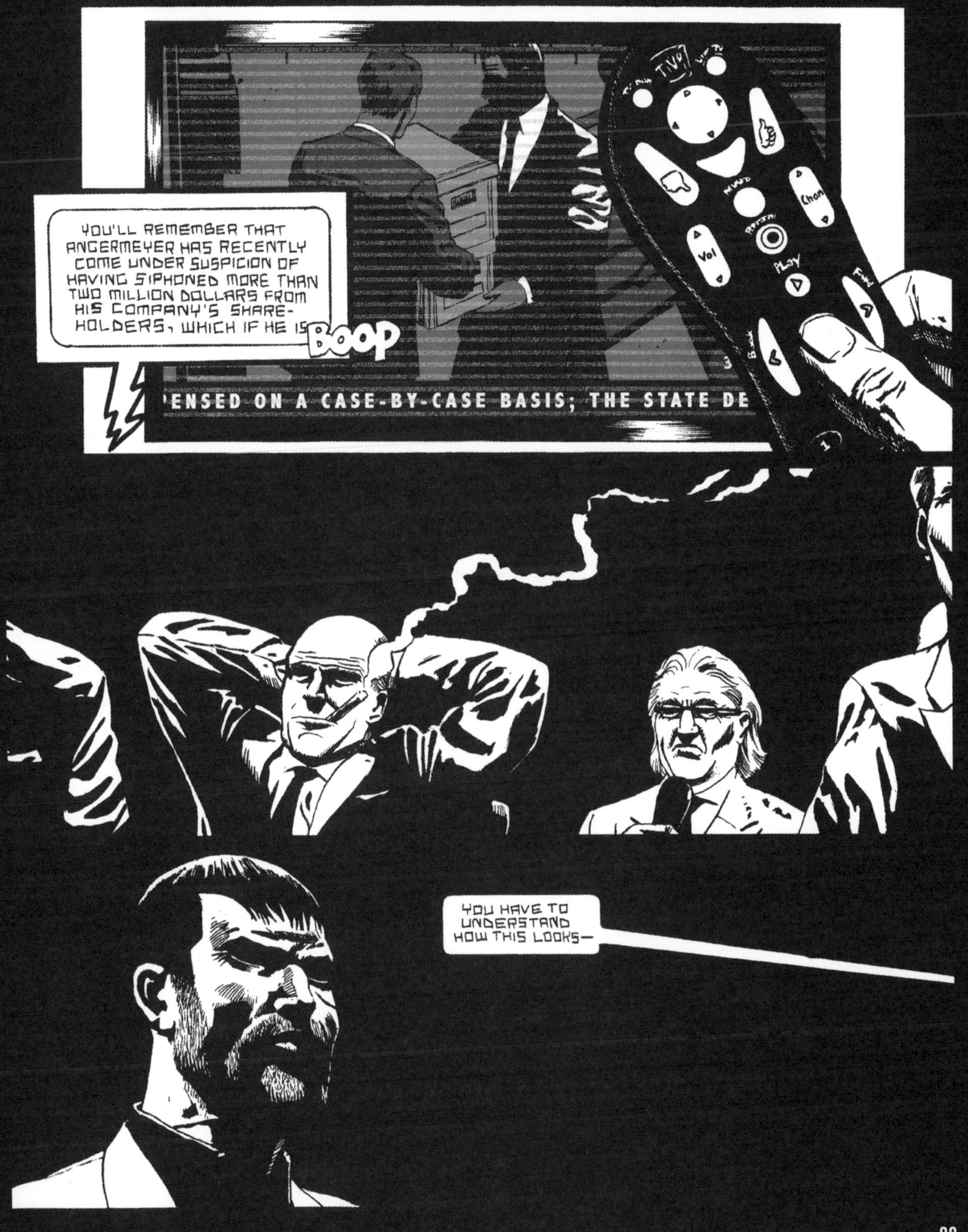
YOU'LL REMEMBER THAT ANGERMEYER HAS RECENTLY COME UNDER SUSPICION OF HAVING SIPHONED MORE THAN TWO MILLION DOLLARS FROM HIS COMPANY'S SHARE-HOLDERS, WHICH IF HE IS
BOOP
PENSED ON A CASE-BY-CASE BASIS; THE STATE DE
YOU HAVE TO UNDERSTAND HOW THIS LOOKS—

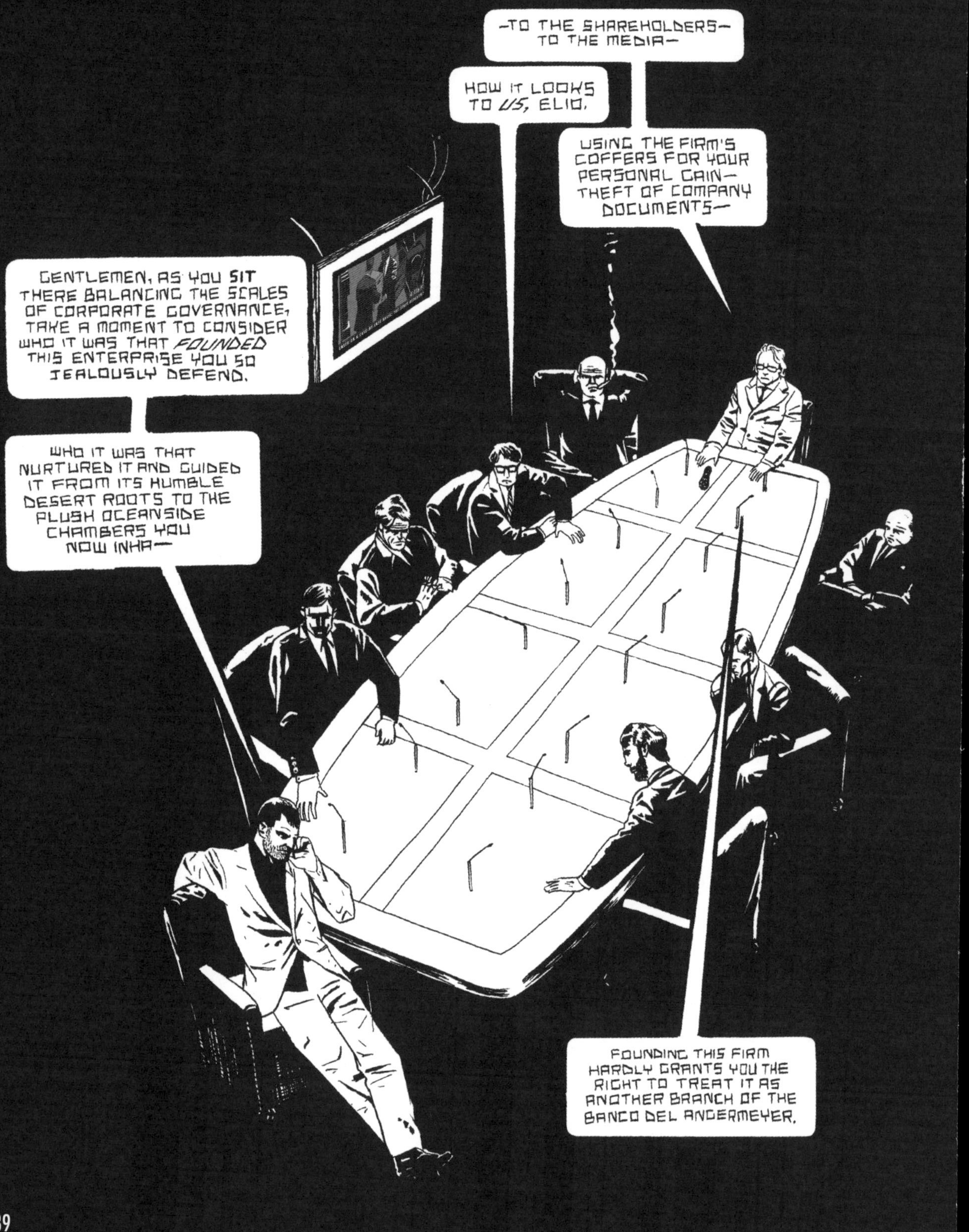
GENTLEMEN, AS YOU SIT THERE BALANCING THE SCALES OF CORPORATE GOVERNANCE, TAKE A MOMENT TO CONSIDER WHO IT WAS THAT *FOUNDED* THIS ENTERPRISE YOU SO JEALOUSLY DEFEND.
WHO IT WAS THAT NURTURED IT AND GUIDED IT FROM ITS HUMBLE DESERT ROOTS TO THE PLUSH OCEANSIDE CHAMBERS YOU NOW INHA—
FOUNDING THIS FIRM HARDLY GRANTS YOU THE RIGHT TO TREAT IT AS ANOTHER BRANCH OF THE BANCO DEL ANGERMEYER.
USING THE FIRM'S COFFERS FOR YOUR PERSONAL GAIN— THEFT OF COMPANY DOCUMENTS—
—TO THE SHAREHOLDERS— TO THE MEDIA—
HOW IT LOOKS TO *US*, ELIO.

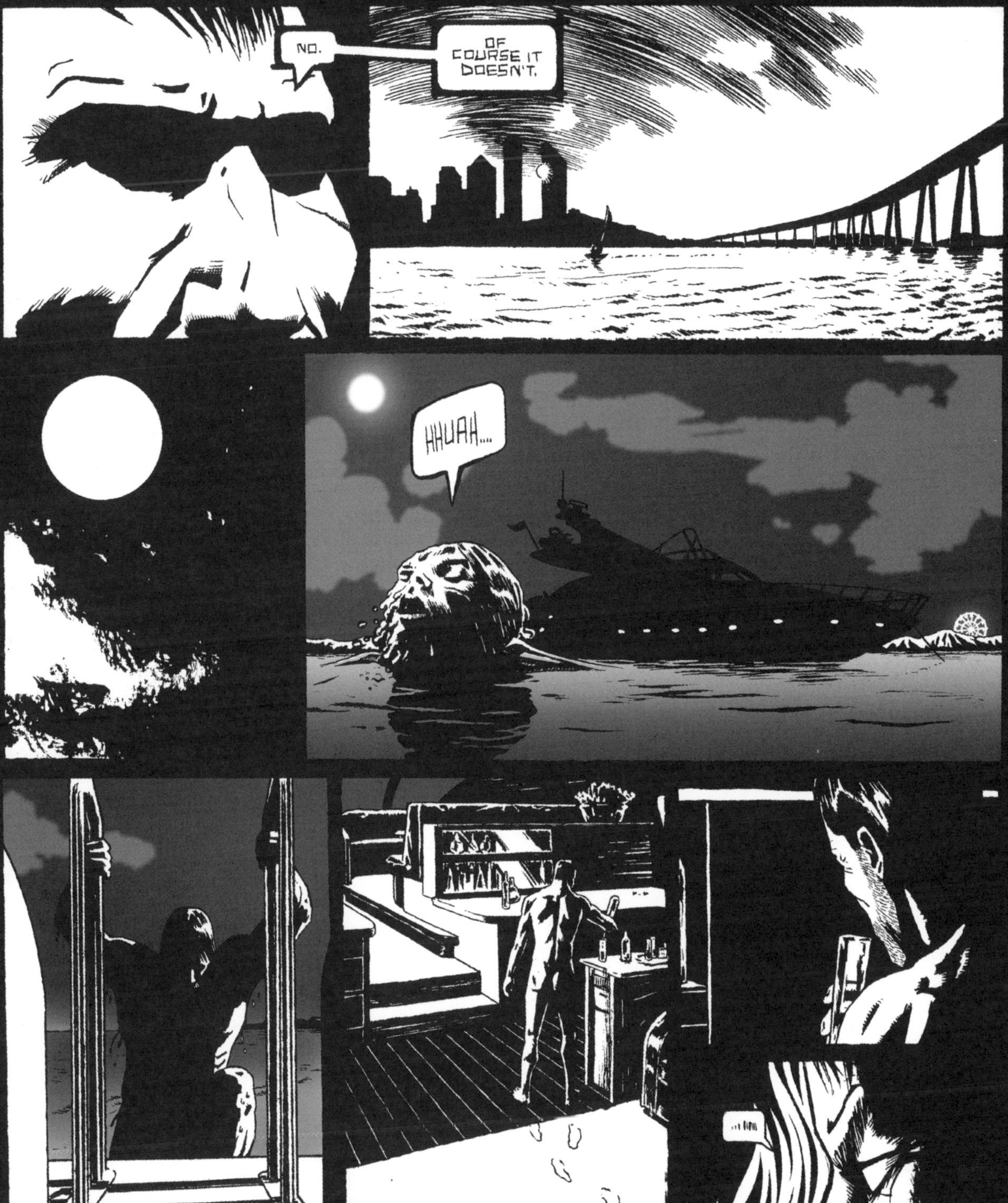
NO.
OF COURSE IT DOESN'T.
HHUAH...

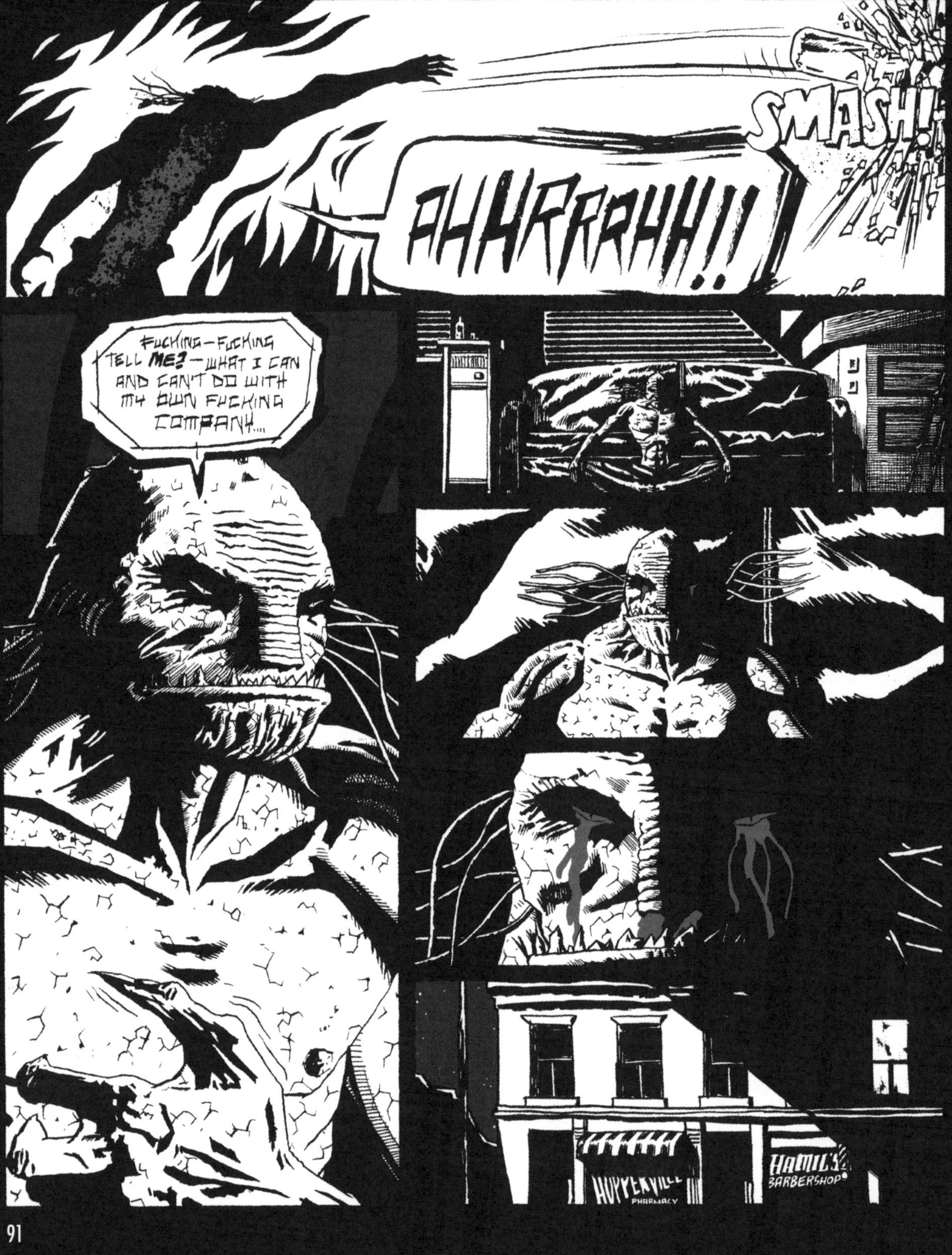

SMASH!
AHHRRRHH!!
FUCKING—FUCKING TELL ME?—WHAT I CAN AND CAN'T DO WITH MY OWN FUCKING COMPANY....
HOPPERVILLE PHARMACY
HAMIL'S BARBERSHOP

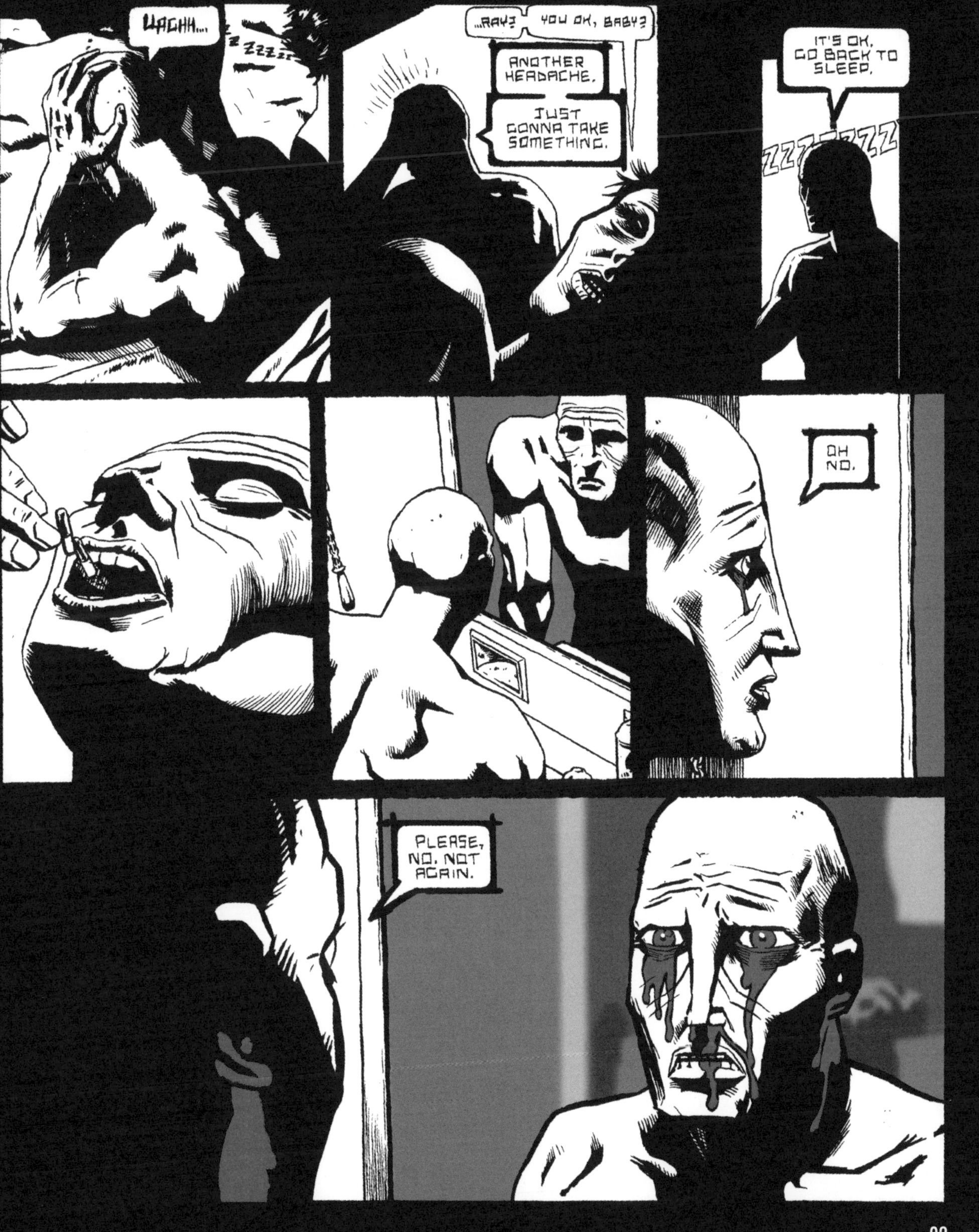
UAGHH...
ZZZZZ
...RAY?
YOU OK, BABY?
ANOTHER HEADACHE.
JUST GONNA TAKE SOMETHING.
IT'S OK, GO BACK TO SLEEP.
ZZZZZZZ
OH NO.
PLEASE, NO. NOT AGAIN.

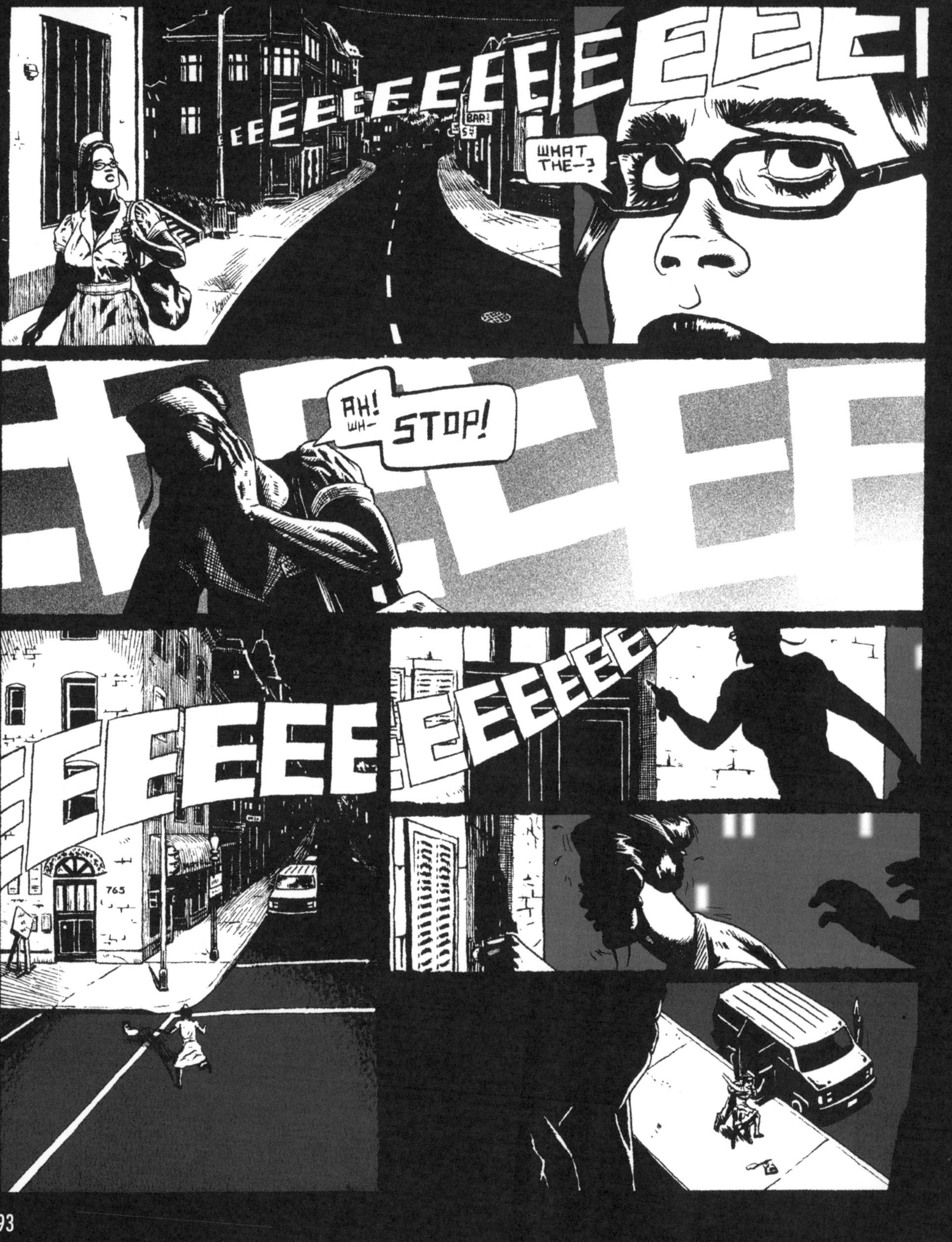
EEEEEEEEEEEEEEEET!
BAR
WHAT THE--?
AH! WH- STOP!
765
EEEEEEEEEEEE

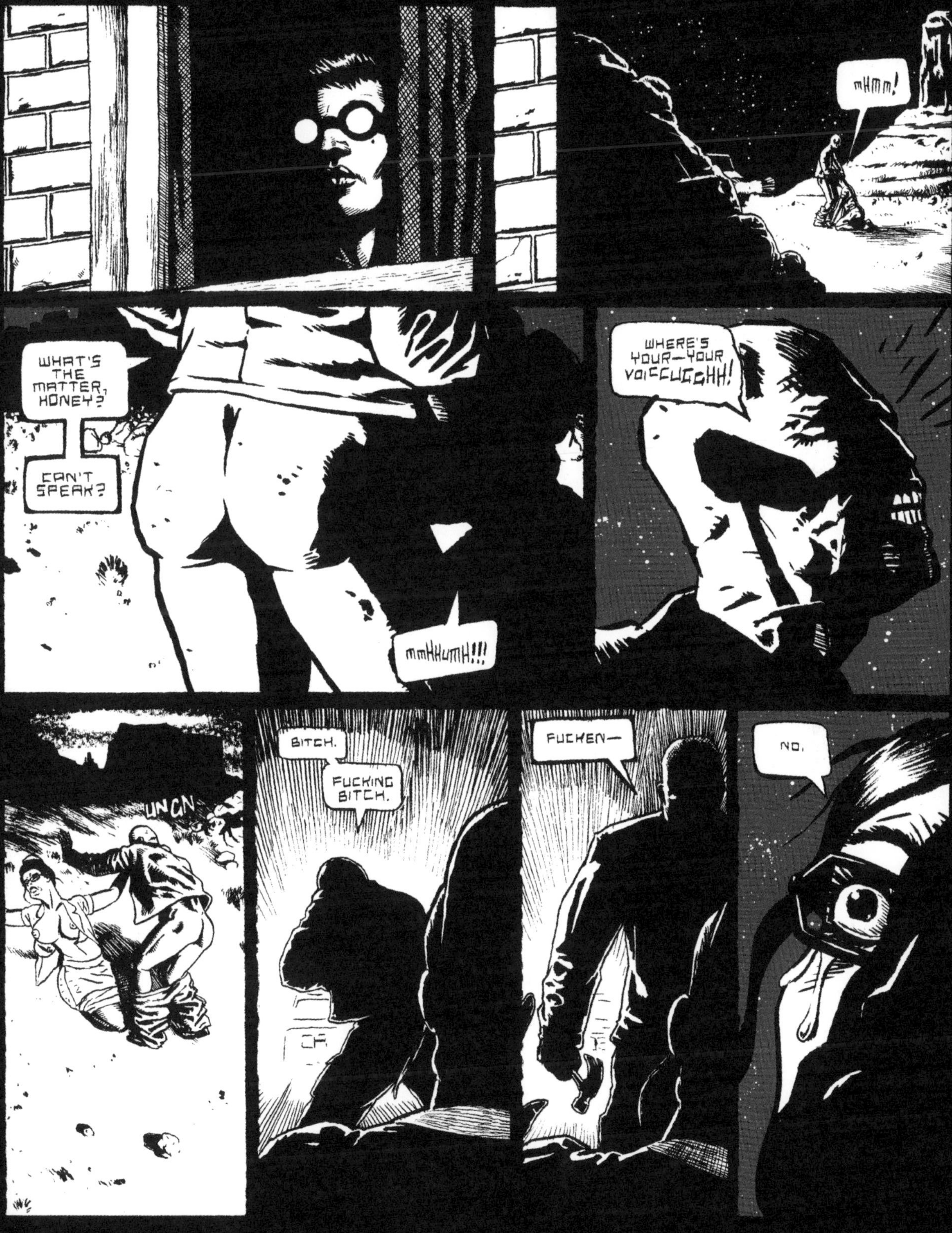
MHMM!
WHAT'S THE MATTER, HONEY?
CAN'T SPEAK?
MMHKUMH!!!
WHERE'S YOUR—YOUR VOICCUGGHH!
UNGN
BITCH.
FUCKING BITCH.
CR
FUCKEN—
NO.

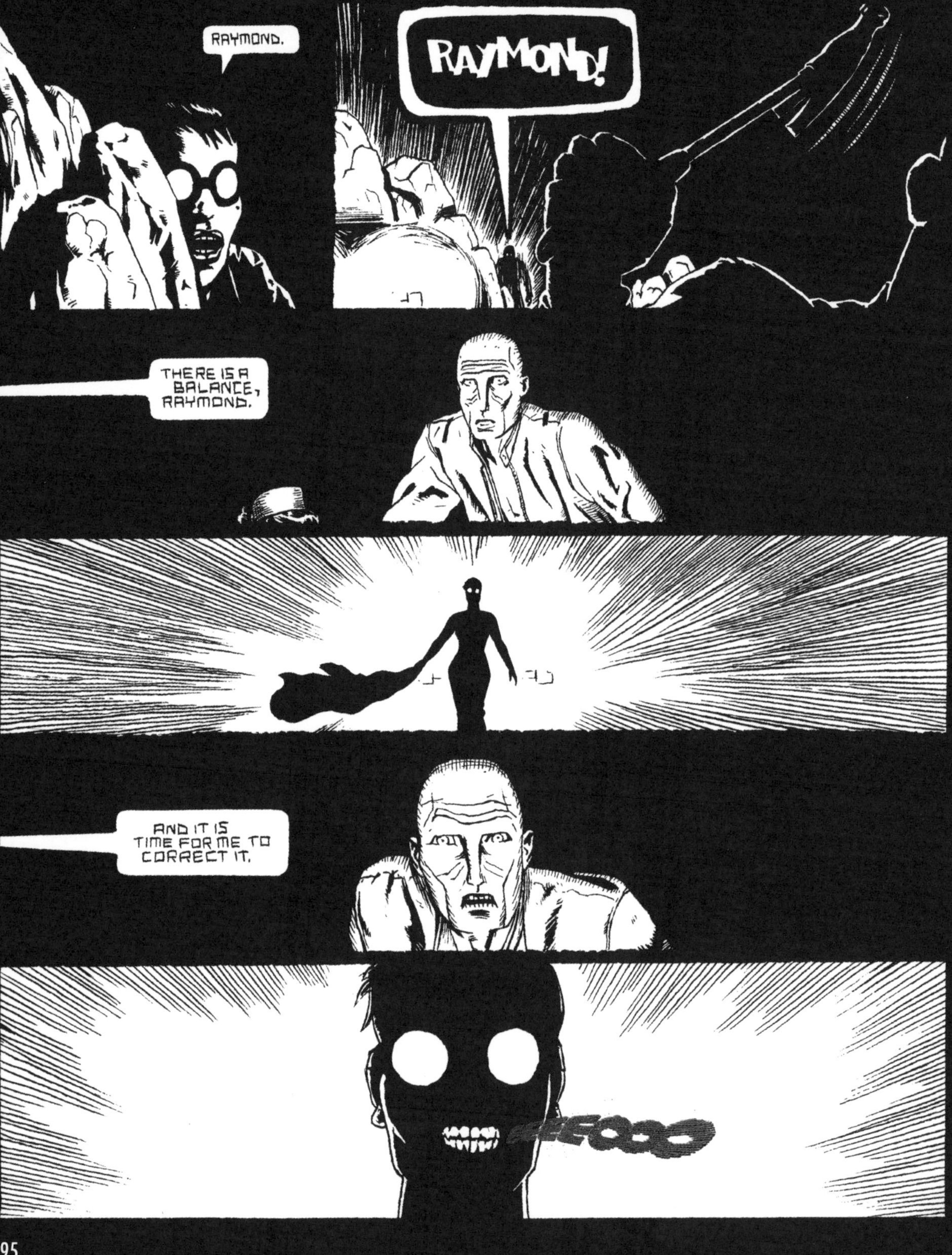
RAYMOND.
RAYMOND!
THERE IS A BALANCE, RAYMOND.
AND IT IS TIME FOR ME TO CORRECT IT.
EEEEOOOO

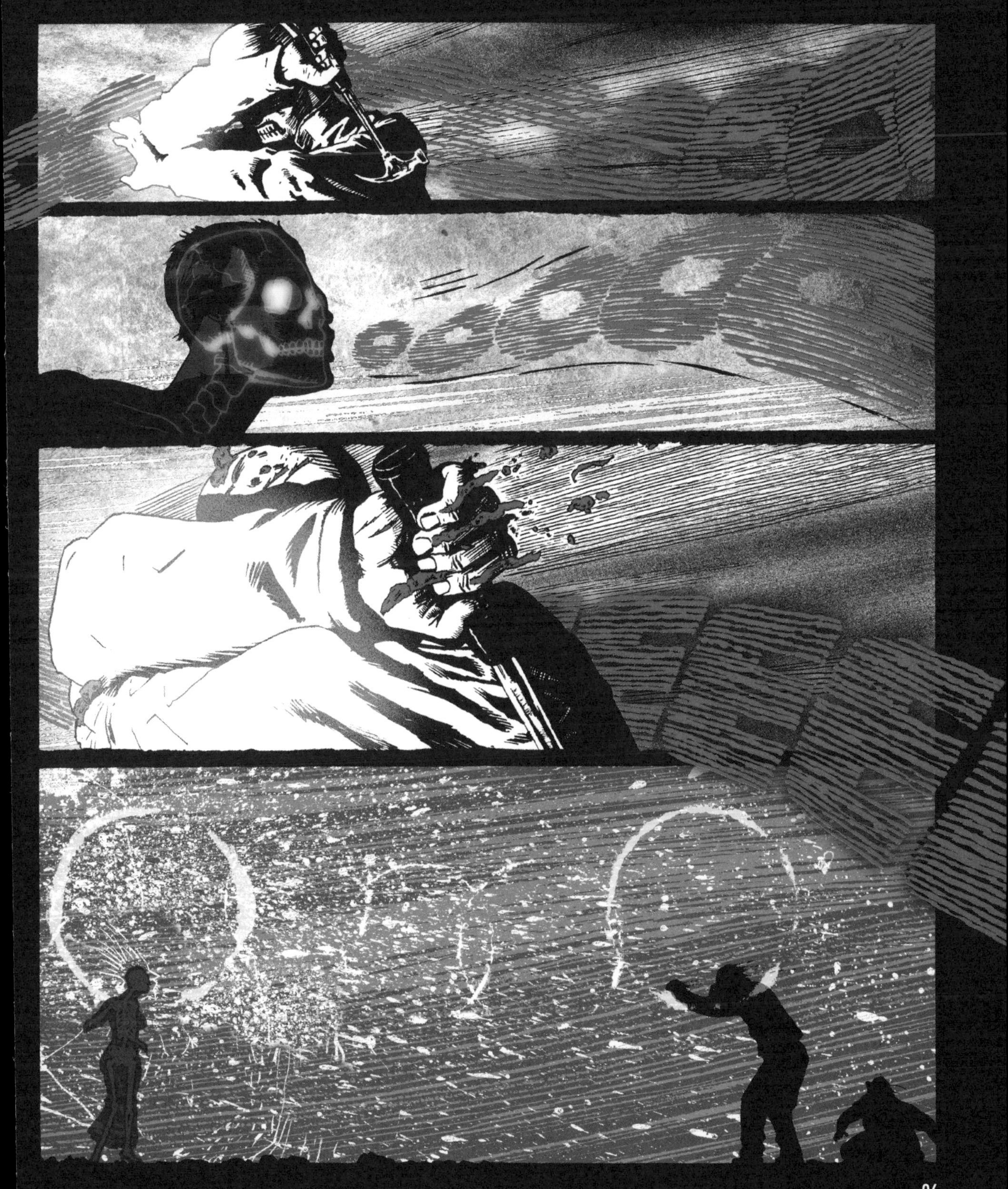

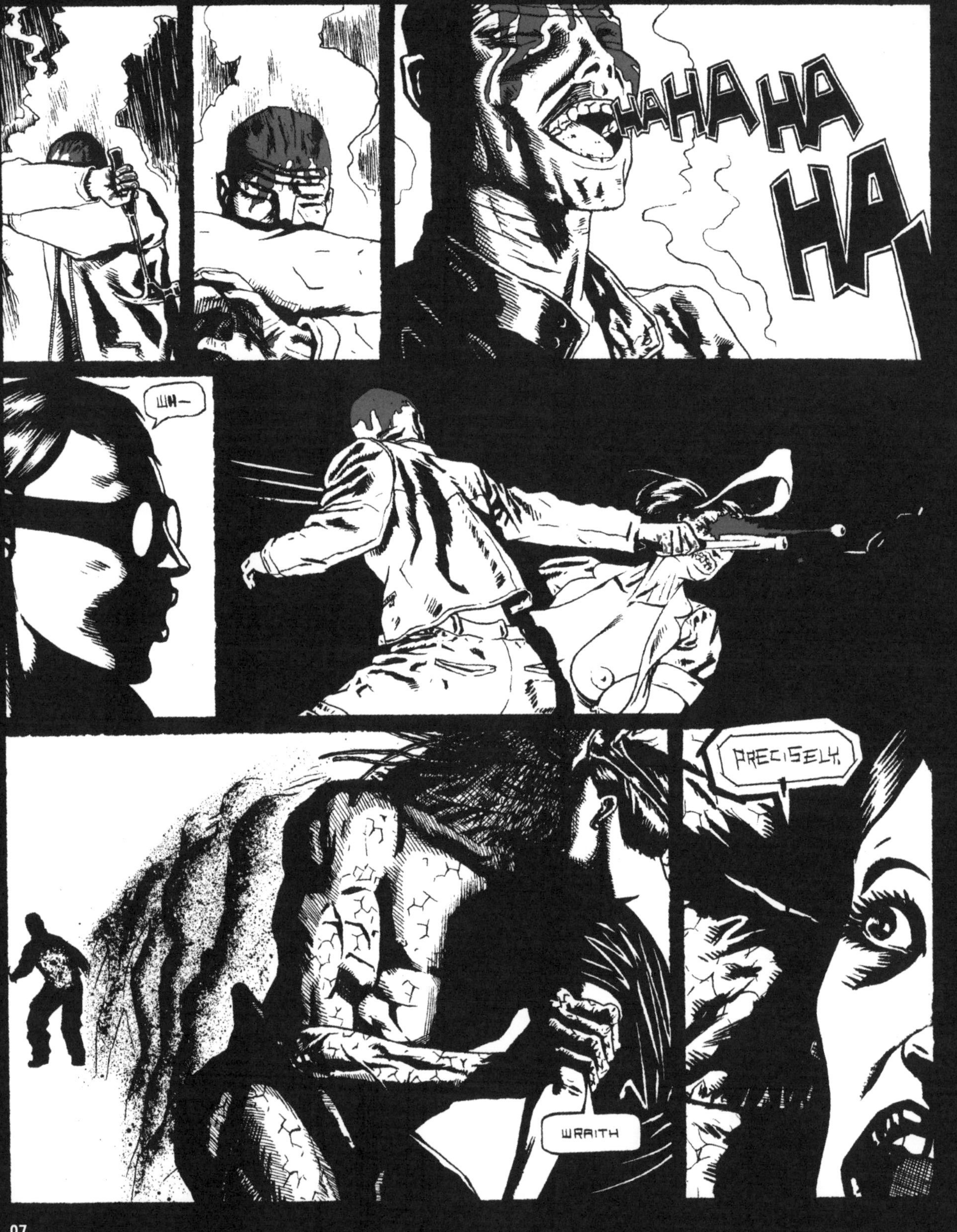
HAHAHAHA
HA
WH—
PRECISELY.
WRAITH

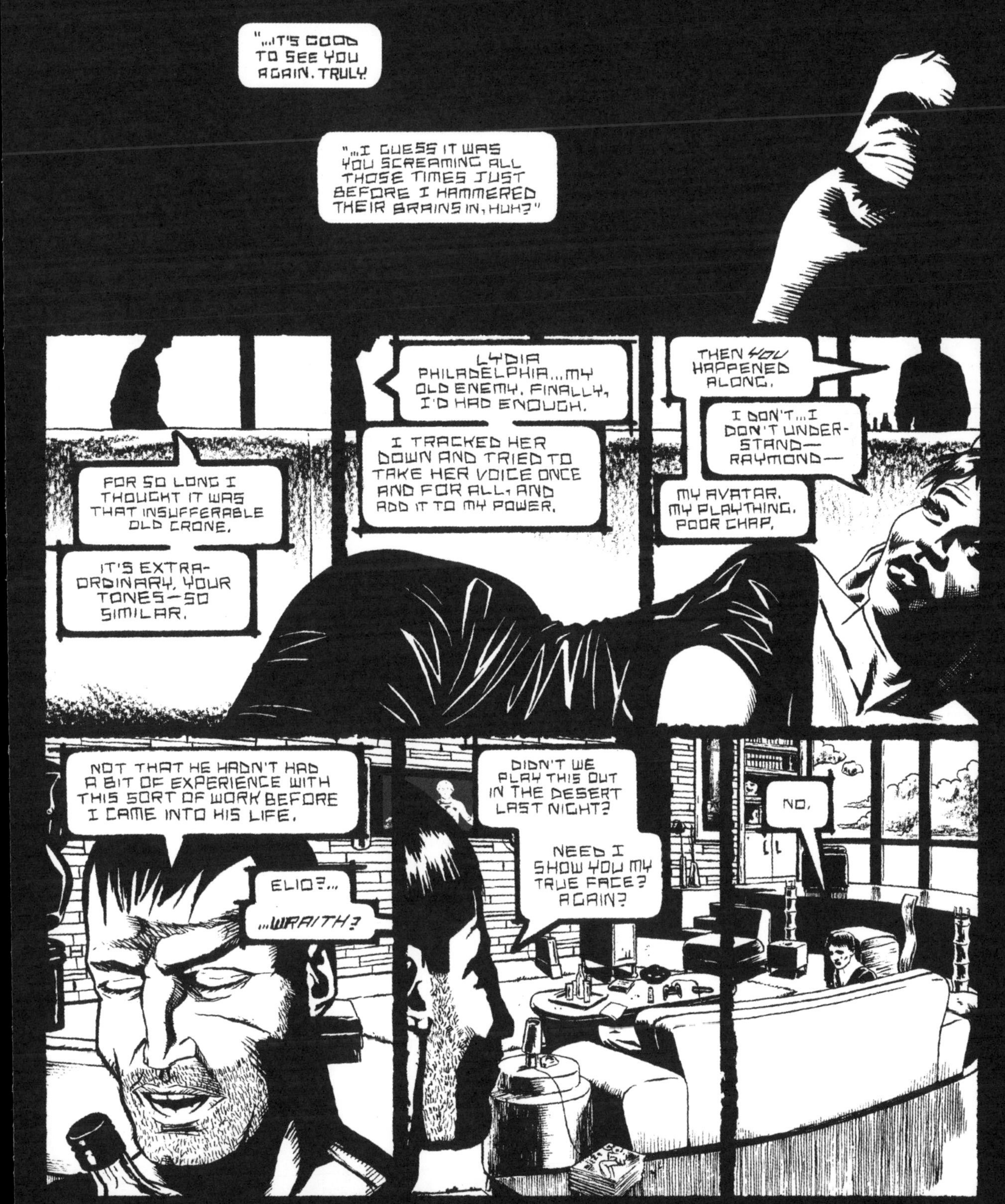
"...IT'S GOOD TO SEE YOU AGAIN. TRULY.
"...I GUESS IT WAS YOU SCREAMING ALL THOSE TIMES JUST BEFORE I HAMMERED THEIR BRAINS IN, HUH?"
FOR SO LONG I THOUGHT IT WAS THAT INSUFFERABLE OLD CRONE.
IT'S EXTRA-ORDINARY, YOUR TONES—SO SIMILAR.
LYDIA PHILADELPHIA... MY OLD ENEMY. FINALLY, I'D HAD ENOUGH.
I TRACKED HER DOWN AND TRIED TO TAKE HER VOICE ONCE AND FOR ALL, AND ADD IT TO MY POWER.
THEN YOU HAPPENED ALONG.
I DON'T... I DON'T UNDER-STAND— RAYMOND—
MY AVATAR. MY PLAYTHING. POOR CHAP.
NOT THAT HE HADN'T HAD A BIT OF EXPERIENCE WITH THIS SORT OF WORK BEFORE I CAME INTO HIS LIFE.
ELIO?...
...WRAITH?
DIDN'T WE PLAY THIS OUT IN THE DESERT LAST NIGHT?
NEED I SHOW YOU MY TRUE FACE? AGAIN?
NO.

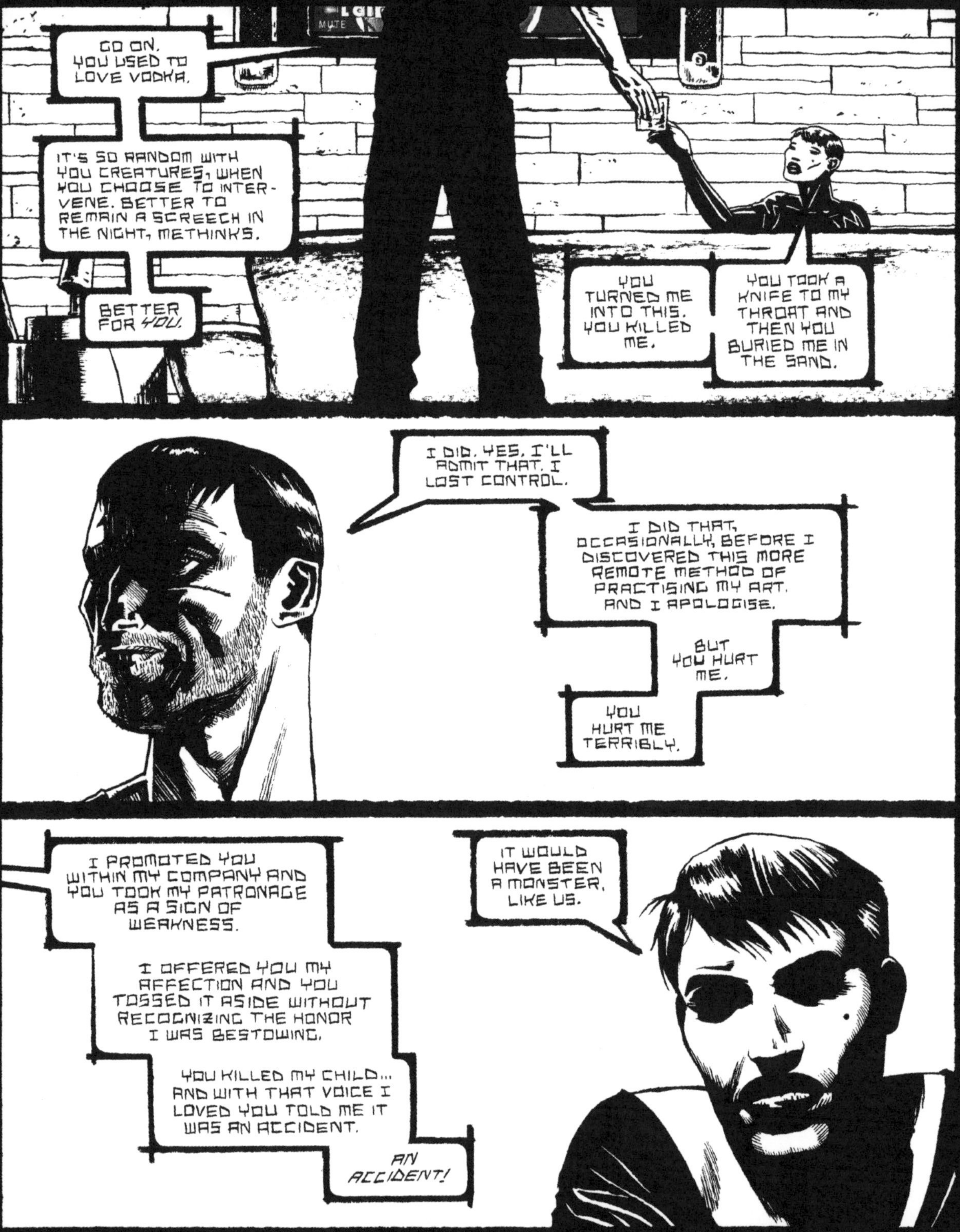
GO ON. YOU USED TO LOVE VODKA.
IT'S SO RANDOM WITH YOU CREATURES, WHEN YOU CHOOSE TO INTER-VENE. BETTER TO REMAIN A SCREECH IN THE NIGHT, METHINKS.
BETTER FOR YOU.
YOU TURNED ME INTO THIS. YOU KILLED ME.
YOU TOOK A KNIFE TO MY THROAT AND THEN YOU BURIED ME IN THE SAND.
I DID. YES, I'LL ADMIT THAT. I LOST CONTROL.
I DID THAT, OCCASIONALLY, BEFORE I DISCOVERED THIS MORE REMOTE METHOD OF PRACTISING MY ART. AND I APOLOGISE.
BUT YOU HURT ME.
YOU HURT ME TERRIBLY.
I PROMOTED YOU WITHIN MY COMPANY AND YOU TOOK MY PATRONAGE AS A SIGN OF WEAKNESS.
I OFFERED YOU MY AFFECTION AND YOU TOSSED IT ASIDE WITHOUT RECOGNIZING THE HONOR I WAS BESTOWING.
YOU KILLED MY CHILD... AND WITH THAT VOICE I LOVED YOU TOLD ME IT WAS AN ACCIDENT.
AN ACCIDENT!
IT WOULD HAVE BEEN A MONSTER, LIKE US.

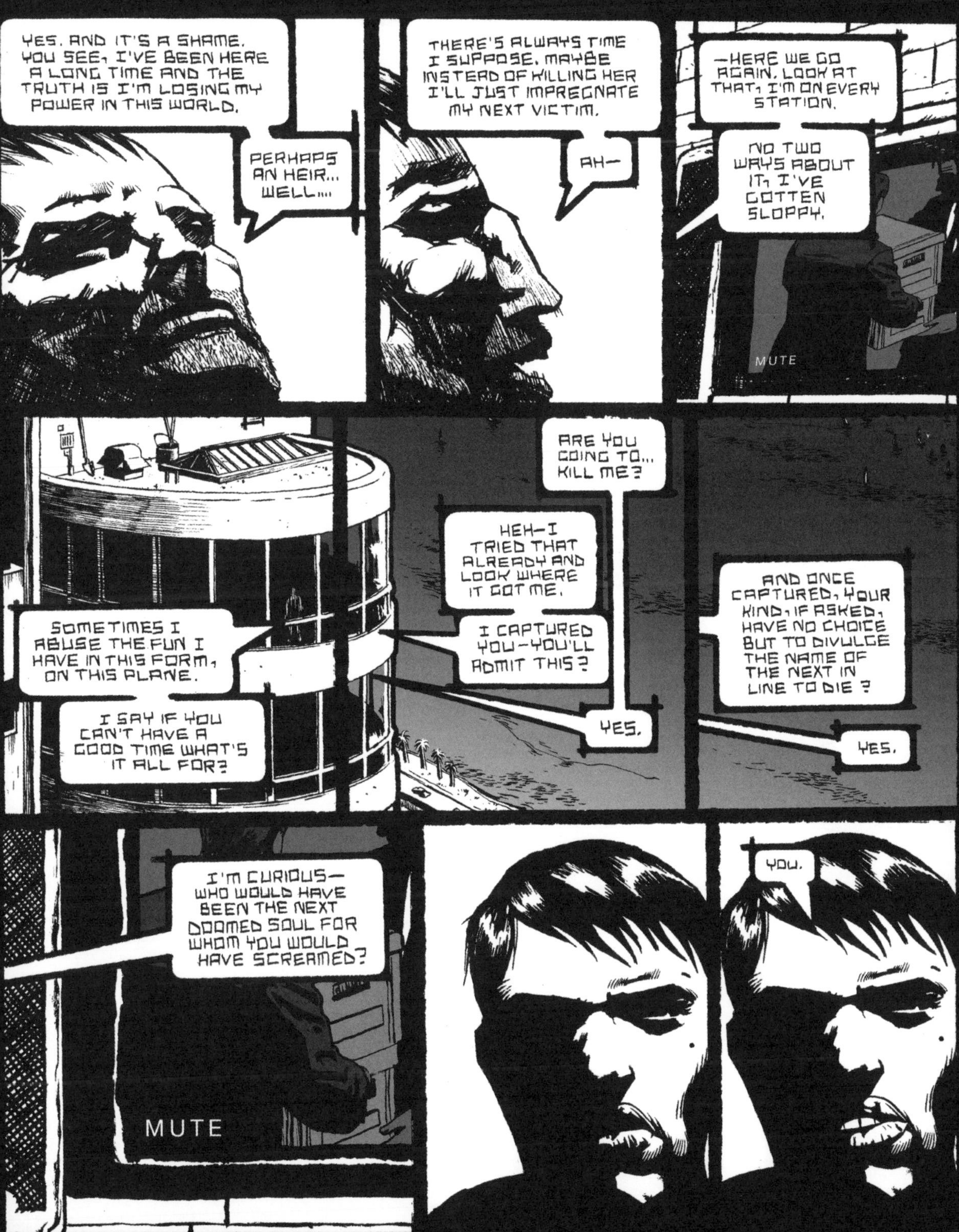
YES. AND IT'S A SHAME. YOU SEE, I'VE BEEN HERE A LONG TIME AND THE TRUTH IS I'M LOSING MY POWER IN THIS WORLD.
PERHAPS AN HEIR... WELL....
THERE'S ALWAYS TIME I SUPPOSE. MAYBE INSTEAD OF KILLING HER I'LL JUST IMPREGNATE MY NEXT VICTIM.
AH—
—HERE WE GO AGAIN. LOOK AT THAT, I'M ON EVERY STATION.
NO TWO WAYS ABOUT IT, I'VE GOTTEN SLOPPY.
MUTE
SOMETIMES I ABUSE THE FUN I HAVE IN THIS FORM, ON THIS PLANE.
I SAY IF YOU CAN'T HAVE A GOOD TIME WHAT'S IT ALL FOR?
ARE YOU GOING TO... KILL ME?
HEH—I TRIED THAT ALREADY AND LOOK WHERE IT GOT ME.
I CAPTURED YOU—YOU'LL ADMIT THIS?
YES.
AND ONCE CAPTURED, YOUR KIND, IF ASKED, HAVE NO CHOICE BUT TO DIVULGE THE NAME OF THE NEXT IN LINE TO DIE?
YES.
I'M CURIOUS— WHO WOULD HAVE BEEN THE NEXT DOOMED SOUL FOR WHOM YOU WOULD HAVE SCREAMED?
MUTE
YOU.

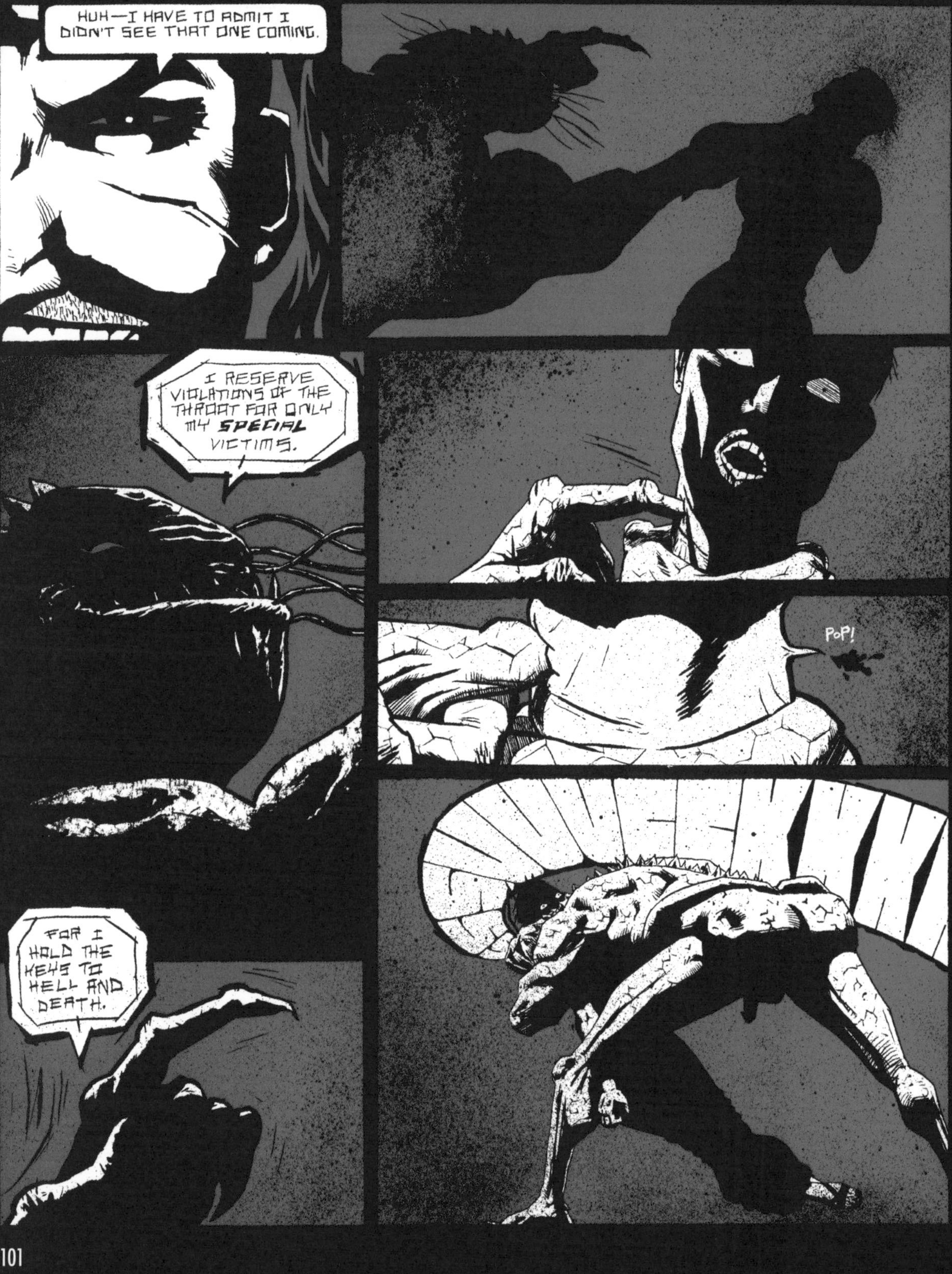
HUH—I HAVE TO ADMIT I DIDN'T SEE THAT ONE COMING.
I RESERVE VIOLATIONS OF THE THROAT FOR ONLY MY SPECIAL VICTIMS.
POP!
FOR I HOLD THE KEYS TO HELL AND DEATH.

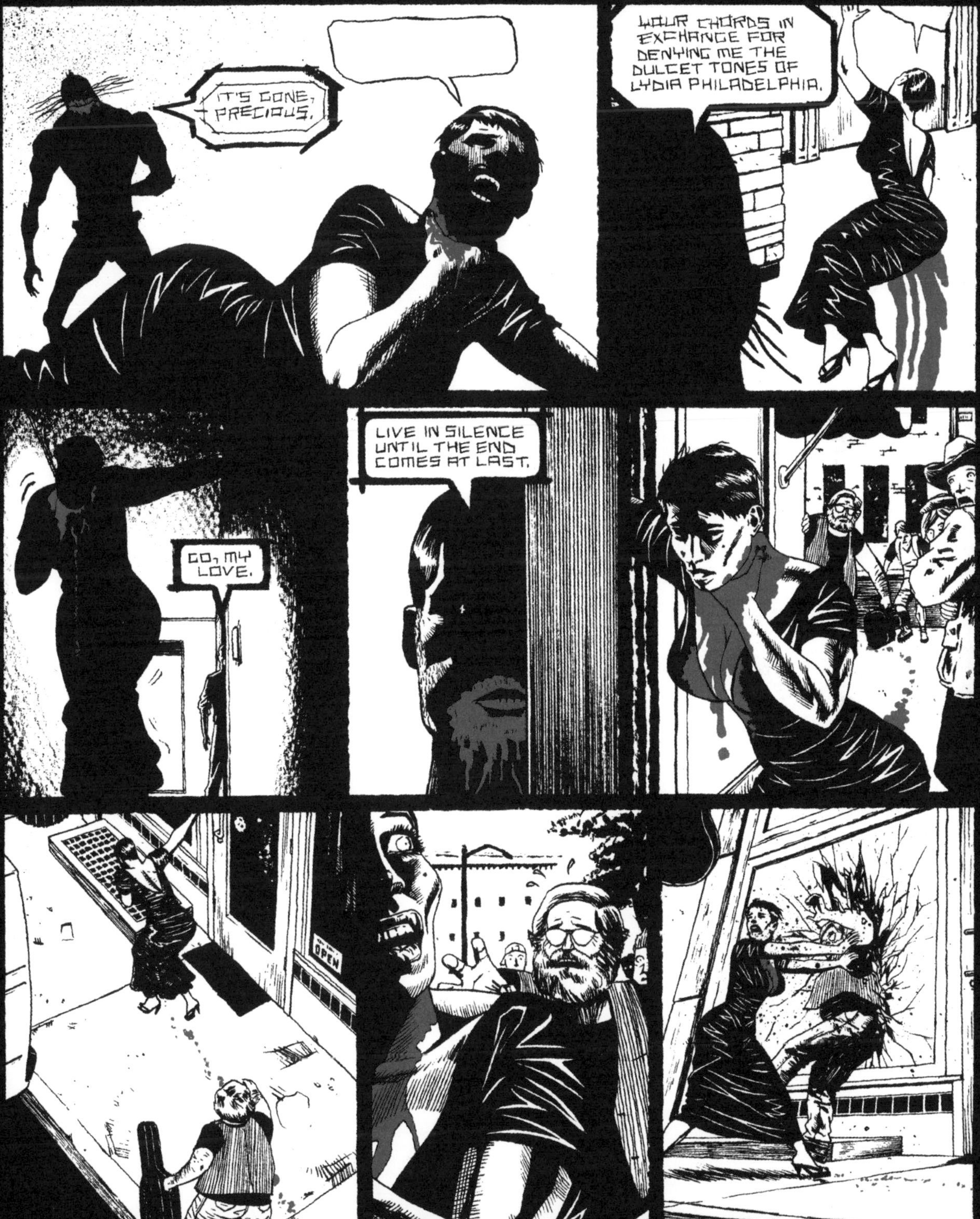
IT'S GONE, PRECIOUS.
YOUR CHORDS IN EXCHANGE FOR DENYING ME THE DULCET TONES OF LYDIA PHILADELPHIA.
GO, MY LOVE.
LIVE IN SILENCE UNTIL THE END COMES AT LAST.
OPEN

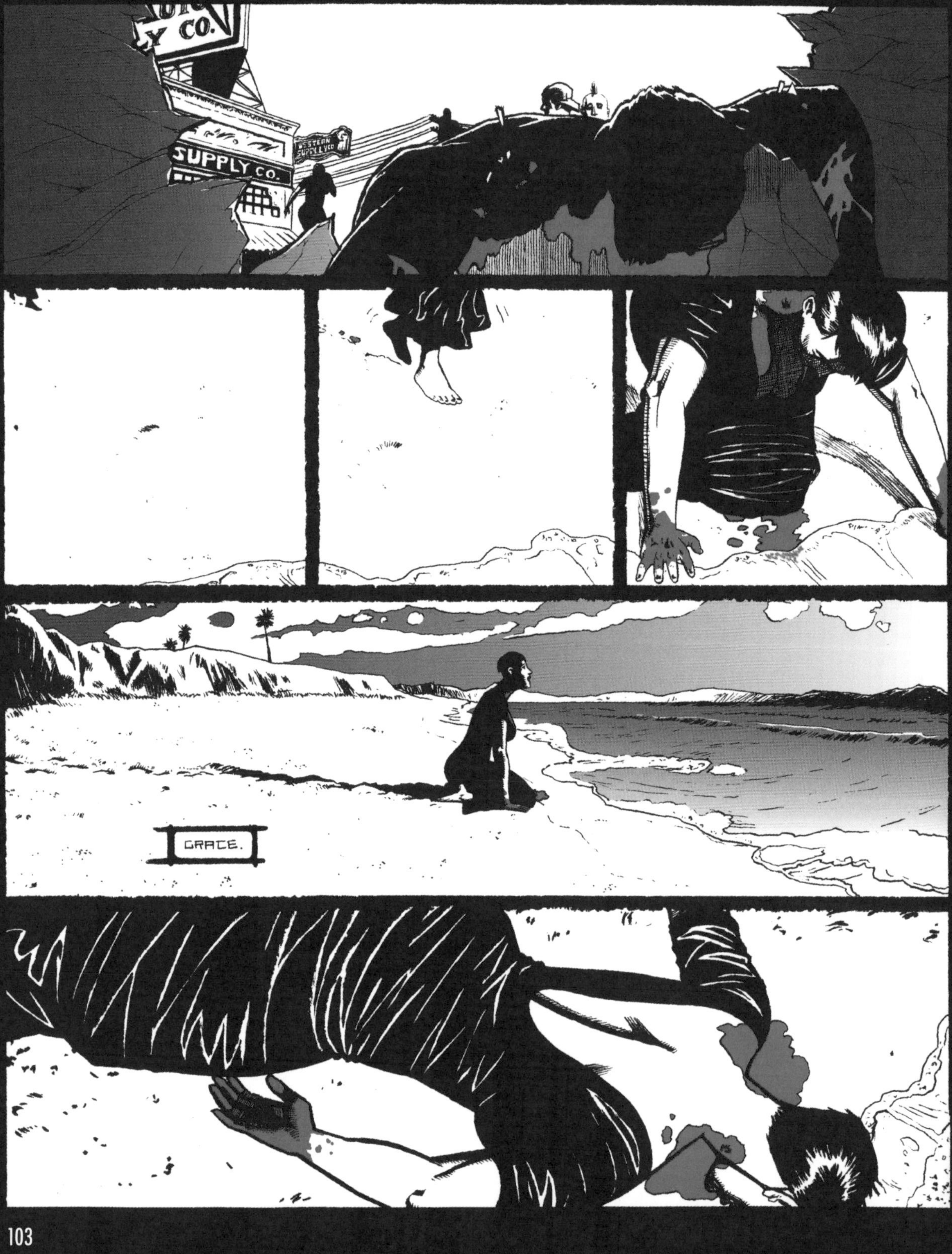
Y CO.
SUPPLY CO.
WESTERN SUPPLY CO.
GRACE.

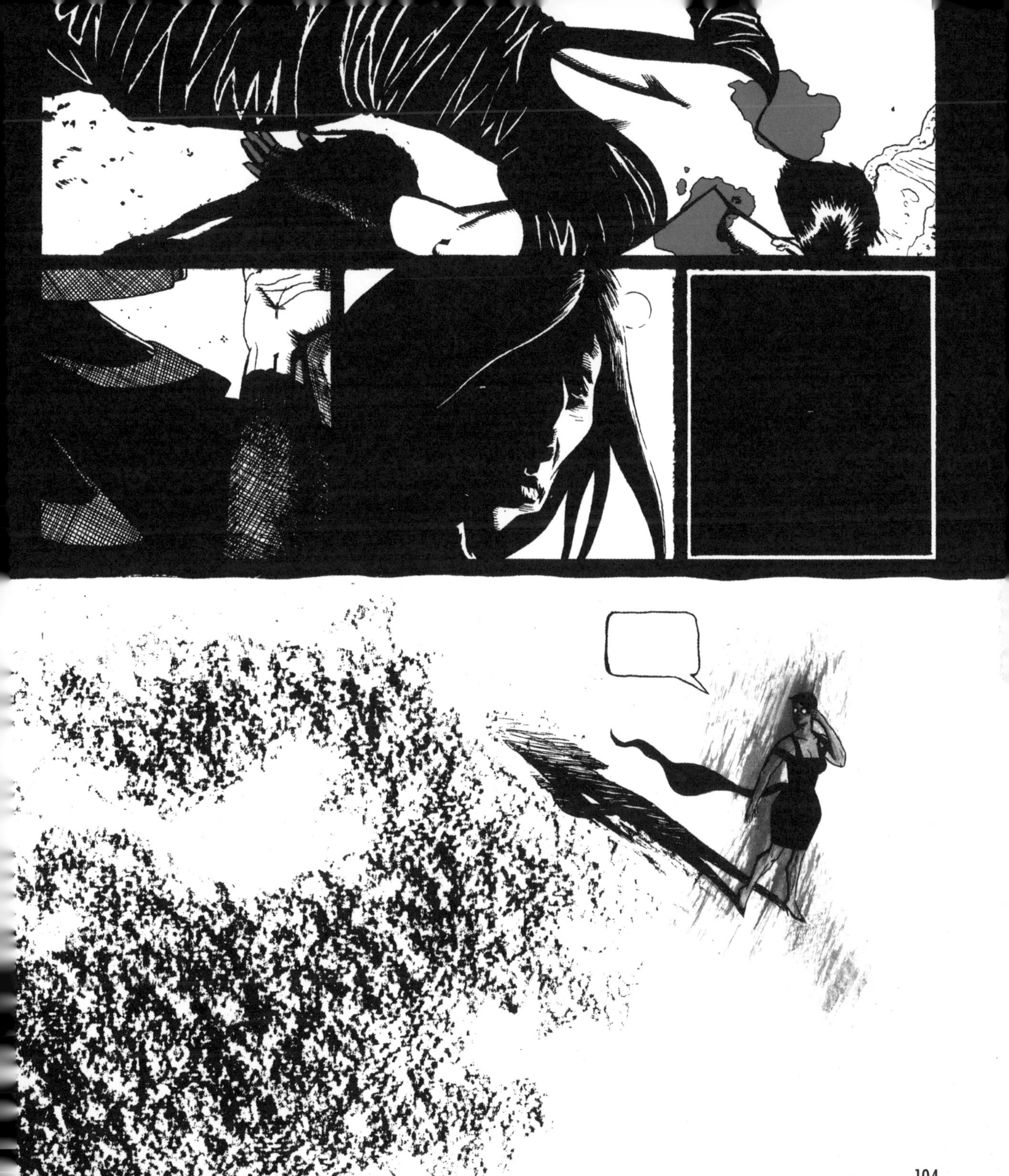

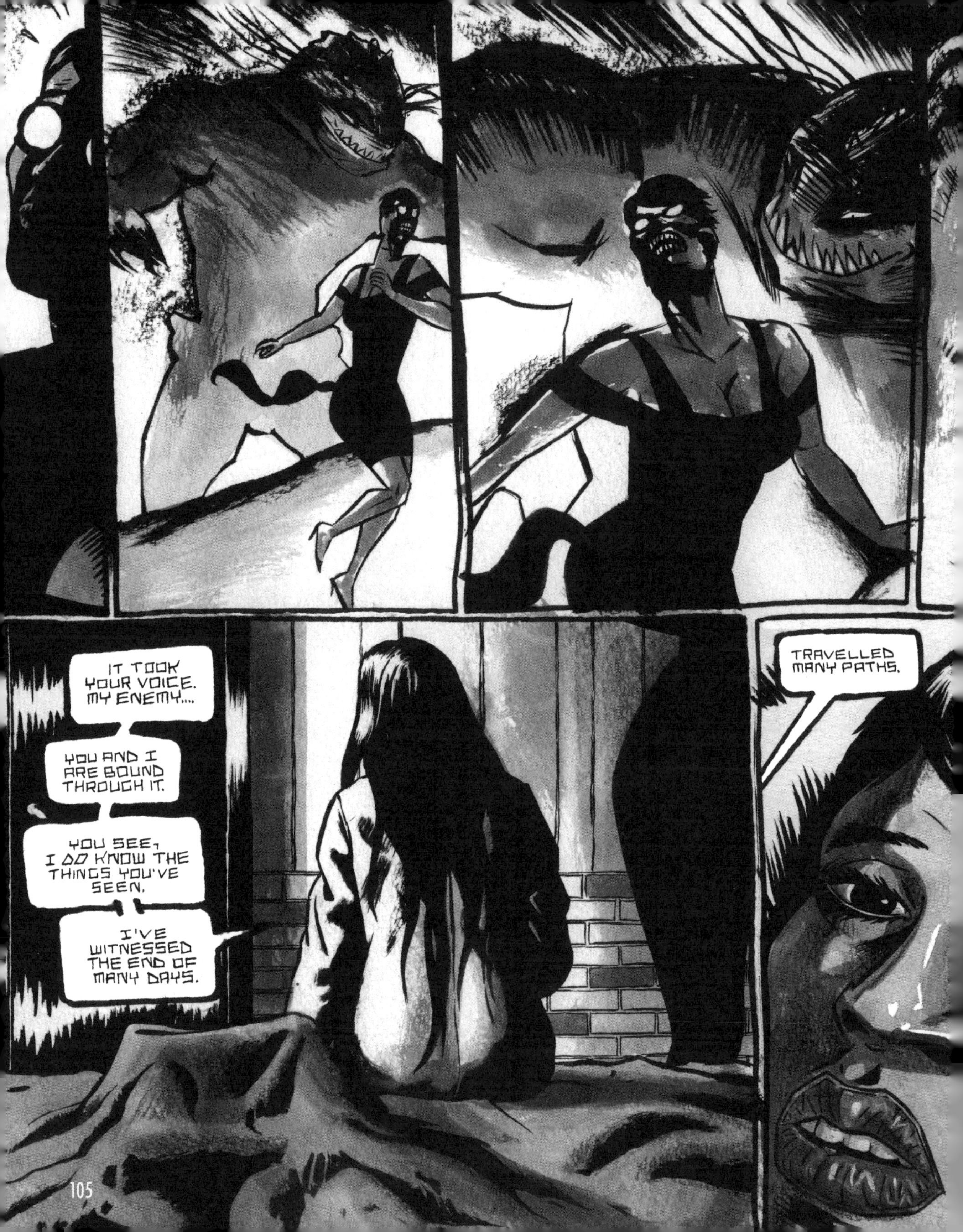
IT TOOK YOUR VOICE. MY ENEMY....
YOU AND I ARE BOUND THROUGH IT.
YOU SEE, I DO KNOW THE THINGS YOU'VE SEEN.
I'VE WITNESSED THE END OF MANY DAYS.
TRAVELLED MANY PATHS.

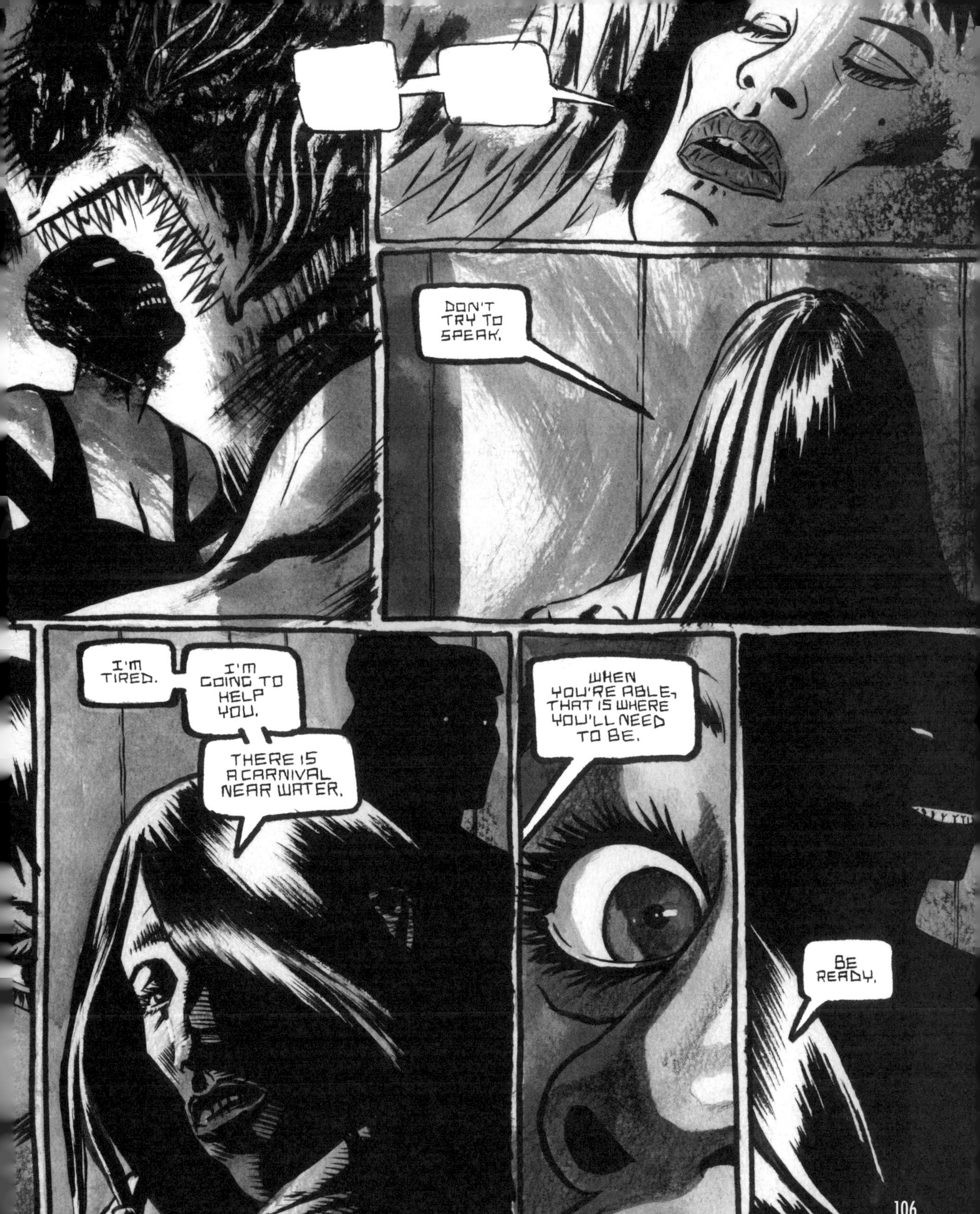
DON'T TRY TO SPEAK.
I'M TIRED.
I'M GOING TO HELP YOU.
THERE IS A CARNIVAL NEAR WATER.
WHEN YOU'RE ABLE, THAT IS WHERE YOU'LL NEED TO BE.
BE READY.

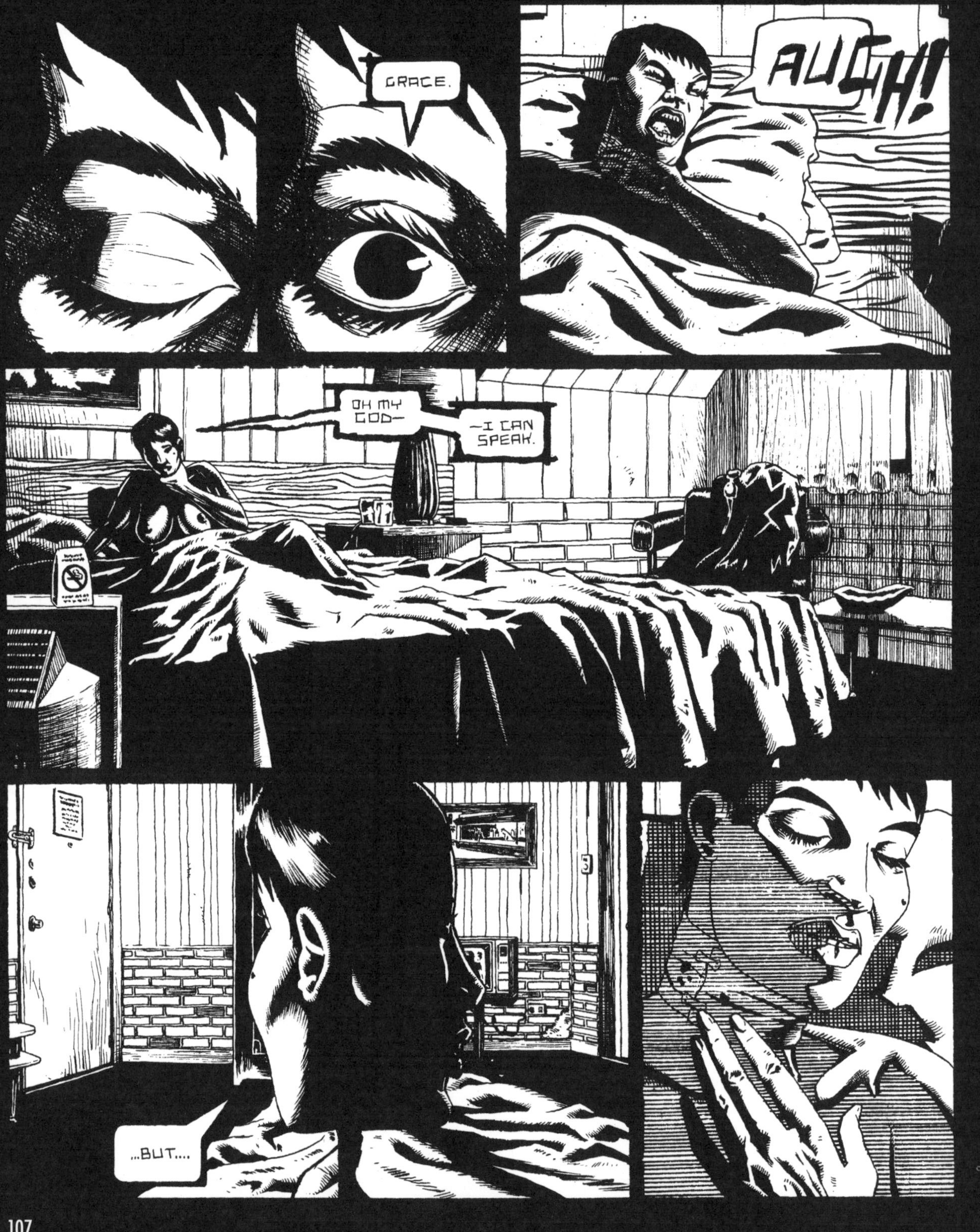
GRACE.
AUGH!
OH MY GOD—
—I CAN SPEAK.
...BUT....

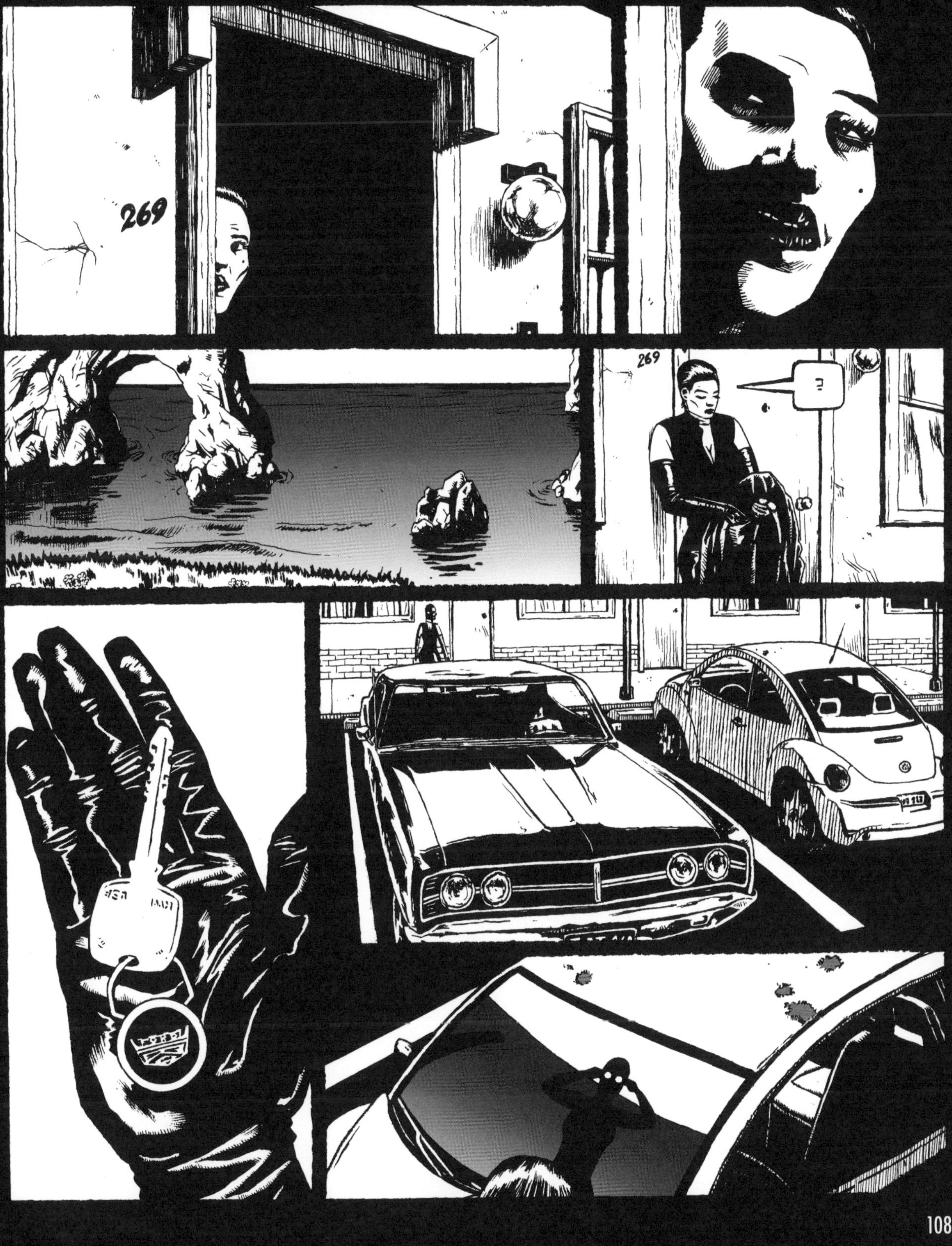
269
?

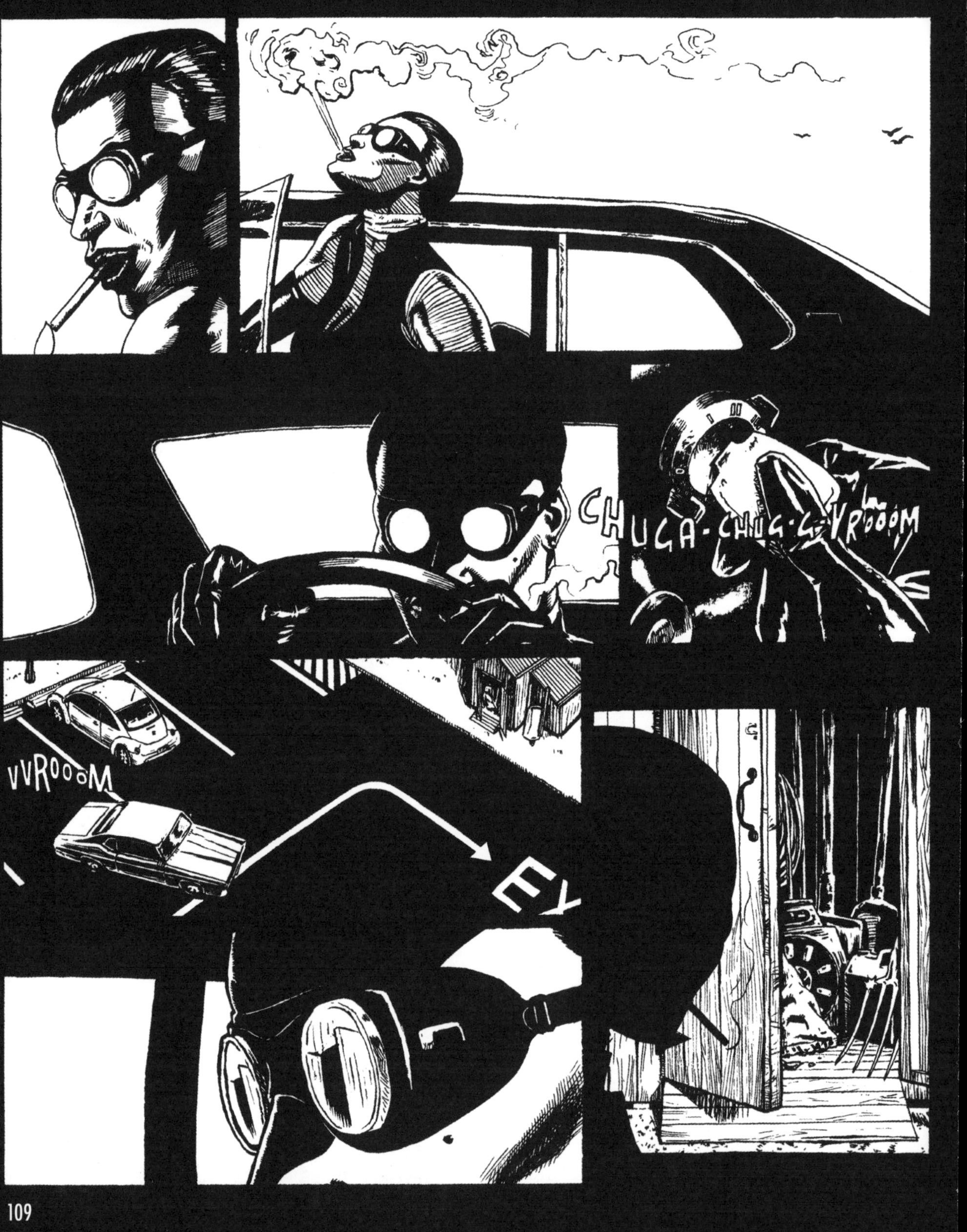
CHUGA-CHUG-G-VROOOM
VVROOOM
EX

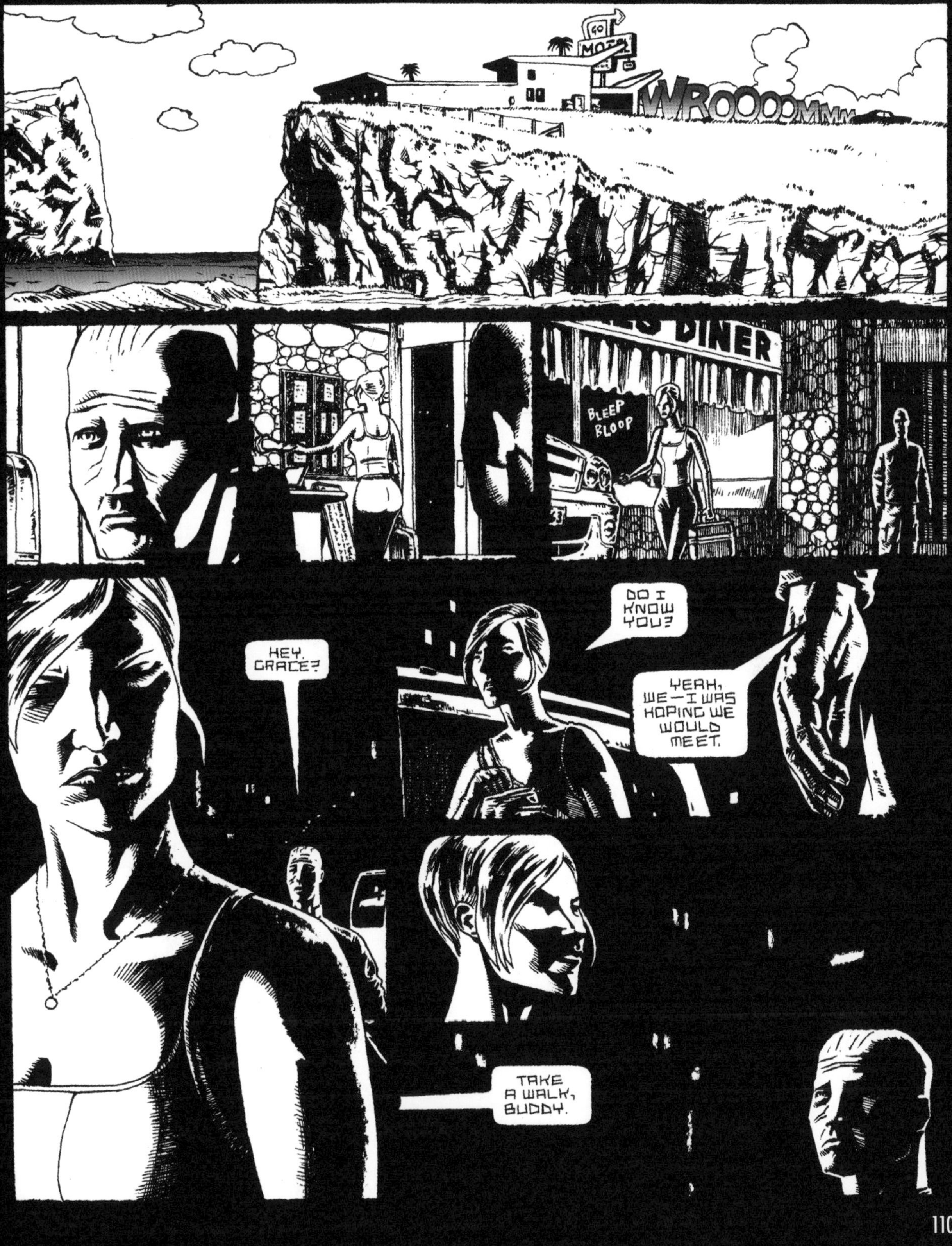

WROOOOOMMM
DINER
BLEEP BLOOP
HEY. GRACE?
DO I KNOW YOU?
YEAH, WE—I WAS HOPING WE WOULD MEET.
TAKE A WALK, BUDDY.

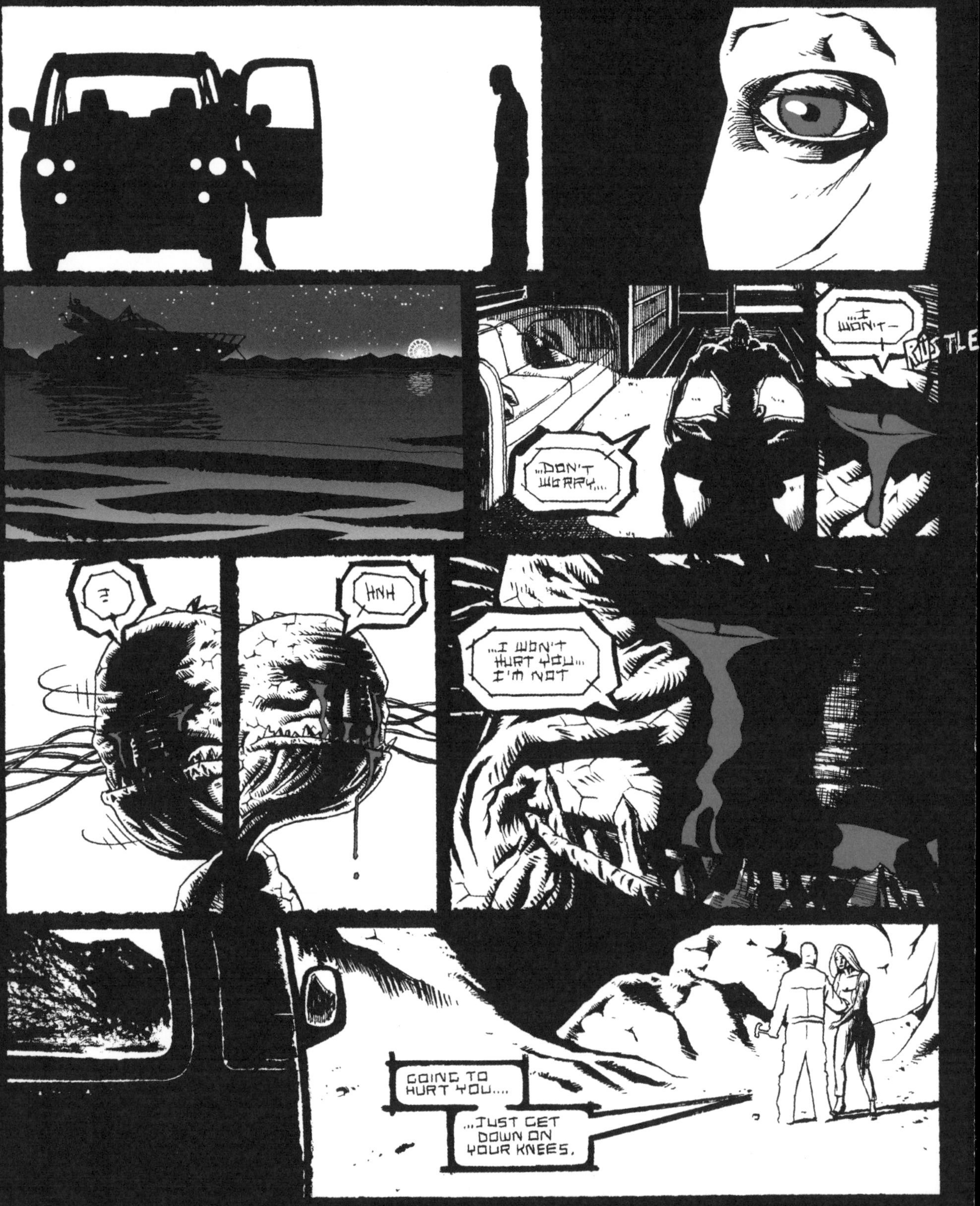

...DON'T WORRY...
...I WON'T-
RUSTLE
HNH
...I WON'T HURT YOU... I'M NOT
GOING TO HURT YOU....
...JUST GET DOWN ON YOUR KNEES.

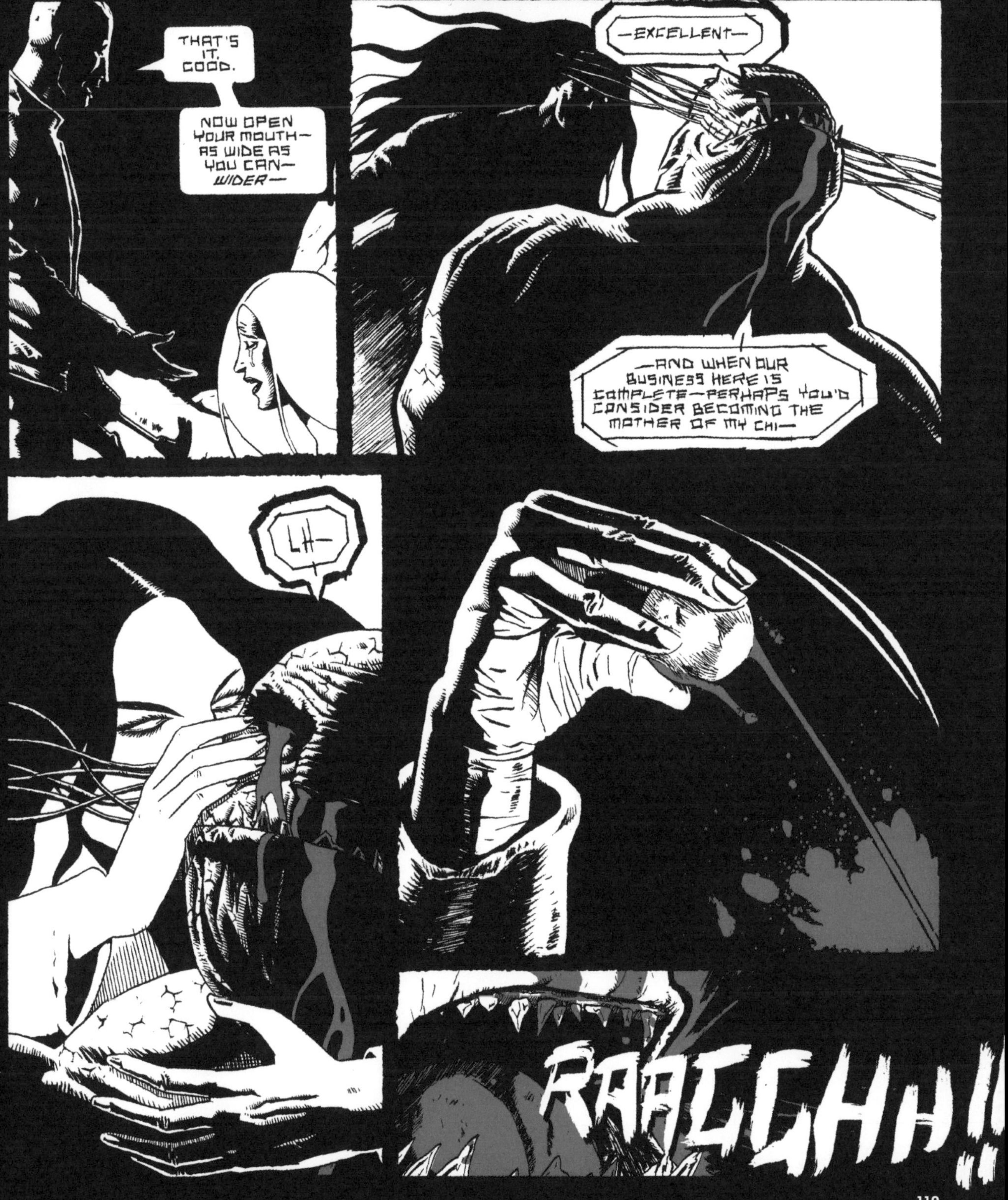
THAT'S IT, GOOD.
NOW OPEN YOUR MOUTH— AS WIDE AS YOU CAN— WIDER—
—EXCELLENT—
—AND WHEN OUR BUSINESS HERE IS COMPLETE—PERHAPS YOU'D CONSIDER BECOMING THE MOTHER OF MY CHI—
LH—
RAAGCHH!!

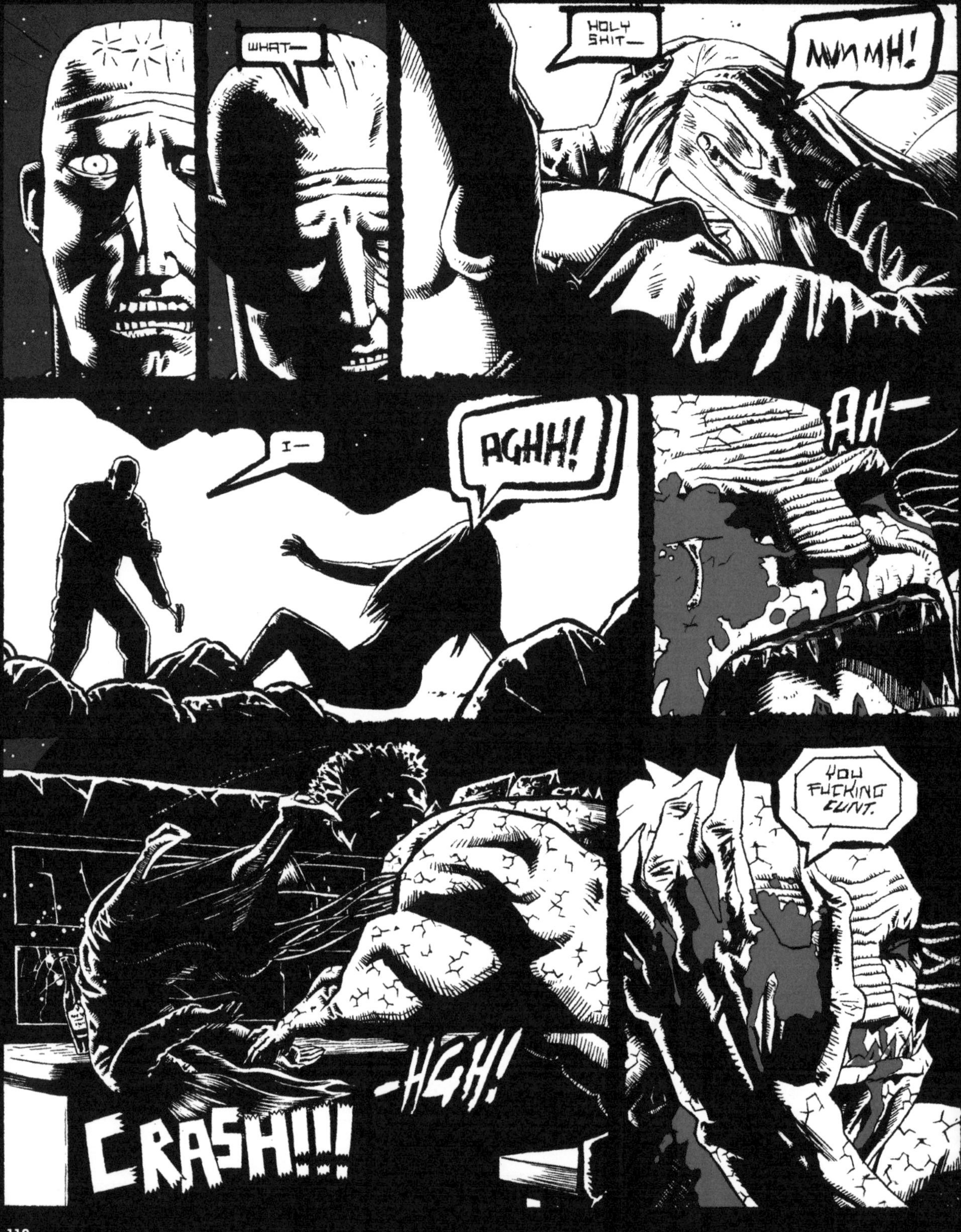

WHAT—
HOLY SHIT—
MMMH!
I—
AGHH!
AH—
-HGH!
CRASH!!!
YOU FUCKING CUNT.

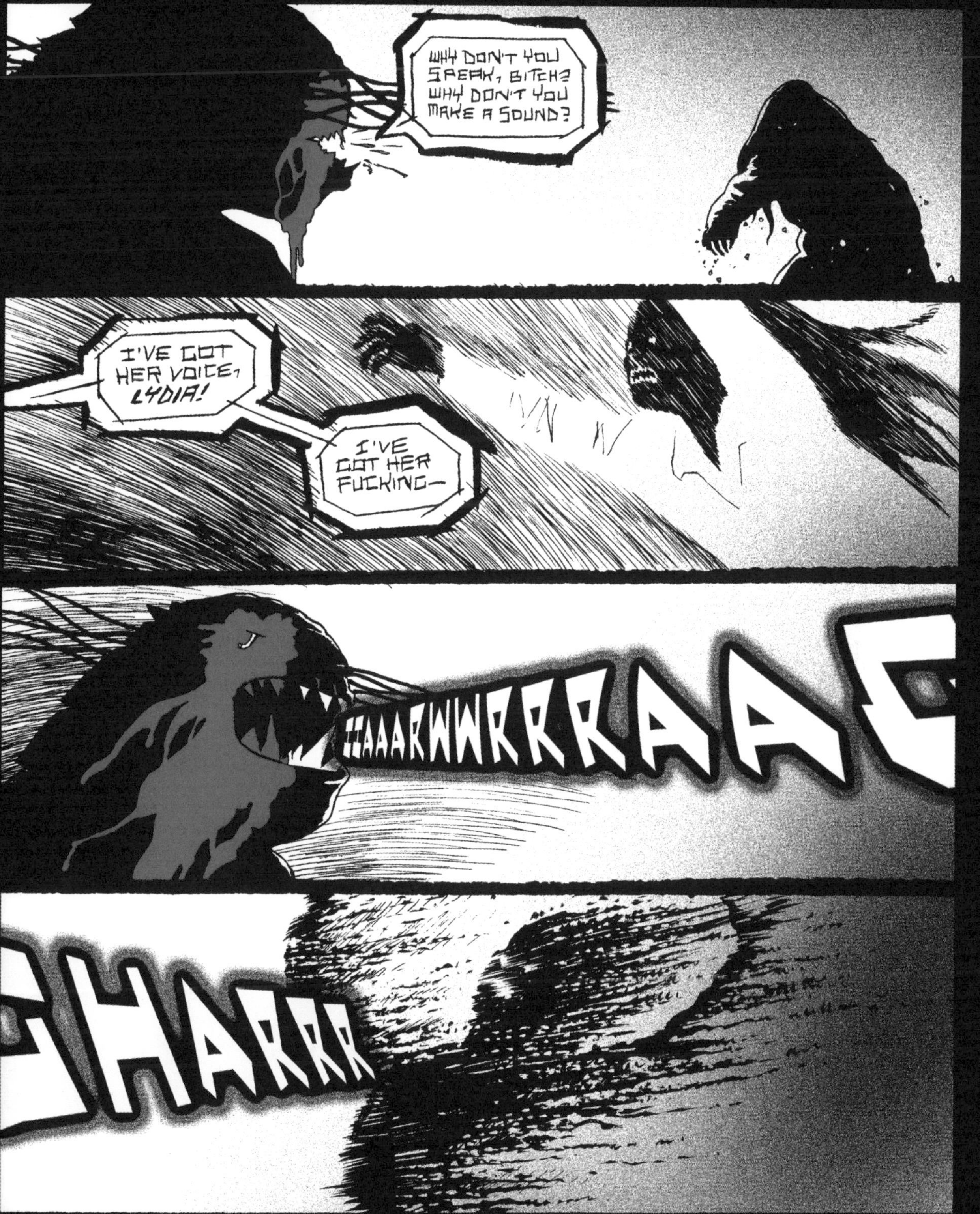
WHY DON'T YOU SPEAK, BITCH? WHY DON'T YOU MAKE A SOUND?
I'VE GOT HER VOICE, LYDIA!
I'VE GOT HER FUCKING—
IIAAARWWRRRAAG
CHARRR

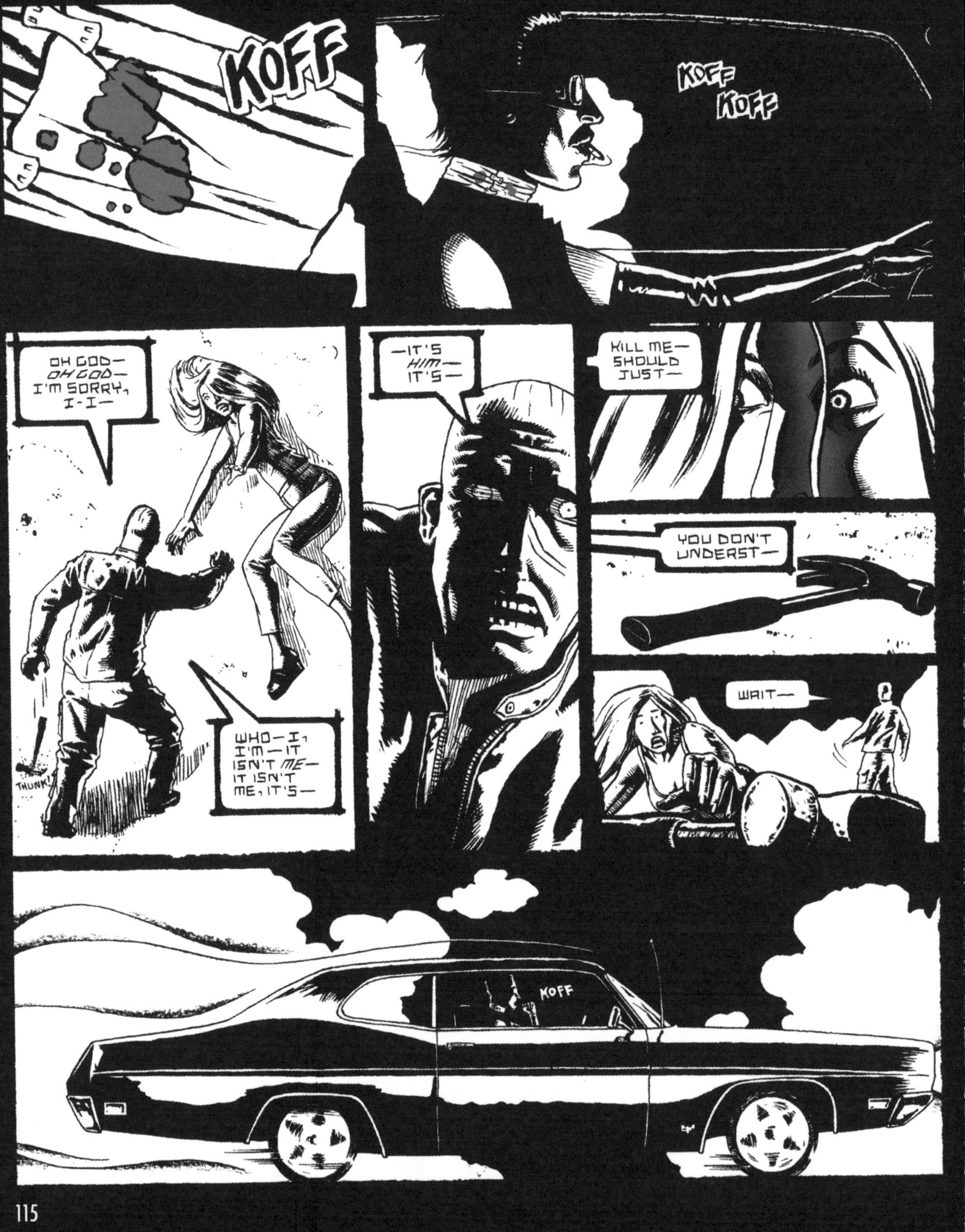
KOFF
KOFF KOFF
OH GOD— OH GOD— I'M SORRY, I-I—
THUNK!
WHO—I, I'M—IT ISN'T ME— IT ISN'T ME, IT'S—
—IT'S HIM— IT'S—
KILL ME— SHOULD JUST—
YOU DON'T UNDERST—
WAIT—
KOFF

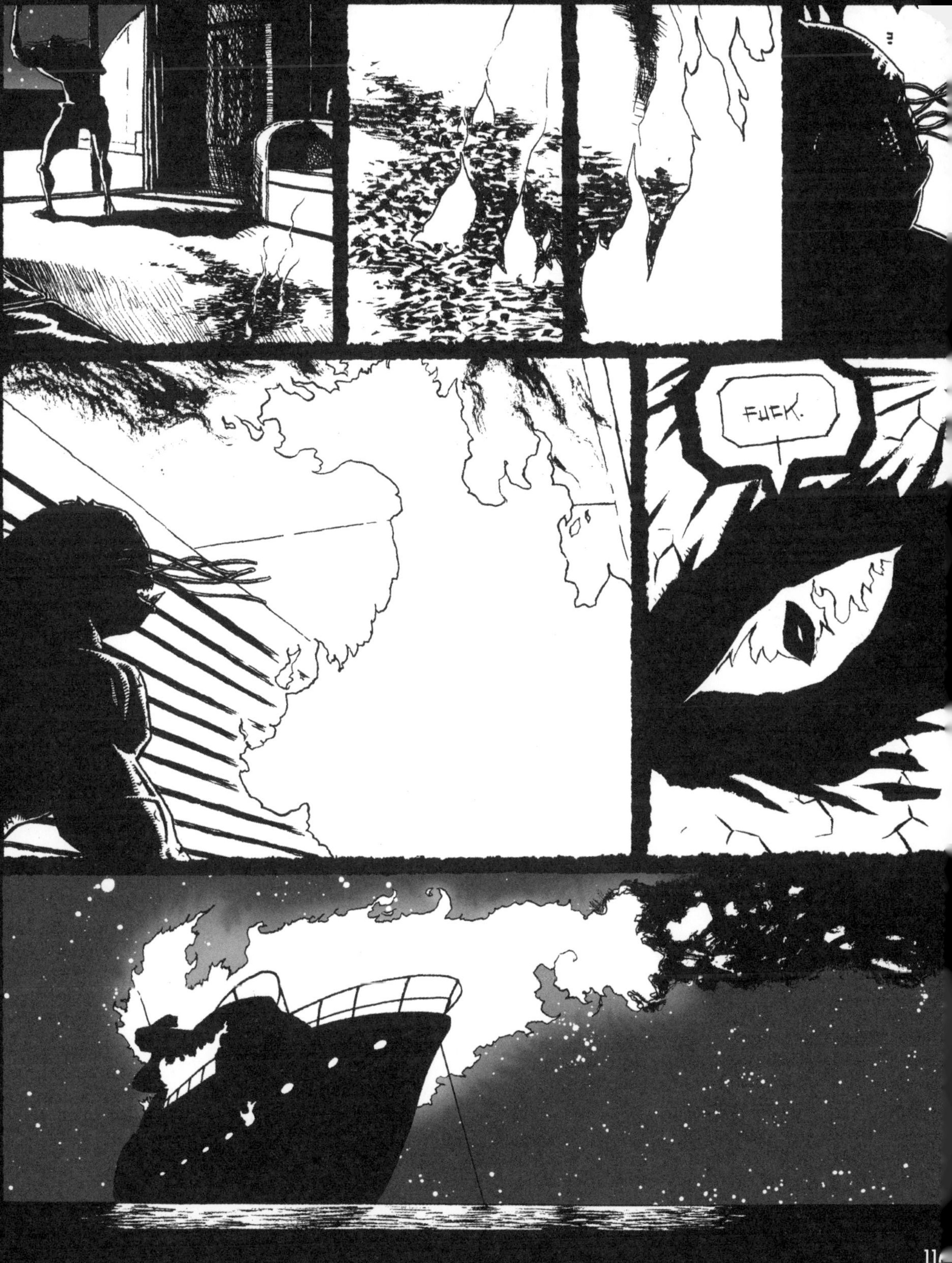
FUCK.

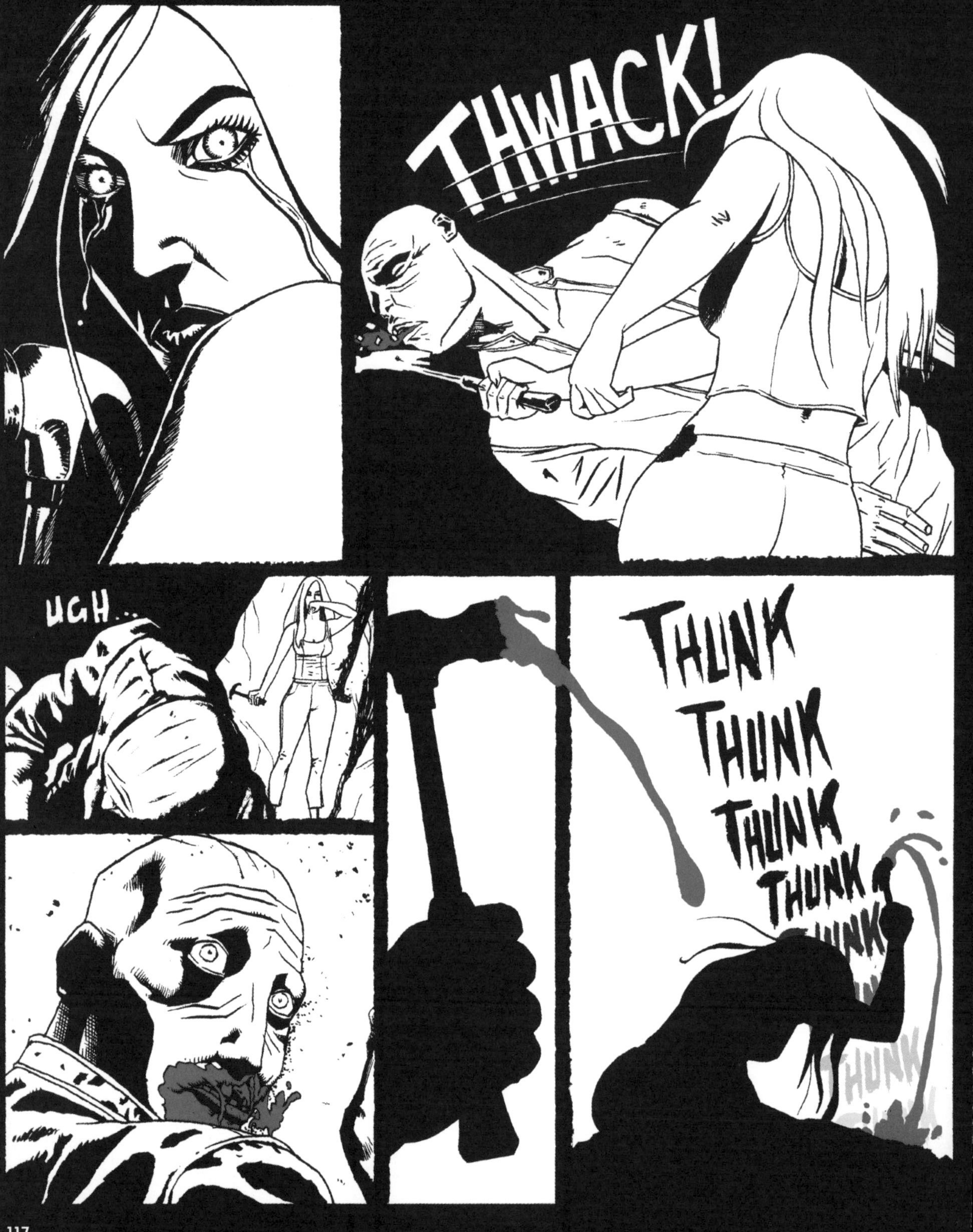
THWACK!
UGH...
THUNK
THUNK
THUNK
THUNK
THUNK

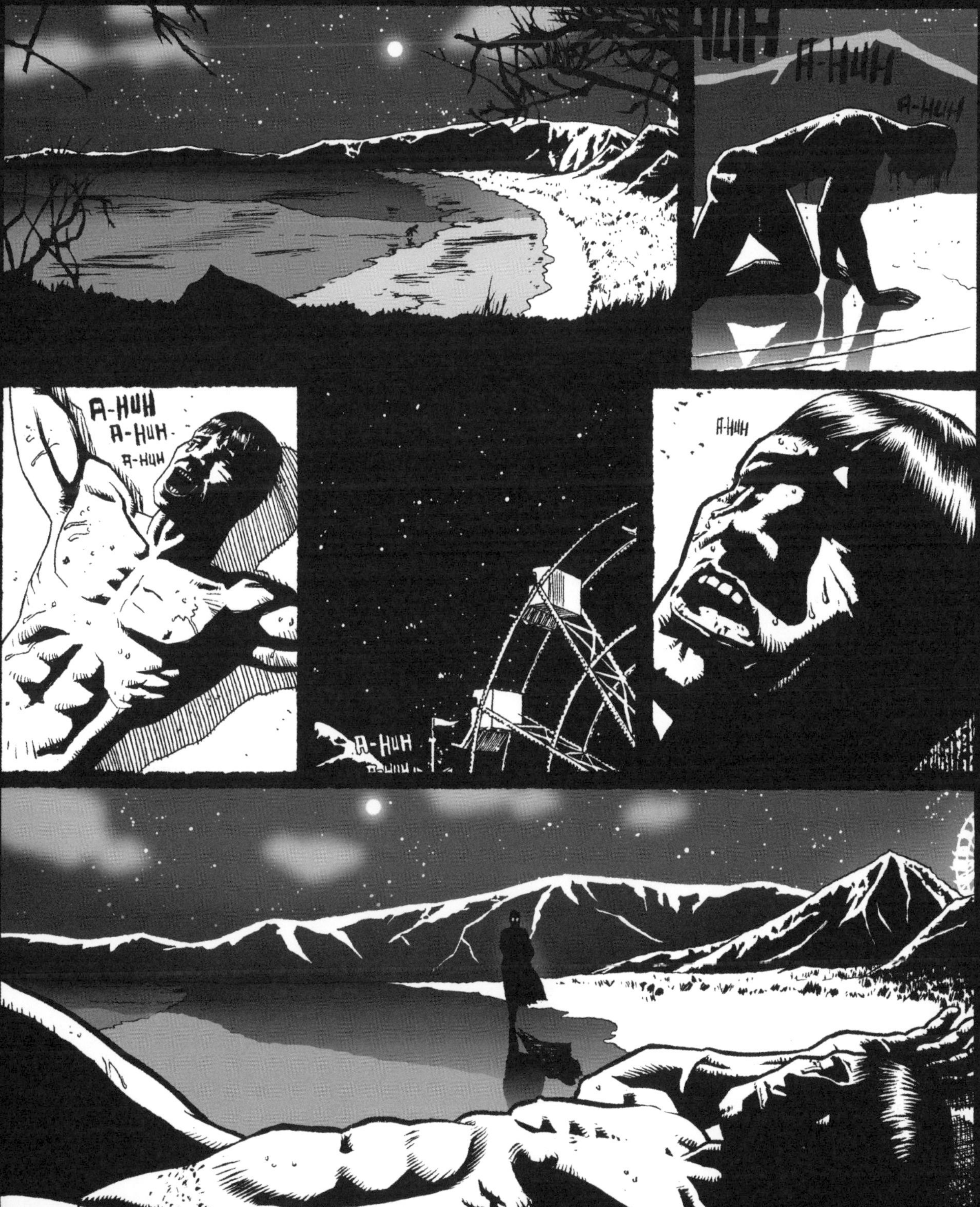
A-HUH
A-HUH
A-HUH
A-HUH
A-HUH
A-HUH
A-HUH

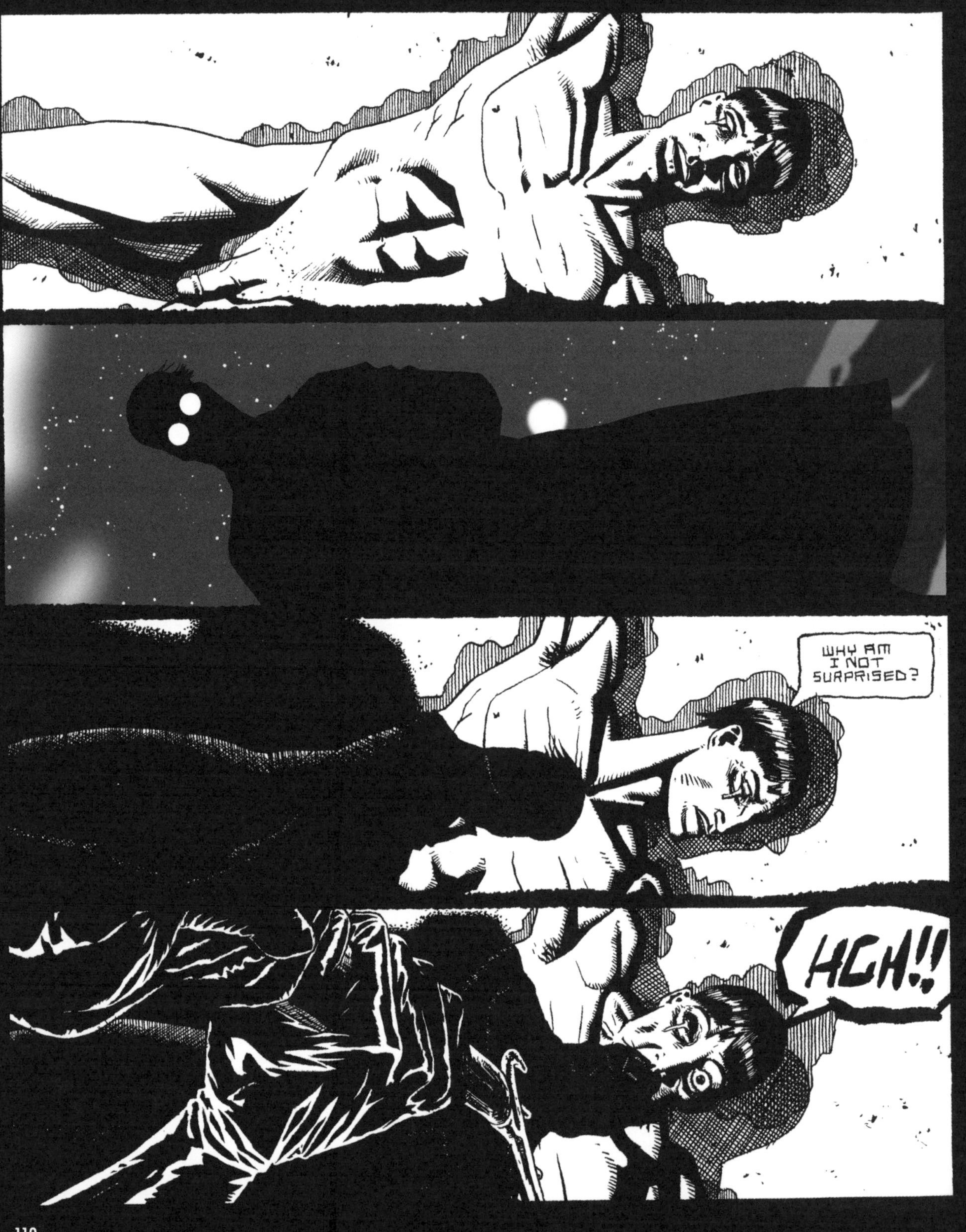
WHY AM
I NOT
SURPRISED?
HGH!!

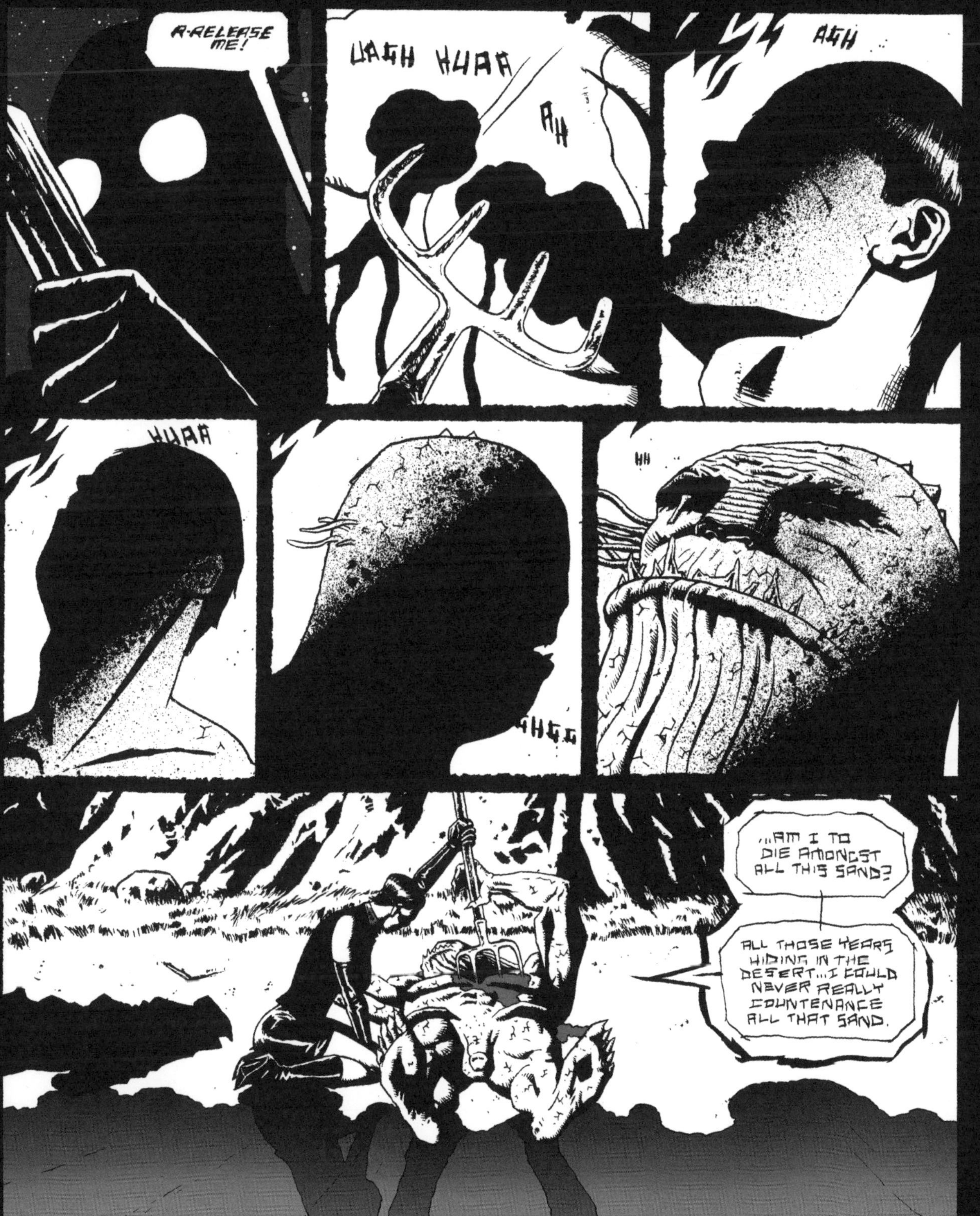
A-RELEASE ME!
UAGH HUAA
AH
AGH
HUAA
HHGG
HH
...AM I TO DIE AMONGST ALL THIS SAND?
ALL THOSE YEARS HIDING IN THE DESERT... I COULD NEVER REALLY COUNTENANCE ALL THAT SAND.

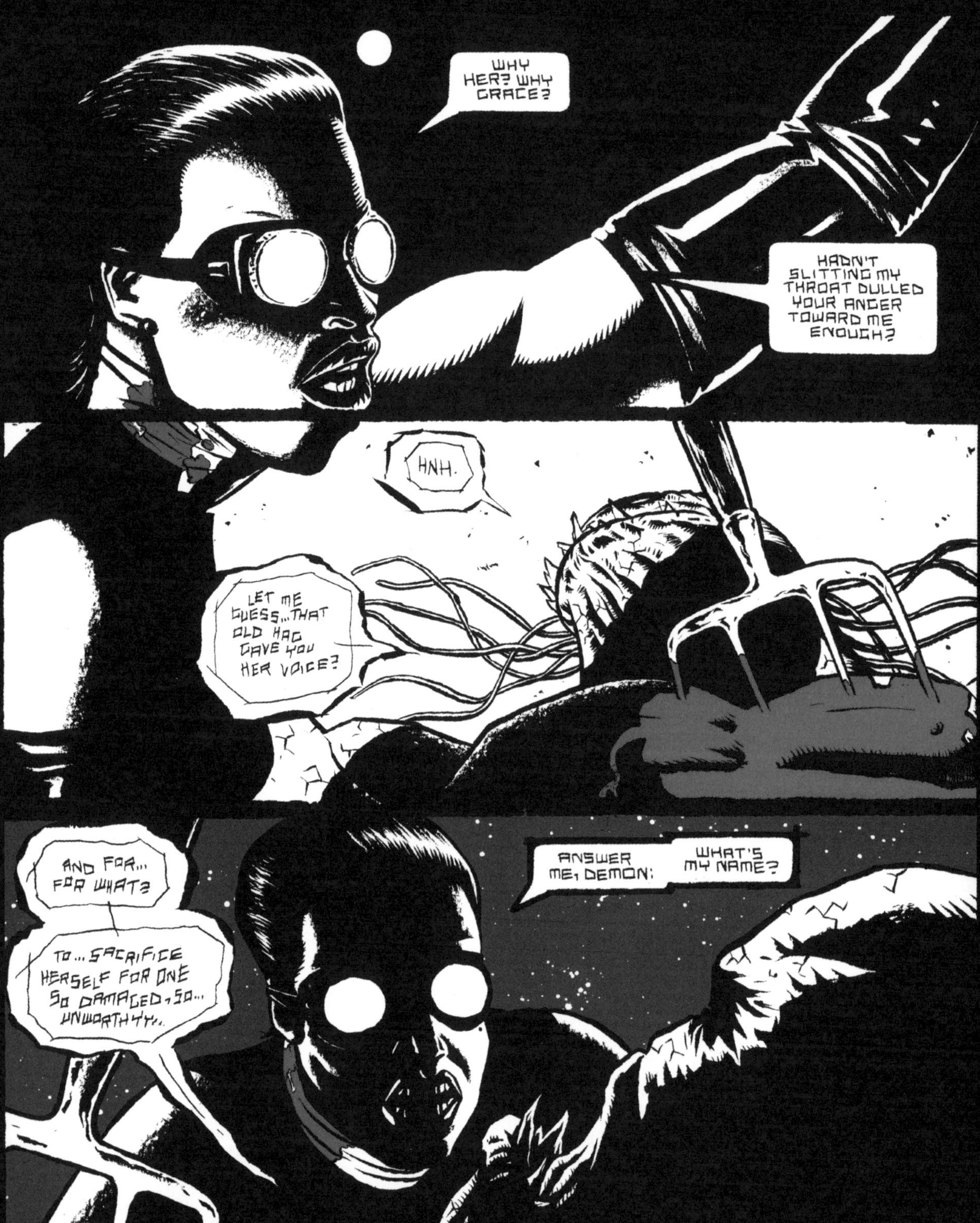
WHY HER? WHY GRACE?
HADN'T SLITTING MY THROAT DULLED YOUR ANGER TOWARD ME ENOUGH?
HNH.
LET ME GUESS... THAT OLD HAG GAVE YOU HER VOICE?
AND FOR... FOR WHAT?
TO... SACRIFICE HERSELF FOR ONE SO DAMAGED, SO... UNWORTHYY...
ANSWER ME, DEMON:
WHAT'S MY NAME?

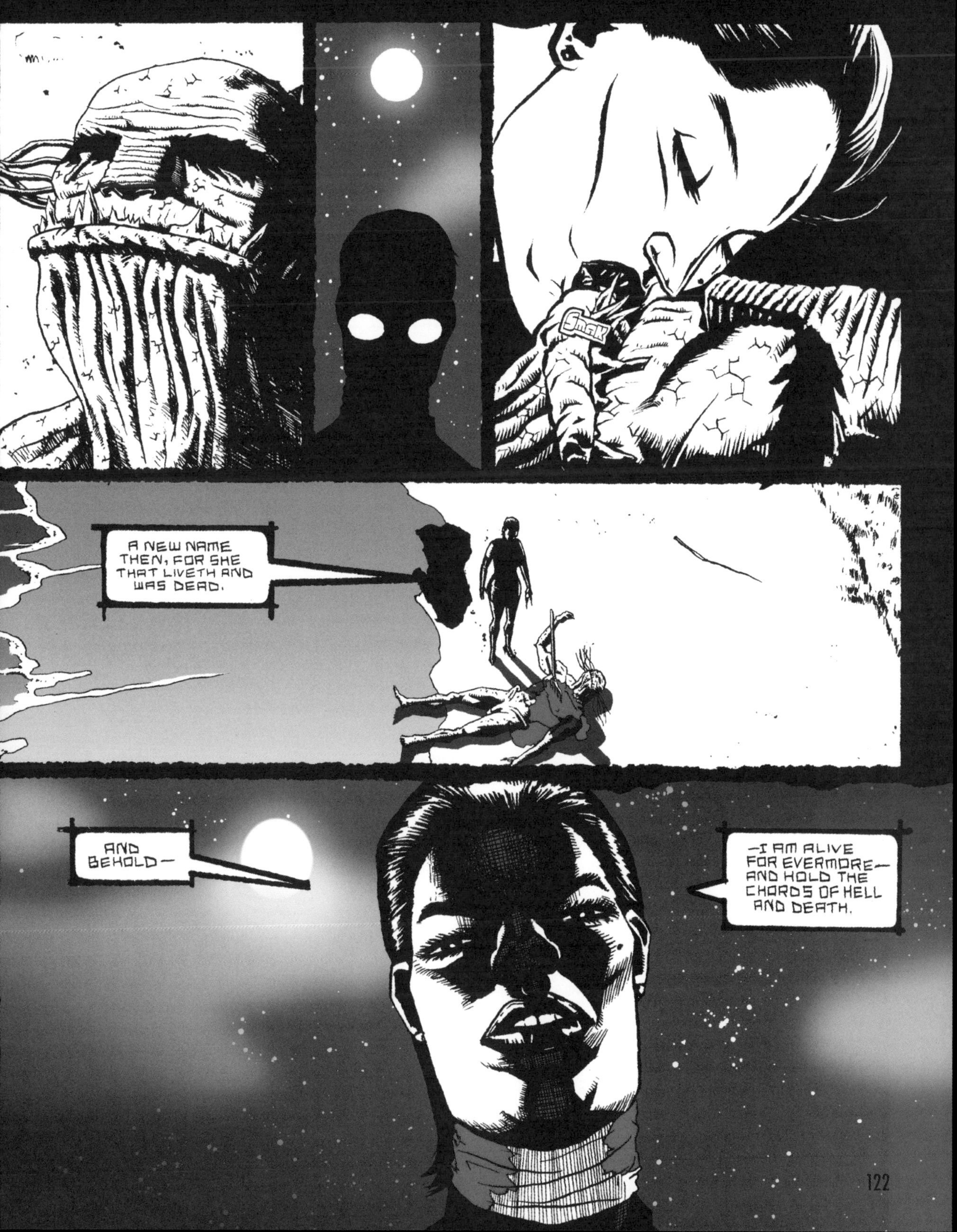
SMAK
A NEW NAME THEN, FOR SHE THAT LIVETH AND WAS DEAD.
AND BEHOLD—
—I AM ALIVE FOR EVERMORE—AND HOLD THE CHORDS OF HELL AND DEATH.

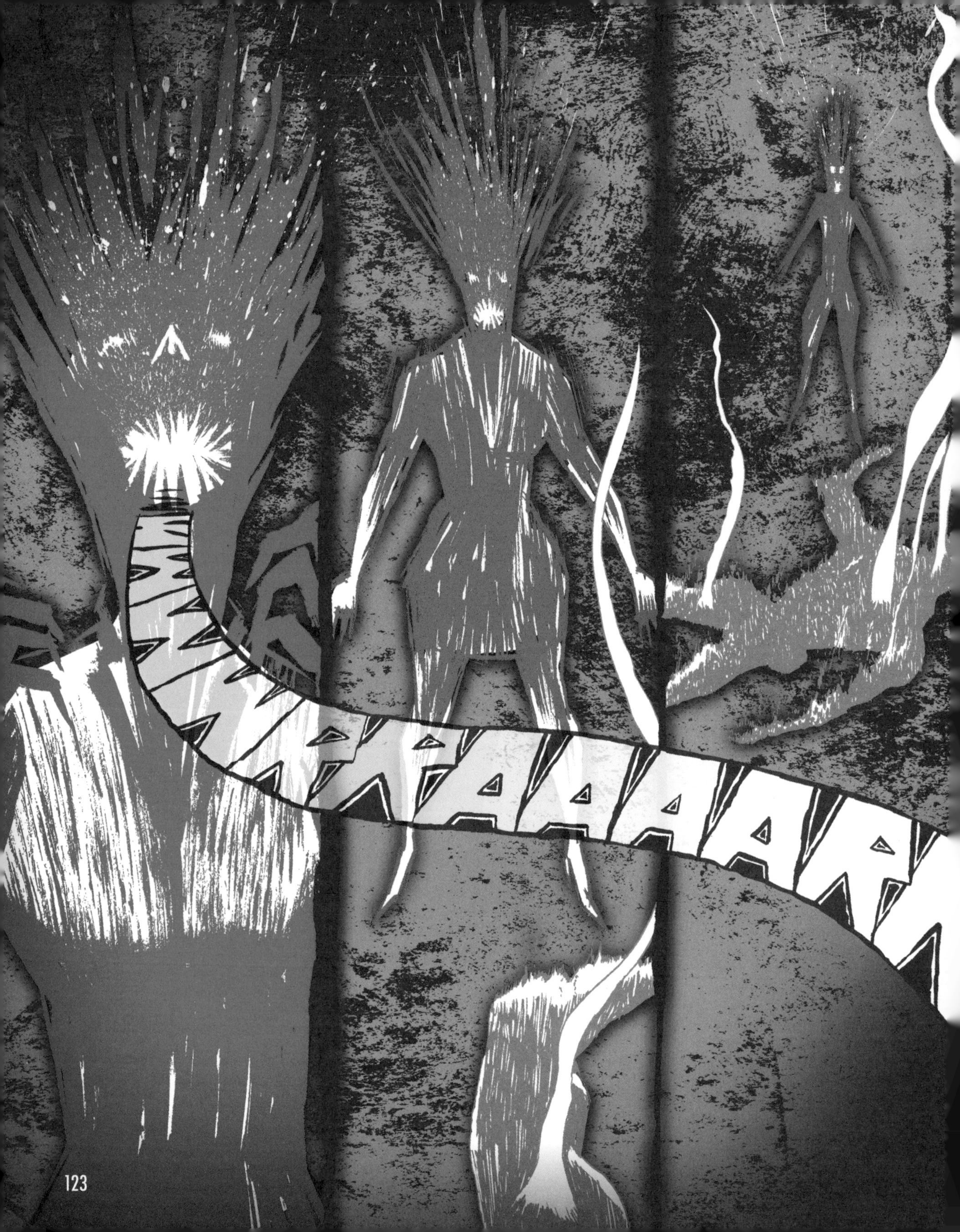

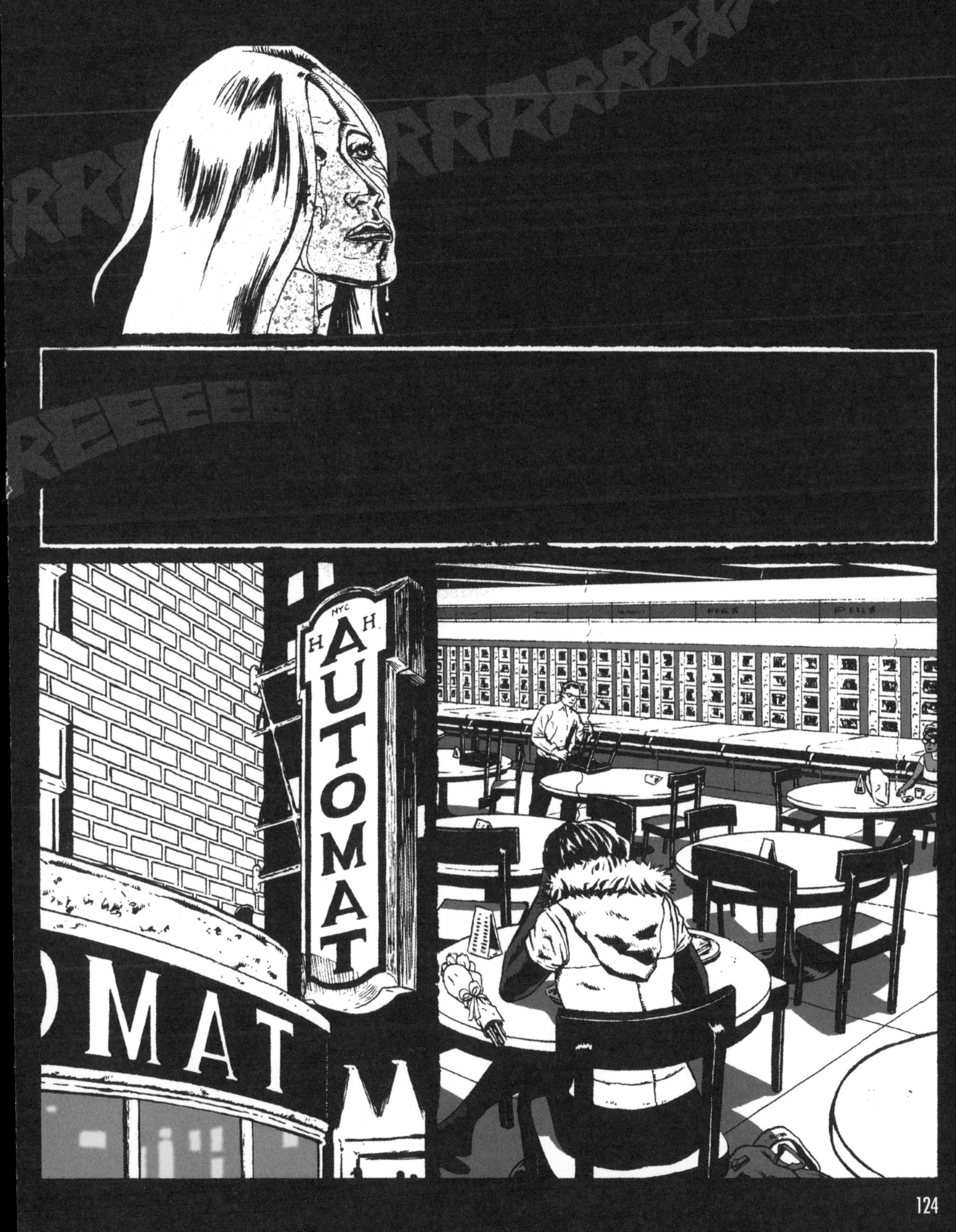
NYC
H H
AUTOMAT
OMAT
M

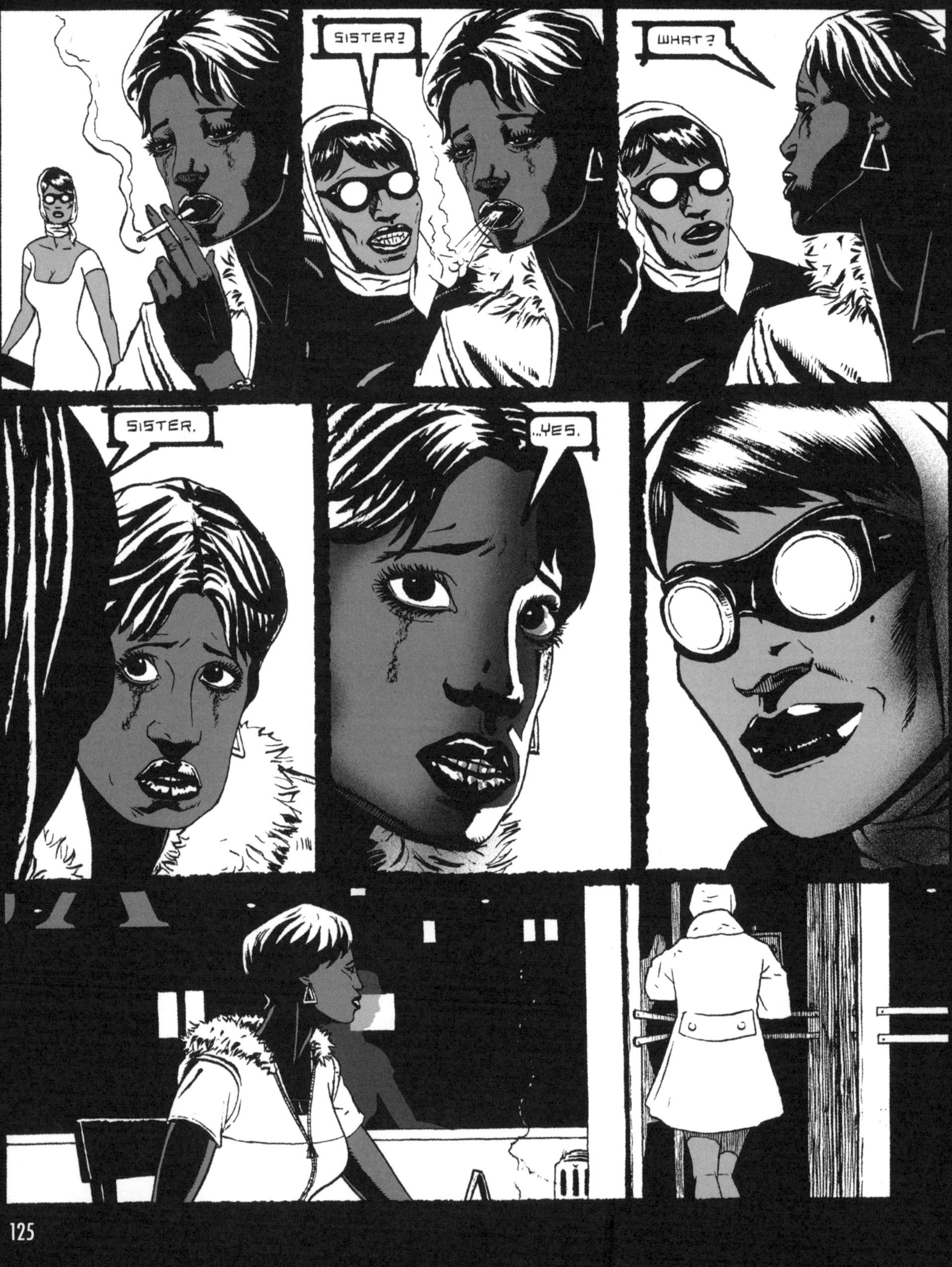
SISTER?
WHAT?
SISTER.
...YES.

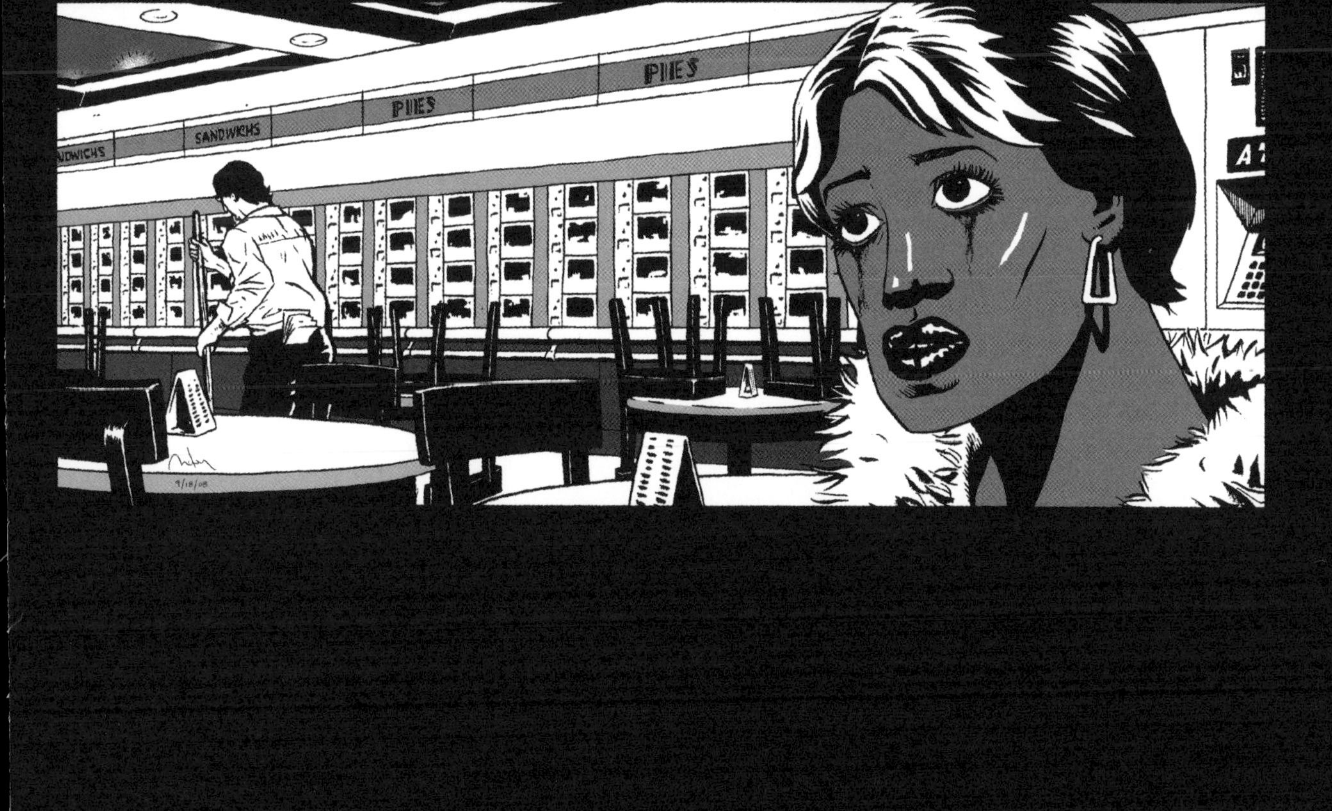

SANDWICHS
PIES
PIES

WRITTEN
&
DRAWN BY HO CHE ANDERSON

EDITOR
**GARY GROTH**
DESIGN
**HCA**
PRODUCTION MANAGER
**ADAM GRANO**
PRODUCTION ASSISTANCE
**PAUL BARESH**
PROMOTION
**ERIC REYNOLDS**
PUBLISHERS
**GARY GROTH**
&
**KIM THOMPSON**

## OL' NEXT SHIT BY HCA

I WANT TO BE YOUR DOG / KING / WISE SON / POP LIFE / THE NO-BOYS CLUB / YOUNG HOODS IN LOVE / STEEL DRUMS AND ICE SKATES / TEMPLE DUNCAN

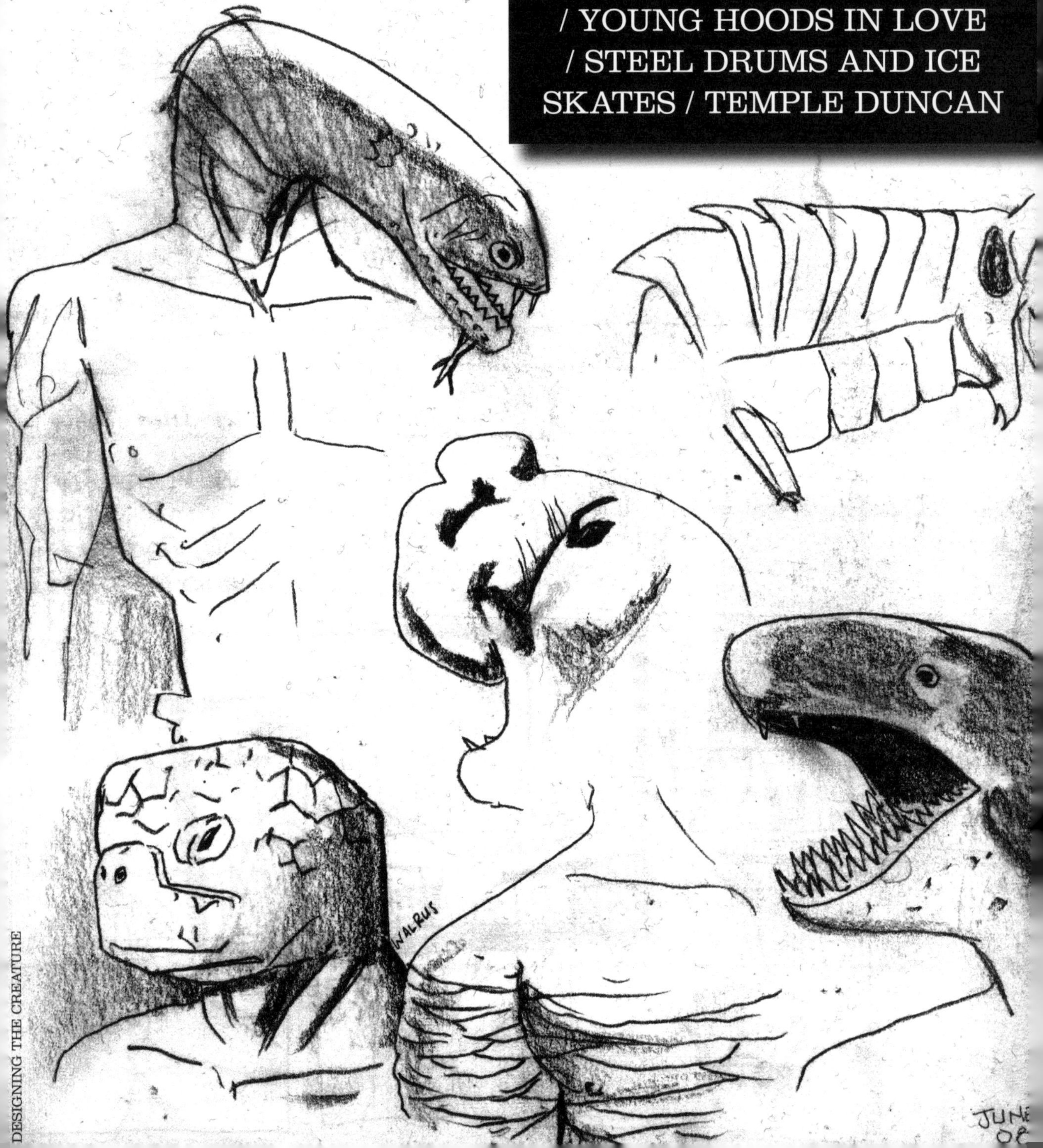
WALRUS

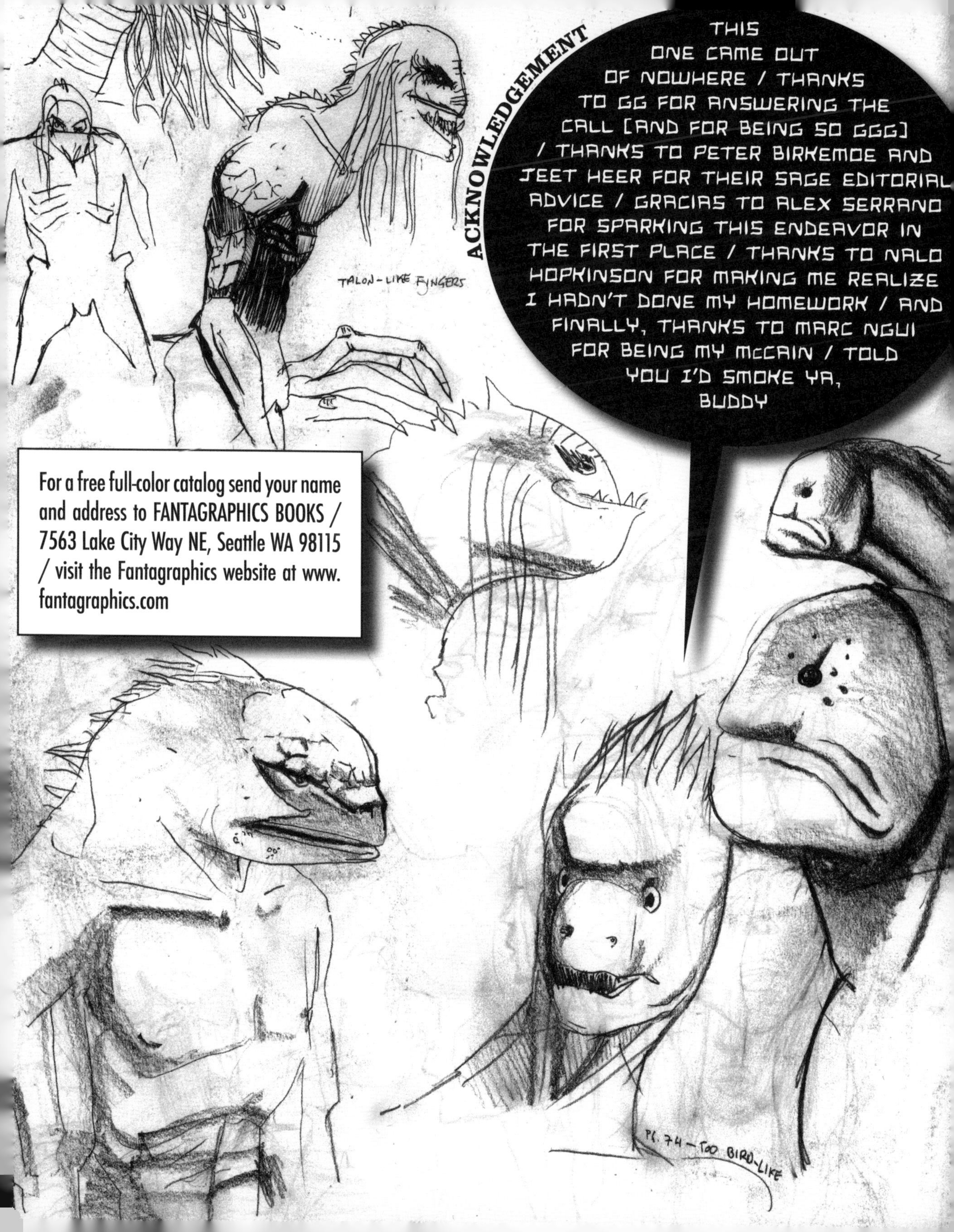
TALON-LIKE FINGERS
PG. 74 — TOO BIRD-LIKE

**ACKNOWLEDGEMENT**

THIS ONE CAME OUT OF NOWHERE / THANKS TO GG FOR ANSWERING THE CALL [AND FOR BEING SO GGG] / THANKS TO PETER BIRKEMOE AND JEET HEER FOR THEIR SAGE EDITORIAL ADVICE / GRACIAS TO ALEX SERRANO FOR SPARKING THIS ENDEAVOR IN THE FIRST PLACE / THANKS TO NALO HOPKINSON FOR MAKING ME REALIZE I HADN'T DONE MY HOMEWORK / AND FINALLY, THANKS TO MARC NGUI FOR BEING MY McCAIN / TOLD YOU I'D SMOKE YA, BUDDY

"All things are changing; nothing dies. The spirit wanders, come now here, now there, and occupies whatever frame it pleases.

"For that which once existed is no more, and that which was not has come to be; and so the whole round of motion is gone through again."

*–Ovid*

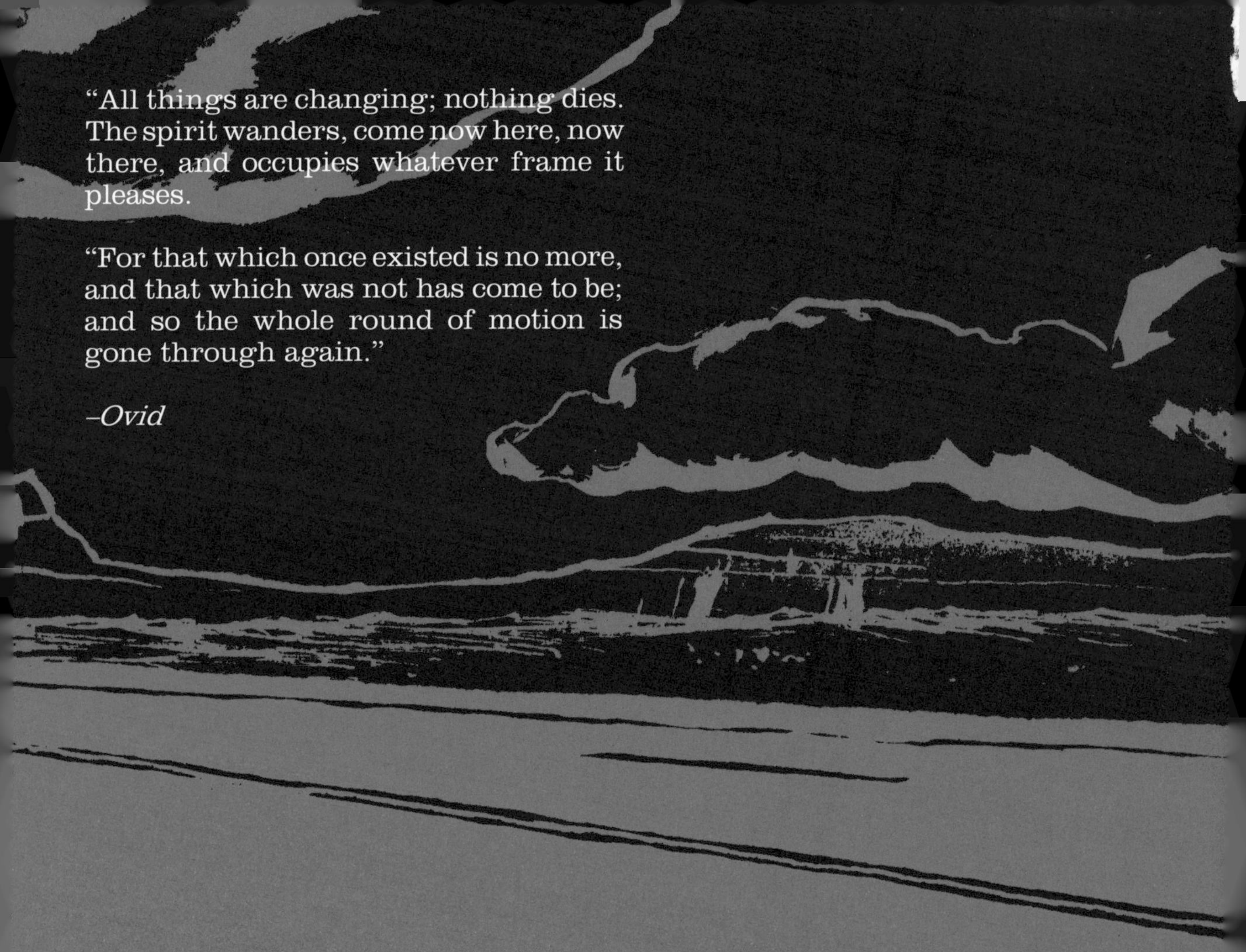